PALGRAVE *Studies in Oral History*

Series Editors: Linda Shopes and Bruce M. Stave

The Order Has Been Carried Out: History, Memory, and Meaning of a Nazi Massacre in Rome by Alessandro Portelli (2003)

Sticking to the Union: An Oral History of the Life and Times of Julia Ruuttila by Sandy Polishuk (2003)

To Wear the Dust of War: From Bialystok to Shanghai to the Promised Land, an Oral History by Samuel Iwry, edited by L. J. H. Kelley (2004)

Education as My Agenda: Gertrude Williams, Race, and the Baltimore Public Schools by Jo Ann Robinson (2005)

Remembering: Oral History Performance edited by Della Pollock (2005)

Postmemories of Terror: A New Generation Copes with the Legacy of the "Dirty War," by Susana Kaiser (2005)

Growing Up in the People's Republic: Conversations between Two Daughters of China's Revolution by Ye Weili and Ma Xiaodong (2005)

Life and Death in the Delta: African American Narratives of Violence, Resilience, and Social Change by Kim Lacy Rogers (2006)

Creating Choice: A Community Responds to the Need for Abortion and Birth Control, 1961–1973 by David P. Cline (2006)

Voices from This Long Brown Land: Oral Recollections of Owens Valley Lives and Manzanar Pasts by Jane Wehrey (2006)

Radicals, Rhetoric, and the War: The University of Nevada in the Wake of Kent State by Brad Lucas (2006)

The Unquiet Nisei: An Oral History of the Life of Sue Kunitomi Embrey by Diana Meyers Bahr (2007)

Sisters in the Brotherhoods: Working Women Organizing for Equality in New York City by Jane LaTour (2008)

Iraq's Last Jews: Stories of Daily Life, Upheaval, and Escape from Modern Babylon edited by Tamar Morad, Dennis Shasha, and Robert Shasha (2008)

Soldiers and Citizens: An Oral History of Operation Iraqi Freedom from the Battlefield to the Pentagon by Carl Mirra (2008)

Overcoming Katrina: African American Voices from the Crescent City and Beyond edited by D'Ann R. Penner and Keith C. Ferdinand (2009)

I Saw it Coming: Worker Narratives of Plant Closings and Job Loss by Tracy E. K'Meyer and Joy L. Hart (2009)

Speaking History: Oral Histories of the American Past, 1865–present by Sue Armitage and Laurie Mercier (2009)

Bringing Desegregation Home: Memories of the Struggle toward School Integration in Rural North Carolina by Kate Willink (2009)

Surviving Bhopal: Dancing Bodies, Written Texts, and Oral Testimonials of Women in the Wake of an Industrial Disaster by Suroopa Mukherjee (2010)

Living with Jim Crow: African American Women and Memories of the Segregated South by Anne Valk and Leslie Brown (2010)

Stories from the Gulag by Jehanne Gheith and Katherine Jolluck (2010)

Speaking History

Oral Histories of the American Past, 1865–present

Sue Armitage and Laurie Mercier

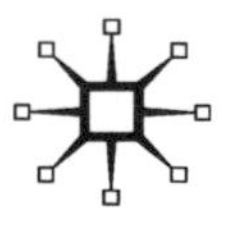

SPEAKING HISTORY

First published in 2009 by
PALGRAVE MACMILLAN®
in the United States—a division of St. Martin's Press LLC,
175 Fifth Avenue, New York, NY 10010.

Where this book is distributed in the UK, Europe and the rest of the world, this is by Palgrave Macmillan, a division of Macmillan Publishers Limited, registered in England, company number 785998, of Houndmills, Basingstoke, Hampshire RG21 6XS.

Palgrave Macmillan is the global academic imprint of the above companies and has companies and representatives throughout the world.

ISBN 978–1–4039–7783–0 (paperback)
ISBN 978–1–4039–7782–3 (hardcover)

Library of Congress Cataloging-in-Publication Data.

Speaking history : oral histories of the American past, 1865–present / edited by Sue Armitage and Laurie Mercier.
p. cm.—(Palgrave studies in oral history)
Includes bibliographical references and index.
ISBN 978–1–4039–7783–0
1. United States—History—1865– 2. Oral history. I. Armitage, Susan H. (Susan Hodge), 1937– II. Mercier, Laurie.

E661.S64 2009
973—dc22 2009023411

A catalogue record of the book is available from the British Library.

Design by Newgen Imaging Systems (P) Ltd., Chennai, India.

First edition: December 2009

10 9 8 7 6 5 4 3 2 1

Printed in the United States of America.

Transferred to Digital Printing in 2011

Contents

Illustrations

Series Editors' Foreword

The history of the United States during the past 150 years is marked by enormous change, but also by more than a modicum of continuity. The tension between the two helps make the history of the period a fascinating chronicle of economic and political transformation, war and peace, racial and ethnic division as well as unity, and cultural cohesion and cleavage. Historians often slice and dice the period covered in this volume with labels such as Reconstruction, the Gilded Age, Populism, Progressivism, the Twenties, the Great Depression and the New Deal, the Cold War, the Age of Reagan, and so on. In *Speaking History*, Sue Armitage and Laurie Mercier divide their work into five chronological periods and bring together some of the best examples of how oral history helps to illuminate the nation's past.

Their emphasis on the role of *ordinary people* reveals one of the several ways that oral history can be useful. It also can be employed to capture the stories of the movers and shakers, such as the decision-makers who govern or who oversee large corporations. Those people often leave written records and have their activities chronicled in newspapers or other media. In their case, the oral history normally attempts to get beyond what already is known, to ask questions not answered by other available information, to fill in the gaps. The people of interest to Armitage and Mercier, the "unfamous," usually don't leave written records, and when they do appear in the public record, it is often as the object of state intervention, not on their own terms. An oral history interview provides the sole opportunity to obtain their version of life stories or accounts of a specific event or activity. Since the middle of the 20th century such accounts have been planned tape recorded, or more recently, digitally recorded interviews. However, because the chronology of this volume extends back to the period of Reconstruction, the editors creatively have included material not captured with the help of audio technology. As this book's early selections reveal, interviews were conducted and recorded in writing long before these devices existed. The resulting transcripts reflected as much the person who wrote down the interview as the individual interviewed. For example, see the first excerpt in this volume with Boston Blackwell, a former slave.

Whatever the means used to obtain them, capturing spoken words brings history alive. Quotes by ordinary people humanize the historical narrative. Among the selected oral histories herein, readers of this volume will find many instances that prove the point. An African American who came to Detroit during the Great

Migration explained how insignificant he felt when he walked through the crowded Detroit Athletic Club: "I thought everybody in the world was looking at me. *There wasn't a soul seeing me.* Who the hell is going to see a busboy?" The implications for issues of race and class at the time are palpable. An Oklahoman, or "Okie," who migrated to California aptly describes the Dust Bowl and remarks, "You couldn't even tell where the sun was." A Japanese American recounts her feelings at the time of internment during World War II: "*I felt like an ant.* I wanted to shrivel up into nothing." Less dramatically, a resident of Fairfax, Virginia incisively portrays everyday, mundane life in an American suburb during the 1950s and 1960s. Those who *speak history* have much to say even when discussing the ordinary.

Beyond giving us new knowledge of those otherwise absent from history and humanizing them, oral history can complicate the generalities with which surveys of United States history necessarily proceed. That is, oral history shows us in a more fine-grained way the continuities and changes of a given period, the fits and starts by which the trajectory of "history" moves, and also the human consequences of the "big events" of the past.

This volume adds a new dimension to the Palgrave Studies in Oral History series, which already includes sixteen books. These ordinarily cover a single topic such as those most recently published about African Americans and Hurricane Katrina or about reactions to the war in Iraq; others concentrate on the experience of a single individual such as Sue Kunitomi Embrey, who led the movement for redress of Japanese Americans interned during World War II. Usually, the interviews on which the books are based primarily come from one oral history collection. *Speaking History*, on the other hand, covers the entire panorama of U. S. history since Reconstruction and mines the collections of a variety of the nation's archives, large and small. It also includes a guide on how to conduct an oral history for those interested in doing so. It will assist those who seek to understand change and continuity in American society over the past century and a half.

Bruce M. Stave
University of Connecticut

Linda Shopes
Carlisle, Pennsylvania

Acknowledgments

Our first thanks go to the people who asked us to undertake this project in the first place, Linda Shopes and Bruce Stave, longtime members and officers of the national Oral History Association and editors of the Palgrave Oral History series. Special thanks are also owed to Chris Chappell at Palgrave for his support, patience, and keeping this book on track; to Tess Rond of Washington State University (WSU) for her computer skills and intelligent questions; and to the WSU History Department for its assistance.

This project would have been impossible without the help of oral historians and archivists all over the country. The long list that follows is one way to say thanks. Oral histories came to us from many individuals and institutions. Listed alphabetically, they are:

American Century Project, St. Andrew's Episcopal School, Potomac, Maryland
American Indian Research Project, University of South Dakota
American West Center, University of Utah
Bancroft Library, University of California Berkeley
Baylor University Institute for Oral History
Center for Documentary Studies, Duke University
Center for Oral and Public History, California State University Fullerton
Center for History and New Media, George Mason University
Center for the Study of History and Memory, Indiana University
Gloria Cuadraz, Arizona State University
Detroit Urban League
Dust Bowl Migration Digital Archives, Walter W. Stiern Library, California State University Bakersfield
Experience Music Project | Science Fiction Museum and Hall of Fame, Seattle
Charles Hardy, "Goin' North: Tales of the Great Migration" radio documentary
Hoover Library, Stanford University
Hudson River Museum, Yonkers, New York
Idaho State Historical Society
Latah County (Idaho) Historical Society
Sydney Lewis, Rochester, Massachusetts
Library of Congress, "Born in Slavery" collection

Library of Congress, American Memory project
Maine Folklife Center, University of Maine
Minnesota Historical Society
Montana Historical Society
Nevada Test Site Oral History Project, University of Nevada Las Vegas
Northwest Women's Oral History Project
Louie B. Nunn Center for Oral History, University of Kentucky Libraries
Oklahoma Historical Society
Oral History Research Office, Columbia University
Sandy Polishuk, Portland, Oregon
Project Jukebox, University of Alaska Fairbanks
Regional Oral History Office, University of California Berkeley
Southern Oral History Program, University of North Carolina
Dan Terkel, Chicago
United States Senate Historical Office
University at Albany, State University of New York
University of Southern Mississippi Oral History Program
Veterans History Project, American Folklife Center, Library of Congress
Vietnam Center and Archive, Texas Tech University
Washington Women's History Consortium, Washington State Historical Society
Women in Journalism Oral History Project, Washington Press Club Foundation
Youngstown (Ohio) State University Archives and Special Collections
Judy Yung, San Francisco

Introduction

This volume of oral histories features the voices of Americans who lived through some of the most critical events shaping the nation's history since the Civil War. Their memories bring history alive, lending an unequalled immediacy to the past. In the process, they give us a glimpse of a new kind of history. Conventionally, we tend to think of History with a capital H: a narrative of great events—wars, elections, and enterprise—decided by the prominent people in charge—generals, presidents, and CEOs. And in most history textbooks, generalizations drown out the particular, the voices of ordinary individuals are lost, and what we remember are the words and actions of the famous (and infamous). This volume seeks to illuminate the particular experiences of ordinary Americans and how they participated in and observed history in the making. Here, they speak to us about themes familiar and unfamiliar: about migration, family life, discrimination, labor, leisure, social movements, depression, and wars. In so doing, they reveal the many ways in which individual experience and historical events intersect. On the one hand, they show us how individuals live through, and affect, great historical events. And at the same time, they aid our historical understanding by providing texture and depth to historians' generalizations.

For thousands of years peoples of the world have relied on the spoken word to understand history. In the late nineteenth century, however, as history became an organized academic discipline, scholars became suspicious of oral sources and considered only written records as reliable. The inevitable result was "top down" history, because records were created only by those who were able to write or who were so notable that others wanted to write about them. Only in the mid-twentieth century did historians begin to rediscover the value of oral reminiscences. In the depth of the Great Depression of the 1930s, the Federal Writers Project employed writers to document American lifeways and culture by interviewing elderly people of special interest—ex-slaves, western pioneers, workers in certain occupations, immigrants, and their children—and then writing up the interviews. What made these interviews unique was precisely the fact that they were not with well-known people, nor about celebrated events. In spite of an obvious bias toward a nostalgic vision of rural America, the interviews provided the first real opportunity for ordinary Americans (especially the 2,000 former slaves) to speak for themselves about their own lives.

Following World War II, the advent of new technology—the tape recorder—and the desire to obtain a more complete record of those who had led notable lives or were eyewitnesses to significant events led to the formal creation of the first academic oral history programs and archives. Allan Nevins founded the Columbia Oral History Research Office in 1948. The University of California at Berkeley, UCLA, and several presidential libraries initiated oral history programs in the 1950s and 1960s. These programs sought to record the memories of the nation's "movers and shakers" about what we might call "the story behind the story." Why did a politician propose a controversial bill? What were his personal, private reasons? What happened behind the scenes? Whom did he contact, make deals with, work against? Who were his rivals, who his collaborators? What was he really like in his unguarded, offstage moments? These kinds of interviews with public figures have added considerably to our understanding of political and institutional history.

It was the social movements of the 1960s and 1970s that spawned new interest in the lives of people formerly ignored by the historical record—women, workers, racial/ethnic minorities, people of different sexual orientations, children—and oral history became a popular method for discovering and capturing those "hidden" histories. An entire generation of historians became motivated to write what is commonly known as social history, by which we mean the history of interactions of different groups in society rather than the more customary narrative of politics and economics. Beginning in the 1970s, large numbers of schools, local historical societies, and university and state programs launched oral history projects to capture the reminiscences of both the known and not-so-well known people. You will find interviews from a number of these projects in the pages that follow. Indeed, there are thousands of oral history interviews stored in archives all over the country; increasingly, these can be found in digital formats on the Internet. A major purpose of this volume is to encourage our readers to appreciate the richness of the source material that these archived oral histories can provide.

What exactly is oral history? It is much more than a conversation between two people about past events. Oral history refers to a planned and recorded interview in which the interviewer helps the narrator recall certain experiences in full detail. For the narrator, the process of reflecting often elicits spontaneous thoughts and emotions, bringing a sense of immediacy that even the best-written recollections lack. Interviewers also have an important part to play in the questions they ask, and in how they encourage full recollection. Narrators often react differently to different interviewers, depending on race, age, gender, and familiarity. You will see many varieties of interviewer-narrator interaction in the following pages, but even in the selections where the questions have been removed, it is important to remember that oral history is a collaboration between two people, not a monologue, and created at a particular point in time.

Using Oral History

What makes oral history such a valuable source for our understanding of history? And what did we mean when we say that these interviews are the building blocks of a new kind of history?

We look to oral histories to answer a number of questions. The first that we all feel is the urge to recapture significant events: what was it like to be there? What did you see when the World Trade Towers collapsed on 9/11? What did you do on 9/11? What was it like to serve as a soldier in World War II or to migrate from China to the United States at the end of the nineteenth century? But we also seek to find out how people lived their lives from day to day. How did you survive on your wages as a domestic worker? What was a typical work day like in the steel mill? What can you recall of the games you played in childhood, or the foods prepared by your parents or grandparents? As narrators remember what happened and what they did, they can make past events come alive again for all of us. Through their eyes we can see the past—or a little slice of it. The memories of individuals contain a wealth of information, information that is usually not available in any other form. By giving voice to people heretofore excluded or ignored in the usual historical sources, oral history can provide a fuller, more honest picture of the past.

But are these memories reliable? Memory is a tricky thing. As we age, some memories become sharper while others dim. Often the popular or collective memory of events such as a natural catastrophe or a labor strike drowns out or alters our own individual recollections. And we know that one single memory can't tell it all. The problem with "eyewitness" oral history, for example, is that no single reminiscence can contain the whole truth. Famously, when Cornelius Ryan decided to write the "truth" of the D Day invasion of Normandy by interviewing survivors, he found so many conflicting stories that he abandoned his goal of writing the absolutely final, definitive "history." In a larger sense, it seems fair to say that oral histories are a way for people to make sense of their pasts, even if all the details are not precisely accurate.

The full possibilities of oral history begin to become clear when we think of all the people who will never write their memoirs, never save their letters or emails and donate them to an archive, never keep a diary or share it with anyone. We have never known how most people lived their daily lives, or what they thought. Today, however, we have the tools to interview almost anyone. We have the means to document a genuine peoples' history. Of course we cannot in fact interview everyone, but we can now realistically aim to write a popular history, based on the idea: we all make history. Each one of us, in our life choices, makes our own history, even if under circumstances inherited from the past. All of us, with our combined choices and reactions, make our national history. Those actions, of course, are shaped by structures often beyond our control, for example the decisions made by officials to go to war, or by corporations to lay off workers and move operations to another country. At any given moment, all that may be obvious is a huge jumble of conflicting actions and opinions, but out of that very diversity emerges a direction that in hindsight we call "history."

Oral history has been a key tool in this exciting process of discovery. All the new voices have vastly complicated any simple version of American history. These reminiscences enrich, illuminate, and often contradict older versions of the meaning of events, and they lead us to ask new questions. Each oral history is individual, and it tells an individual story. As our experiences have differed, so have our beliefs, values, and perceptions. Some people find this diversity of viewpoints upsetting, fearing that we are losing the unity and shared beliefs that hold us together as a nation. But for many others, the diversity is the story. New viewpoints challenge us to think of the past in wider and more comprehensive ways, and in their complexity, make history more compelling. In that spirit, we offer a variety of perspectives in the following pages. We invite you to hear the past speak in many voices.

Navigating Speaking History

In the following pages we present excerpts from fifty oral history interviews that exemplify major themes in American history since 1865. We chose them from among the thousands of interviews in oral history archives all over the country. Recognizing the fallibility of memory, we make no claim that the oral histories we have chosen "tell the whole truth." We chose interviews that, in our view, seemed accurate to the facts of history as we know them, but our primary purpose was to select interviews that provided more than usual depth of insight into the life of an individual and his or her times. There are many other interview examples that could not be included because of space limitations. We urge you to explore the rich variety of the country's oral history archives, many of which have excellent indexes and substantial collections available through the Internet.

The five sections that follow are divided chronologically: 1865–1900; 1900–1920; 1920–1945; 1945–1965; 1965–2000. Beginning with a very brief introduction to the major events of the period, each section offers about ten oral histories, drawn from archives all over the country, to illuminate major themes. Five of the constant themes across all sections are war, migration, race, culture, and work, while within each section other themes will be prominent as well. To a large extent, we let each oral history "speak for itself," while also pointing out specific characteristics of each interview. Each example comes from a longer interview; many of the transcribed interviews are available in their entirety in electronic form on the Internet or from the institution noted. We have lightly edited most interviews by removing repeated phrases, eliminating some questions, and indicating by ellipses where we made cuts. Brackets indicate editorial clarifications, either by the interviewer, transcriber, or by us.

In each thematic section, we ask questions to guide you in thinking about how these oral histories expand, modify or challenge our current historical understanding. In this way, we encourage you to join us in thinking about history as the ongoing story of people shaping their own lives. As they speak history, they point the way to a new sense of the past.

Finally, the Appendix gives you the tools to undertake an oral history yourself. There you will find a brief "how to" guide for conducting and preserving an interview, as well as a bibliography and list of websites with further helpful information. The opportunity to interview a person about historical events through which they lived is a way in which you personally can bring history alive. You will probably hear things you did not expect to hear—the surprise value of oral history is one of its greatest pleasures! Many people have a lot to tell us about their pasts. By helping them speak their histories they enrich our own.

ONE

1865–1900

The consequences of the Civil War shaped every aspect of American life in the second half of the nineteenth century. The South had to be rebuilt and the fate of four million African-American former slaves decided. Race relations were the paramount, and the most controversial, southern concern. Race was also an issue in the vast new western territories that the United States had taken in 1848 at the end of the Mexican-American War. Many Americans believed that westward expansion required control over the American Indian and Mexican inhabitants of the region and its resources.

Another consequence of the Civil War was a fundamental change in size and organization of society. Large industries originally created by wartime needs now contributed to a vastly accelerated rate of industrialization that attracted massive immigration from Europe and Asia. The growth of industrial capitalism provoked unprecedented conflict about wages, working conditions, and power in American society. At the very moment when individual homesteaders were establishing farms and ranches in the West, a new, larger scale of organization—what one historian has called "the incorporation of America"—was transforming the society of small towns and small businesses that had been the norm before the Civil War.

The nine interviews in this section introduce you to the voices of nineteenth century Americans as they coped with these major adjustments in their lives. The first five interviews concern different aspects of *race relations* in the period 1865–1900, in the South and in the West, followed by two interviews about *work on the western agricultural frontier*, by a farmer and a cowboy. Two *immigration* accounts, one from the East Coast, one from the West, follow. Finally, this section concludes with an account of a battle that epitomized the bitter nature of the *industrial war* of the period. Each thematic section provides questions that focus on what these oral histories add to our sense of history.

None of the interviews in this section were preserved with mechanical recording devices. Unlike later sound recordings, in the nineteenth century the accuracy of an interview depended on the interviewer and how well he or she listened and transcribed. Accuracy also depended on the interviewer's intent: sometimes it seemed important to reproduce exact words and speech patterns; in other cases interviewers paraphrased the spoken narrative. When reading the interviews in this section, the reader should always keep in mind that the very words the narrator "speaks" come to us literally through the interviewer as that person decides how to write down the narrator's words. The selections that follow introduce the reader to various choices made by interviewers about how they present the reminiscence.

Race Relations

In the South, federally imposed Reconstruction following the Civil War intended to give four million ex-slaves political and civil rights. In 1865 General William T. Sherman granted economic independence, represented by land and the means to cultivate it—the famous "forty acres and a mule"—to black families on the coasts of South Carolina, Georgia, and Florida. But Andrew Johnson revoked the provision when he became president after the assassination of Abraham Lincoln. As a result, few ex-slaves were able to withstand the violence and coercion of the Ku Klux Klan and economic pressures from landowners, who quickly established the labor system known as sharecropping. Although no longer enslaved, African Americans were forced to sign contracts with white landowners for land and tools, and in return paid the owner a share of each year's crop. Many soon found themselves in debt to their landlords. White southerners claimed that former slaves were too ignorant and indolent to survive without this strict control. In the decades after Reconstruction ended in 1877, whites established a system of segregation (Jim Crow), and denied voting rights to African Americans as well.

In the lands that the United States had conquered from Mexico, two groups came under American control: the Mexicans in California, Arizona, New Mexico, and Texas; and American Indians. The Mexicans lost their lands and influence, and few were able to become U.S. citizens, although the Treaty of Guadalupe Hidalgo technically guaranteed citizenship. American Indians, overwhelmed by Euro-American settlers and the United States military, were confined to reservations. In effect, both groups were racially marked as inferior. When most Americans thought about Mexicans and American Indians at all, they echoed journalist John O'Sullivan, who claimed that it was "our manifest destiny to overspread the continent allotted [to us] by Providence," ignoring the rights of the people who were already there.

Questions to Consider: The first three interviews, one by an ex-slave and another by two members of the next generation of African Americans, illustrate how the initial hopes of freedom were lost. The last two interviews, from an elite Spanish Mexican woman and from a survivor of the Wounded Knee massacre of 1890, illustrate different kinds of conquest and resistance. Note how language matters in these interviews. Beulah Hagg probably believed that she was "authentic" when she wrote Boston Blackwell's interview in dialect. Thomas Savage, the interviewer of Doña Angustias, was proud of his ability to transcribe Spanish at high speed word for word. James McGregor interviewed Dewey Beard through an interpreter.

1. In what ways do the first three narrators contradict the southern stereotype of former slaves as ignorant and childlike?
2. How do these five narrators demonstrate resistance?
3. In what ways does language itself affect the interview? Can we regard these interviews as authentically "in their own words?" And even when we hear the recorded voices of Hughsey Childes and Minnie Whitney, do we know enough about them from these brief excerpts to be able to fully understand their testimony?

The End of Slavery: Boston Blackwell

Source Note: The first interview is from the nation's most famous oral history collection, the slave narratives collected by the Federal Writers Project in the 1930s. Over 2000 former slaves were interviewed and their memories preserved in the Library of Congress. For years the collection was controversial. Many historians questioned the accuracy of the accounts. After all, by the 1930s, ex-slaves were elderly and their memories faded. Historians also questioned how well the interviews represented former slaves. Although 2,000 was a large sample, it was only 2 percent of the total slave population. Also, would elderly black people speak frankly with the interviewers, most of whom were white? For these and other reasons, scholars generally ignored the interviews until the 1970s, when as a consequence of the civil rights movement, historians came to realize that the interviews contained valuable insight into the day-to-day reality of slavery as it was experienced by those who endured it. Today *Born in Slavery: Slave Narratives from the Federal Writers' Project, 1936–1938* is a major online resource of the Library of Congress at http://memory.loc.gov/ammem/snhtml/.

Boston Blackwell was 98 years old when he was interviewed in 1938 in Little Rock, Arkansas, but his energetic recollections show that he was neither senile nor intimidated by his interviewer, Beulah Hagg, who was white. He tells a vivid story of hard work, hope, and disappointment: "That old story 'bout 40 acres and a mule, it make me laugh." Blackwell describes several experiences typical of ex-slaves, including escape to Union lines, being welcomed as a "contraband" and put to work, and that he had pension and voting rights. The interviewer chose to convey the voice and style of this narrator by the use of dialect in her transcript of the interview, a choice that was common in the 1930s but can seem demeaning today.

Make yourself comfoble, miss. I can't see you much 'cause my eyes, they is dim. My voice, it kinder dim too. I knows my age, good. Old Miss, she told me when I got sold "Boss, you is 13—borned Christmas. Be sure to tell your new misses and she put you down in her book." My borned name was Pruitt 'cause I got borned on Robert Pruitt's plantation in Georgia,—Franklin County, Georgia. But Blackwell, it my freed name. You see, miss, after my mammy got sold down to Augusta—I wisht I could tell you the man what bought her, I ain't never seed him since—I was sold to go to Arkansas; Jefferson county, Arkansas. Then was when old Miss telled me I am 13. It was before the Civil War I come here. The onliest auction of slaves I ever seed as in Memphis, coming on to Arkansas. I heerd a girl bid off for $800. She was about fifteen, I reckon. I heard a woman—a breeding woman, bid off for $1500. They always brought good money. I'm telling you, it was when we was coming from Atlanta.

Do you want to hear how I runned away and jined the Yankees? You know Abraham Lincoln 'claired freedom in '63, first day of January [the Emancipation Proclamation]. In October '63, I runned away and went to Pine Bluff to get to the Yankees. I was on the Blackwell plantation south of Pine Bluff in '63. They was building a new house; I wanted to feel some putty in my hand. One early morning I clim a ladder to get a little chunk and the overseer man, he seed me. Here he come, yelling me to get down; he g'wine whip me 'cause I'se a thief, he say. He call a slave boy and tell him cut ten willer whips; he gwine wear every one out on me. When he 'a gone to eat breakfas', I runs to my cabin and tells my sister, "I'se leaving this here place for good." She cry and say, "Overseer man, he kill you." I says, "He kill me anyhow." The young boy what cut the whips—he named Jerry—he come along wif me, and we wade the stream for long piece. Heard the hounds a-howling, getting ready for to chase after us. Then we hide in dark woods. It was cold, frosty weather. Two days and two nights we traveled. That boy, he so cold and hongry, he want to fall out by the way, but I drug him on. When we gets to the Yankee camp all our troubles was over. We gets all the contraband we could eat. Was they more runaways there? Oh, Lordy, yessum. Hundreds, I reckon. Yessum, the Yankees feeds all them refugees on contraband. They made me a driver of a team in the quartermasters department. I was always keerful to do everything they telled me. They telled me I was free when I gets to the Yankee camp, but I couldn't go outside much. Yessum, iffen you could get to the Yankee's camp you was free right now.

That old story 'bout 40 acres and a mule, it make me laugh. Yessum, they sure did tell us that, but I never knowed any pusson which got it. The officers tolled us we would all get slave pension. That just exactly what they tell. They sure did tell me I would get a passel [parcel] of ground to farm. Nothing ever hatched out of that, neither.

When I got to Pine Bluff I stayed contraband. When the battle come, Captain Manly carried me down to the battle ground and I stay there till fighting was over. I was a soldier that day. No'um, I didn't shoot no gun nor cannon. I carried water from the river for to put out the fire in the cotton bales what made the breas' works. Every time the 'Federates shoot, the cotton, it come on fire; so after the battle, they transfer me back to quartemaster for driver. Captain Dodridge as his name. I served in Little Rock under Captain Haskell. I was swored in for during the war (Boston held up his right hand and repeated the words of allegiance). It was on the corner of Main and Markham street in Little Rock I was swored in. Year of '64. I was 5 feet, 8 inches high. You says did I like living in the army? Yes-sum, it was purty good. Iffen you obeyed them Yankee officers they treated you purty good, but iffen you didn't, they sure went rough on you.

You says you wants to know how I live after soldiers all go away? Well, firstes thing, I work on the railroad. They was just beginning to come here. I digged pits out, going along front of where the tracks was to go. How much I get? I get $1.00 a day. You axes me how it seem to earn money? Lady, I felt like the richess man in the world: I boarded with a white fambly. Always I was a watching for my slave pension to begin coming. 'Fore I left the army my captain, he telled me to file. My file number, it is lll585... Lady, that number for me is filed in Washington. Iffen you go there, see can you get my pension.

After the railroad I went steamboating. First one was a little one; they call her Fort Smith 'cause she go from Little Rock to Fort Smith. It was funny, too, her captain was name Smith. Captain Eugene Smith was his name. He was good, but the mate was sure rough. What did I do on that boat? Missy, was you ever on a river boat? Lordy, they's plenty to do. Never is no time for rest. Load, onload, scrub. Just you do whatever you is told to do and do it right now, and you'll keep outen trouble, on a steamboat, or a railroad, or in the army, or wherever you is. That's what I knows.

Yessum, I reckon they was right smart old masters what didn't want to let they slaves go after freedom. They hated to turn them loose. Just let them work on. Heap of them didn't know freedom come. I used to hear tell how the govmint had to send soldiers away down in the far back country to make them turn the slaves loose. I can't tell you how all them free niggers was living; I was too busy lookin out for myself. Heaps of them went to farming. They was share croppers.

Yessum, miss, them Ku-Kluxers was turrible, what they done to people. Oh, God, they was bad. They come sneaking up and runned you outen your house and take everything you had. They was rough on the women and chilren.

People all wanted to stay close by where soldiers was. I sure knowed they was my friend.

Lady, lemme tell you the rest about when I runned away. After peace, I got with my sister. She's the onliest of all my people I ever seed again. She telled me she was skeered all that day, she couldn't work, she shake so bad. She heerd overseer man getting ready to chase me and Jerry. He saddle his horse, take his gun and pistol, bofe. He gwine kill me on sight, but Jerry, he say he bring him back, dead or alive, tied to his horse's tail. But he didn't get us, ha, ha, ha. Yankees got us.

Now you wants to know about this voting business. I voted for Genral Grant. Army man come around and registered you before voting time. It wasn't no trouble to vote them days; white and black all voted together. All you had to do was tell who you was vote for and they give you a colored ticket. All the men up had different colored tickets. Iffen you're voting for Grant, you get his color. It was easy. Yes Mam! Gol 'er mighty. They was colored men in office, plenty. Colored legislaturs, and colored circuit clerks, and colored county clerks. They sure as some big officers colored in them times. They was all my friends. This here used to be a good county, but I tell you it sure is tough now. I think it's wrong—exactly wrong that we can't vote now. The Jim Crow law, it put us out. The Constitution of the United States, it give us the right to vote; it made us citizens, it did.

Image 1 An African American sharecropper (Library of Congress).

Sharecropping and Violence: Hughsey Childes and Minnie Whitney

Source Note: In 1984, when oral historian Charles Hardy interviewed African Americans who had left the South for Philadelphia, he recorded vivid memories of sharecropping. These two short interviews with Hughsey Childes and Minnie Whitney can be heard in the first program of Hardy's radio documentary Goin' North: Tales of the Great Migration at http://www.talkinghistory.org/hardy.html.

Hughsey Childes: There was a man had been, was working sharecrop for a gentleman and naturally, he couldn't read or either write. And every year, regardless of how much cotton he made he would just bring him out so he would have just a little bit left. So he got kinda wise and where he would get at the harvest time. And he made six bales of cotton that year, and he took four to count on the wagon. And his white landlord that he was renting, he was sharecropping with, met him. And there are cotton bales on the street.

When the four bales of cotton was sold the amount of money they came to, they went to the bank. And naturally in sharecropping, the man that you sharecrop with, he pays for half and you pay for half. So when everything was over, he told him, he said, "You did marvelous this year, you cleared $350." But now this 350 dollars got to last him till they start to farm again.

So the colored fellow didn't say anything at all, but in a couple of weeks he took two more bales of cotton to town. So when he [the white owner] met him he called him up and told him he wanted to see him in town. So when he met him, he said, "I had an idea that you had been cheating me, but I didn't have no way of knowing it." He said, "Now you say I don't owe you anything?" He says, "No, you paid off and you cleared $350." He said, "Now when we sell I got two more bales of cotton." So, he says, "Why didn't you tell me that at first? Now, I got to go over all these figures, and you might clear just a little something."

So anyway from that they started a argument. And this white man jumped on him, and hitched the horses to him, like he was a wagon and drove him, and drug him through the street—in Abbeville, South Carolina—and took him down in the park, and hung him. Now that's just as true as I'm looking at you. But you wasn't allowed to say anything about it.

Minnie Whitney: Papa raised everything that we ate, even to cows, hogs, chickens, and he raised corn that we could make cornmeal out of, bread and everything else. He didn't have to go to the store and buy too many. He raised the potatoes—two kinds—greens, beans, cabbage, everything. And also strawberries, he had that. And when I was a kid, we used to—what they call the blueberries now, every time I have blueberries—they used to grow wild and we'd go through the woods and pick them. In the summertime, you'd have to be careful, otherwise, a snake would drop down on your head.

And well, it—I would say—my life with my parents, it wasn't too hard like. Because see, my father was a, he was a good sharecropper. And the children that come up with those parents that had a farm...you didn't know too much about hard times, you know like for food and clothes. Because two things my father always made up his mind to do: he was gonna feed us and give us some clothes on our back, even if it was something was left over from somebody else that my mother would fix. But I see so many there was rougher than ours. Because their parents wasn't progressive to go out and they just lived for whatever.

The white man would say, "Well, come and work for me, and I'll give you this, and give you that." They lived for that. They didn't try to make a farm for anything for themselves. But my father always kept hogs and he kept a cow for milk and they had horses to truck the farm.

You see my father, his mother and father both were slaves. And my mother's father and mother both were slaves. And, you know, was a rule they say that whatever the white man would tell them, they believed him. And if he says, "Well, you didn't earn but five dollars this year," they believed him. So see someone was still livin' under the bonds of slavery.

...Then when we would get together on Sunday, when we meet we say a whole lot of things which we wish we could do [to resist]. And say "When we do get grown, we're gonna do somethin'." But I didn't. But some of them did go back and do some of the things they said they were gonna do. But I didn't because I thought about my parents and I know—if I did somethin' that wasn't right down there to them people or say too many things—they would get my father...

I was very careful in what I did, because I didn't want my parents to get hurt. Because they would hurt them. They would hurt them. I'm tellin' you those Southern people, them white Southern people where I came from, they were rough. And if you meet them on a road, and if you, if it was a road, and you had to go by—it was a little small—if you was there first you better wait there until they come by. It was just somethin' that now I begin to understand, how I felt about it. And I always said, "If I'd knowed then what I know now I guess I wouldn't be here." Because you know you speak out, you get hurt.

A *California* Remembers the War: Doña Angustias de la Guerra

Source Note: In California, the historian/entrepreneur Hubert H. Bancroft made his fortune publishing a series of histories of the states and provinces of the Far West. Gathering a large collection of primary documents, Bancroft hired assistants to write 39 separate histories, published between 1874 and 1890 on the peoples and politics of the western states and territories from Mexico to Alaska. To supplement the written materials, interviews were conducted with local political figures. In California, this included interviews in Spanish with *Californios,* the Spanish Mexican residents and rulers of Alta California before the U.S. conquest. Most of the Bancroft interviews lay quietly in the library named for him (Bancroft Library, University of California at Berkeley) until the growth of Chicano history in the 1970s. Today there are several printed versions of the interviews, among them the one used here: Rose Marie Beebe and Robert M. Senkewitcz, translators, *Testimonios: Early California through the Eyes of Women, 1815–1848* (Berkeley: Heyday Books and The Bancroft Library, University of California, Berkeley, 2006).

Doña Angustias de la Guerra was typical of Bancroft's narrators in that she was a member of the Californio elite (her father, husband, and brothers were all prominent political figures). Women had no official role in Californio politics, but the fact that Doña Angustias was able to fully answer the detailed political questions of her interviewer, Thomas Savage, might have made him wonder whether (as Doña Angustias herself believed) women were more active in politics than he had assumed. At the beginning of this excerpt, Doña Angustias refers impatiently to the complicated regional and colonial struggles Savage had asked about earlier in the interview but then she launches into an account of her own very female act of resistance. She was interviewed in 1878, when, as she was well aware, the land holdings and privileged status of Californios had been lost to the Americans.

The taking of California [by the United States] was not at all to the liking of the Californios and least of all to the women. But I must confess, California was on the road to utter ruin. On the one hand, the Indians were out of control, committing robberies and other crimes at the ranchos. Little or nothing was being done to curb their pillaging. On the other hand, there was discord between the people of the north and the south [of California]. In addition, both north and south were against the Mexicans from the mainland [Mexico]. But the worst cancer of all was the widespread thievery. There was such squandering of government resources that the funds in the treasury office had bottomed out...

The Americans took the entire country [in 1846–1847]. They occupied the ports and the pueblos and even the city of Los Angeles. When Commodore [Robert] Stockton withdrew from Los Angeles, he left a small garrison there under the command of Señor [Archibald] Gillespie... The Californios from that area, and many from the north who had headed south with [Jośe] Castro, raised the banner of revolution and forced Gillespie and his troops to head to San Pedro and board ship there. The Californios retook control of Los Angeles, where they began to make the necessary preparations for a strong defense. Captain José Maria Flores was in charge as governor and commander general, and my uncle Don José Antonio Carrillo was major general... After the reoccupation of Los Angeles, certain individuals from the north who were in the southern ranks formulated a plan to create a diversion in the north that would undermine the enemy... Their plan was to descend upon the [Americans] at San Juan de Castro and take all of [John] Frémont's horses as well as those belonging to the rest of the American leaders. Thus the Americans would be left to travel on foot and it would be impossible for them to move quickly... [But the plot was discovered] A rather hard-fought battle [between the Californios and the Americans] took place [near San Juan de

Castro] in which two American officers and some other men died. Several others were injured. On the Californio side, two men died (one Chilean and another man). Several men were injured, among them José Antonio Chávez and the standard bearer, *Alférez* Juan Ignacio Cantúa...

After the battle, Chávez was hidden in the home of some Indians who lived in those parts... From there Chávez went to Monterey to the home of Francisco Day, an American. Day was married to a Californio woman. She was loyal to the Californio cause but her husband was a bitter enemy of the Californios. At that time, however, Day was at his rancho near Tehama...

One night, when the owner of the house [Day] arrived, Chávez was there and he knew it. Because he was such an enemy of the Californios, Day tried to catch Chávez by surprise, but he was not able to. Instead of entering through the door, Day jumped over the adobe wall. Chávez found out in the nick of time that Day had returned and jumped over the wall to another house. Day fired his pistol at him but missed. Chávez fell into the yard of the other house and dislocated his foot. This little house belonged to an old Mexican soldier. The house consisted of two very small rooms where the family lived. The soldier had several children. The soldier did not know what to do with Chávez, so he wrapped him up in a blanket and stuck him under a bed. He told Chávez that he could not keep him in his house because his children might let on that he was there. Chávez thought it over and remembered that of all the people he knew, I was the one who lived the closest. He told the soldier to go and speak with me.

I was in bed because I had just given birth to a daughter a few days before. I was very surprised that the old soldier was so determined to speak with me in private. He told me what had happened to Chávez. He asked me, for the love of God, to come and take Chavez and hide him in house. The words "for the love of God" had a tremendous impact and they forced me to stop and think. My husband was away at our Rancho del Pájaro. Even though it was raining hard, I decided to get dressed and go see my brothers Pablo and Miguel, who were prisoners. I wanted their opinion as to what I should do, since I could not consult with my husband, because he was not there. Pablo told me that the first thing I should consider was that the American authorities probably knew where Chávez was and they would come after him. But if I believed that I could bring him back and hide him so he would not be found, then it would be an act of charity to do so. I was so angry with the Americans for mistreating my brothers and keeping them imprisoned for no rhyme nor reason. I angrily asked my brother if he really believed the Yankees could find someone I had hidden.

In short, I personally went to the soldier's house. Chávez and I talked about ways to take him to my home, since he was not able to walk because of his dislocated foot. The soldier's son-in-law was a short Portuguese man and Chávez was also short. So, if the two of them were put together they would form a man of normal height. The Portuguese man carried Chávez on his back. Chávez had a Spanish cape wrapped around him and was wearing a top hat which I had provided him with. That is how they got by my "señores Yankees" and by the guards and arrived at my home without being discovered. I had already returned home and had gotten back in bed, but before getting to bed I mentioned that I had gotten a chill from the dampness and needed two more narrow, lightweight blankets so that my bed would feel warmer. The space left without a blanket could be filled with more blankets. I did not tell anybody about my plan and nobody suspected a thing...

There was a full moon and during the night I heard a noise in the little den. Some sheep I owned had wandered in. I ordered a young Indian to go and tell the cook to remove those sheep. She had no more than opened the door when she saw armed soldiers. She immediately closed the door and came to warn me.

...And then we heard a knock at the door. I then told my servants that Chávez was hidden in my room because the Americans wanted to kill him... In the meantime, the Indian girls took out the blankets that had been used to fill the opening in my bed. We put Chávez inside that opening, with his face toward the wall so he could breathe easily. And since he was so very thin, the empty space around him was filled with blankets so that it would all look even. We placed my baby, Carolina, on top of the bed...

I should explain that there were powerful reasons to fear that Chávez would be killed if the Americans caught him. He was accused of being a spy... Besides, if the troops stationed in Monterey had been the regular, disciplined troops, perhaps there would not have been any reason for so much fear. But the garrison was comprised of people from every class, picked up from here and there, from land and sea. They were almost all adventurers who lacked discipline and a sense of responsibility. These were the people, fifty in number, who came to my home under the command of Lieutenant Baldwin...

Silva opened the door and said that he was not the owner of the home and that the lady of the house had retired to her bed. Lieutenant Baldwin said that it did not matter to him. They searched all the rooms and left a soldier on guard in each one... The lieutenant and his people finally came into my bedroom without uttering a single word. Baldwin had a pistol in one hand and a candle in the other. He searched underneath my bed and did not find a thing. Then he came close to where I was and put the candle and the pistol to my face. He told me that he had come looking for a man that was said to be hiding in my home. I asked him if he had found him and he said no. I told him that I was very pleased because I never had planned on lying to them. Then he said that he was rather tired and was very sorry that he had come and bothered me. He figured that I was probably somewhat scared and he wanted to grab a chair and sit down. I replied that nothing frightened me and he could go and rest in his own home, because only my family and friends were allowed to rest in my room. He said good night, but we did not respond in kind. The Americans left and Captain Silva accompanied them until they were out the door...

That search and military occupation of my home lasted from ten o'clock at night until about two or three o'clock in the morning. Chávez then came out from his hiding place and Silva's wife treated his injured foot. He told me, "Señora, I am alive today because of you." To which I replied, "What I did for you today, I would do for an American tomorrow if you were to unjustly do him harm." Chávez left my home two days later dressed as a woman. Around the Point of Pines, he got on a horse and then headed for Santa Barbara.

A Wounded Knee Survivor Remembers: Dewey Beard

Source Note: The massacre at Wounded Knee, South Dakota in December 1890 culminated more than twenty years of military efforts to confine western Indians to reservations. As their cultures disintegrated, some Indians turned to the Ghost Dance religion, which frightened the military authorities because they recognized the defiance embodied in the trancelike intensity of the dancing. Forbidden to practice it, some groups of Sioux at first fled the Pine Ridge reservation. Later, ill and starving, one band headed by Big Foot was returning to surrender when they encountered troops of the Seventh Cavalry at Wounded Knee. Soldiers killed at least 250 Indians. Although many people at the time deplored the scale of the massacre, the event effectively ended American Indian resistance to United States control. Fifty years later, James McGregor, "in the interest of justice [and] a duty toward the survivors" interviewed twenty-five Sioux about the event and published the interviews in *The Wounded Knee Massacre from the Viewpoint of the Sioux* (Rapid City SD: Fenske Printing, 1940).

One of the survivors, Dewey Beard, spoke to James McGregor in 1940, when Beard was 77 years old. Beard offers a very clear and detailed account of Sioux actions and expectations at the moment of encounter, but it should be remembered that he was speaking 50 years after the event. William Bergen served as the interpreter.

I was a member of the band that was killed here. Just a little beyond Porcupine Butte we were coming this way when we were met by the soldiers. Big Foot, who was sick and had been sick then for four days, had a hemorrhage, came up with a flag of truce tied to a stick. We were traveling in a peaceful manner, no intention of any trouble. I was told that this was an officer that came around to where Big Foot was laying, so I followed him up possibly a yard right behind him. I wanted to know what his intentions were. This officer asked Big Foot, "Are you the man that is named Big Foot and can you talk?" He asked him where he was going. I am going to my people who are camped down here. The officer then stated that he had heard that they had left Cheyenne River and the Army was on the lookout for him. "I have seen you and I am very glad to have met you. I want you to turn over your guns." Big Foot answered, "Yes, I am a man of that kind." The officer wanted to know what he meant by that, so the interpreter told him that he was a peaceful man. He says, "You have requested that I give you my guns, but I am going to a certain place and when I get there I will lay down my arms."

"Now, you meet us out here on the prairie and expect me to give you my guns out here. I am a little bit afraid that there might be something crooked about it, something that may occur that wouldn't be fair. There are a lot of children here." The officer then said they are bringing a wagon and I want you to get in that and they will take you down to where we are camped. Shortly a wagon drew up and they wrapped a blanket around him and placed him in the wagon and started to camp, so we followed. This side of the store, where you see these houses, is where we were camped and right this way is where the soldiers were camped. In the evening they unloaded some bacon, sugar and hardtack in the center and stated that someone should issue this out, so the women all came into the center and I am the one that issued it out to them. We heard a mule braying over this way and also heard the soldiers making a complete circle from the south to the north direction... That evening I noticed that they were erecting cannons up here, also hauling up quite a lot of ammunition for it. I could see them doing it. Shortly after we erected our camp, guards were stationed around. They were walking their beat. I also noticed that night besides the store there was some fires built there and we knew that they were the Indian Scouts. The following morning there was a bugle call shortly after that another bugle call, then I saw the soldiers mounting the horses and surrounding us. Even though they had surrounded us and we noticed all these peculiar actions, I never thought there was anything wrong. I thought it wouldn't be no time until we could be starting towards the Agency. It was announced that all men should come to the center for a talk and that after the talk they were to move on to Pine Ridge Agency. So they all came to the center. Shortly after that I also followed and came to the center where they all were gathered. After I got there and looked around and the men were just sitting around unconcerned. Big Foot was brought out of his tepee and sat in front of his tent and the older men were gathered around him and sitting right near him in the center. The interpreter said that the officer said that yesterday we promised some guns and that he was going to collect them now. I don't remember how many soldiers there were, but these soldiers were climbing on top of wagons, unpacking things, taking axes and other things, and they were taking them to where the guns were already laid down. Some of the Indians were further east that had guns in their arms but were not seen [by the soldiers] for some time... finally [the soldiers] called to them to bring their arms to the center and put them down. One of them started towards the center with his gun. This fellow that started said: "Now it was understood yesterday that we were to put down our guns after we reached the Agency, but here you are calling for our guns" so he took the gun and showed it to them.

He started towards the guns where they were laid down and one soldier started from the east side towards him and another from the west side towards this Indian. Even so, he was still unconcerned. He was not scared about it. If they had left him alone he was going to put his gun down where he should. They grabbed him and spinned him in the east direction. He was still unconcerned even then. He hadn't his gun pointed at anyone. His intention was to put that gun down. They came on and grabbed the gun that he was going to put down. Right after they spun him around there was the report of a gun, was quite loud. I couldn't say that anybody was shot but following that was a crash. The flag of truce that we had was stuck in the ground right there where we were sitting. They fired on us anyhow. Right after that crash, that is when all the people were falling over. I remained standing there for some little time and a man came up to me and I recognized him as a man known as High Hawk. He said, come on they have started this way, so let's go. So we started up this little hill; coming up this way, the soldiers started to shoot at us and as they did High Hawk was shot and fell down. I wasn't so [I] started back and then they knocked me down. I was alone so I was trying to look out for myself. They had killed my wife and baby. I saw men lying around, shot down. I went around them the best I could, got down in the ravine, then I fell down again. I was shot and wounded at the first time I told you that I fell. I went up this ravine and could see that they were traveling in that direction. I saw women and children lying all over there. They got up to a cut bank up the ravine and there I found a great many that were in there hiding. We were going to try and go on through the ravine but it was surrounded by the soldiers, so we just had to stay in that cut bank. Right near there was a butte with a ridge on it. They placed a cannon on it pointing in our direction and fired on us right along. I saw one man that was shot with one of these cannons. That man's name was Hawk Feather Shooter.

Work on the Western Agricultural Frontier

With the Mexicans deprived of political power and American Indians restricted to reservations, millions of white settlers made their way west between 1865 and 1900. By 1900, in spite of the drought and depression of the 1890s, three million people populated Kansas, Nebraska, North and South Dakota, Montana, Wyoming, Colorado and New Mexico. The 1862 Homestead Act, which promised free land to individuals and families that "proved up" by living on the land and farming for five years, attracted most of these migrants. Many families, including hundreds of thousands of new immigrants from northern and eastern Europe, were recruited by the new transcontinental railroads, who wanted settled land along their routes. The railroads were also responsible for many of the cattle drives of the 1870s and 1880s, in which cattle companies and their hired cowboys drove thousands of Texas cattle north to railheads in Kansas to be shipped to slaughterhouses in Chicago. The scale and speed of the westward migration and the drama of the cattle drives fed the popular imagination, and the figures of the cowboy and the homesteader quickly became symbols of the freedom and opportunity the West seemed to offer.

Questions to Consider: These two narrators exemplified two western occupations, farming and ranching, that came to symbolize the independence and opportunity of the rapid western settlement. In reality, many led lives of uncertainty and grinding hardship. These interviews raise questions about the relationship between the popular image of the West and the reality of individual lives.

1. What do these men choose to emphasize in their narratives? Why? What was important in their lives? Why do you think Will Berger's account jumps back and forth in time?
2. Note that oral histories like the previous interviews with Doña Angustias and Dewey Beard, who also lived in the West, were not included in the Federal Writers Project collection. Who was considered "western" and why?

A Homesteader's Account: Will H. Berger

Source Note: This interview with a farmer in Nebraska and the one that follows with a Texas cowboy were conducted by the same New Deal program, the Federal Writers Project, that produced the Boston Blackwell interview about slavery. The FWP interviewed "pioneers" and old timers as part of the larger project of writing guides to every state in the nation. These interviews, over 3000 of them, are now online at http://memory.loc.gov/ammem/wpaintro/wpahome.html. Together with the slave narratives, they form the largest collection of interviews with Americans prior to the use of the tape recorder, and the first significant collection to focus on daily life rather than on exceptional events.

Will H. Berger, a Nebraska farmer, was born in 1859. He shared his memories of his parents' homesteading and his own childhood with interviewer Edna B. Pearson in 1938. He most vividly remembers the natural challenges that early farmers faced and the yearly differences in crops.

In 1856 my father came to this country from Germany; he was six weeks crossing the ocean. He stopped in New York about a year and a half, then got the western fever and came as far as Chicago, and later wound up in Dubuque. There he met my mother and they were married in 1857. He then came on to Sioux City where he put in the winter of 1858 working at his trade of shoe maker…They came across the state of Iowa in an old spring wagon hitched to one horse; it took them almost half the summer to get across the state as there were no roads and no tiling, and the state of Iowa was just one big swamp. There were several families in the caravan; they landed at Sioux City [Nebraska]. In

1859 he came to Dakota County and homesteaded in Omadi precinct, on the place now known as the old Rymill place. My father's homestead joined the north line of the Winnebago reservation.

He gave up his homestead and enlisted in Company I in 1862 and went north to help take care of the Indians who perpetrated the Minnesota Massacre. [The Santee Sioux uprising of August, 1862.] When he was mustered out of the army in the fall of 1863 or 1864 he bought this quarter section in Townships 24 and 25, Range 8, and 80 acres adjoining. From then on he lived on the farm and worked at his trade some in the winter time, making shoes for the family and the neighbors.

It seemed as though they had one hardship after another for years. The years 1872, 1873 and 1874 were the grasshopper years; 1874 being the bad year. The grasshoppers came so thick. We were harvesting the oats and they had just left a narrow strip, about an acre, to thresh after dinner. When they came back to the field after dinner the stalks were stripped. They would come over in great clouds. That was the worst I ever saw. They would take everything except sugar cane. Of course the fields at that time were very small; that was the reason they could clean up a field so readily...

The winter of 1869–1870 a large number of Texas cattle were sent up here; the government was transporting them by foot; they were driving them; there was less then 25 per cent went through the winter. About 75 per cent froze to death. I have seen four or five stand in a bunch and freeze.

The winter of 1880 and spring of 1881 was the hardest winter that was experienced in Dakota County. Snow came on October 14th, 1880 and stayed on the ground until the next May. We didn't start to sow wheat until May 5th; the corn was left in the fields all winter, under three feet of snow, as the snow came so early, before we had done our husking. We husked corn the next spring and put in the next crop of corn right away; finished planting corn the 13th of June, 1881.

From 1880 to 1890 was not easy sledding. In the early 70's and until about 1880 they used to haul surplus grain to [the] Winnebago [reservation] and sell it to the government and it was issued to the Indians. Winnebago was our main market because we could get more there than any other place. People would sit up nights on the lookout for the Indians but they never harmed anyone around here. They would go past, fifty or a hundred, going back and forth visiting, from the Sioux and Wisconsins to the Winnebagoes and Omahas; a caravan would go back the next year, returning those visits. The early settlers used to have the Indian men work on the farms, binding grain and doing such work. In 1877 or 1878 the St. Cyr boys and an Indian by the name of Crow used to bind wheat here and shock it and help stack and pass bundles. They were nice boys and good help.

The spring of 1881 was the high water year, following that hard winter. We had a thaw in April for a couple of weeks of warm weather which took part of the three feet of snow they had had all winter, then following the thaw they had a fall of about two feet more of snow on top of that; then all went off, with about four feet of ice in the river breaking up, and then we did have water. From about three quarters of a mile west of me, west to the hills, was a solid mass of water.

In 1894 it was exceptionally dry; that year corn was practically a failure all over the country; oats was so short it couldn't be stacked; prices weren't very good. In 1896 we had ten cent corn; from that on until 1898 had pretty slow sledding; prices were poor. In 1898 things began to look up; prices began to advance, and from that time until 1914, up until the war, times were the best this country ever saw...

A Cowboy's Story: Richard Phillips

Source Note: This interview, like the one with Will Berger, was conducted by the Federal Writers Project in the 1930s. Apparently each state was free to decide who should be interviewed. Texas, for example, conducted more than 400 interviews with cowboys, creating a rich record of detail but perhaps overlooking other occupations.

Richard Phillips, a Texas cowboy, described himself to his interviewer as "a yarn-spinner". Although very well aware of his hard and poorly paid life as a cowboy hired by a big cattle company, he was nevertheless proud of his skills and recounts them here. Orphaned at the age of twelve, Phillips describes what happened to him:

"I was left a dogie [orphan calf] when my mother died, and I wasn't but twelve at the time. You know, even though we had tried to get along, we didn't have much stuff when she died, and I sold out for $100.00 and lit out for the West. I wanted to get away from the place where I'd had so much trouble.

A couple of months later, I lit in Fort Stockton, and met Tom Bailey. He was ram rodding for the Western Union Beef Co., and was in town right then, a-looking for cow punchers. [I] told him I could ride and rope, and he gave me a chance. I was told to beat it out to the ranch, and when he came out, he'd see what I could do.

When he got out there, he put me through my paces, and hired me. I got $15.00 a month and chuck. Now the Western Union Beef outfit [was] a big spread, going from Fort Stockton to the mouth of the Pecos River. It was a big outfit, and had ranches from below Uvalde to clean up in Montana. A couple of bankers, R.T. and N.T. Wilson were the ones that owned the [outfit]. They ran the Alamo National bank in San Antonio, and that's where all our checks come from...

In them days a man had to be a man every day without no layoffs. Every day! You take in a stampede now, and I've seen a hundred or more. The boys that are out with a herd must be real good riders willing to take chances with their lives. When a herd starts to running, it goes hell-bent-for-election and will run over anything it can unless it's too big, then the herd'll run 'til they run up against something they can't run over, then they'll split and go around but keep a-running. [That's] the way them ornery critters'll do every time. Well, when a herd gets to running, it'll run 'til it runs down, or gets so tired it can't run anymore. [The] thing a cowhand has to do, is to get that herd to milling, and then they'll run in a circle 'til they get run down. If they're not put into a mill, they'll run over some bank of a crick, or a cut, or even a canyon if there's one in the way. [Then] there'll be a lot of beef killed and lost, which can run up into the thousands of dollars.

Now then, I want you to picture a herd on the stomp, and realize that any human or hoss that gets in the way, that the herd'll run over them and stomp them into the very ground if it possibly can. Get that picture, then realize that the only possible way to turn a herd into a mill is to get right out in front and beat the lead steer 'til he starts turning and trying to get away from you. That away, the rest of the herd'll follow him, and the herd'll then go into a mill. When you get that picture, then you'll see and understand why men had to be he men in them days. Not now, because these fine cattle are hard to put into a stomp, and when they are, they don't run long because they're not grown for strength, but for fat. They didn't grow them in the old days for strength, but them old long horns just naturally growed like a hoss, without any help from man . . .

Now, what I'm telling is what actually happened to me and not something I've read. Truth of the [matter] is that I can't read nor write. Reason being because I was raised a dogie, and had to hustle for my bread and meat all my life. I just want to tell about one of them stomps we had on one of the last trail drives to Amarillo with 7D, while it was still owned by the W.U.H. Co. I'm standing night herd, and its been raining pretty hard. Whenever it goes to raining, a herd'll stand up and go to shifting around, trying to got their tails and backs to the wind and rain. [That's] their nature, but they're also ready to run in case anything makes the [least?] little old bobble. Well, sir. Instead of the rain getting harder, it began to lighten, and the night itself got lighter. [We] could see a heap better'n when it was raining, and all of a sudden, we heard a shot from the camp where the rest of the boys'd gone to sleep.

The herd heard it too, and were off like a shot, running right towards me and the other night rider. We'd stopped for a but of talk and a cigarette, but was in the wrong spot at the right time. If it hadn't have been that the night was pretty light, and we were able to see the leaders, we'd have been stomped right into the ground. Instead, we could see the leaders, and he and me turned [that] herd into a mill in less then five minutes after it got started. Five minutes! [I'll] bet that'd have made some kind of a record if records had been kept, because five minutes is a wonderful time.

[We] had a lot of good times, there on the 7D, what with our contests we had every time we weren't pushed with the work and all, but along came the thing that spoilt it all when John T. McElroy of Pecos City made a deal with the W.U. Beef Co., and bought the ranch. I don't know just what kind of a deal was made, but I do know that the cowhands were given the order to round up every head on the ranch, and bring it to the chutes at the headquarters for a tally. Well, on the day we were to have the herd there, there was a stranger there with [McElroy], nobody paid no attention to him, because we were all busy with the herd.

Finally came the order to [shoot the] chutes, and we started the cattle through. Hugh Boles made the count for the W.U. Beef Co., and John T. made his own count in the middle of the chutes as the critters passed him by. The stranger made the count at the end of the chutes as the critters all passed out and into the new herd. 28,000 head passed through the chutes in that one day, and, this stranger was Segal Saunders, of the Kansas City Saunders Cattle Commission Co. He bought every head that came through, and paid John T. $4.00 a head for every one of them 28,000 critters. Figure it yourself.

Then the real work started. Segal Sanders gave the order to have the critters road branded, and I myself put a seven on 13,000 of them critters. 13,000! You see, all I had to do was put the iron as the other boys downed them, and there were three [crew] working with me. It certainly kept us all busy. After the cattle were all branded, then they roaded to Amarillo, and shipped to different points. I myself left Amarillo with a train load for Terre Haute, Ind., to be fed out.

When I returned from working with that herd, I quit the range for good and never went back. Man could really save his money and be healthy in it, but it just didn't appeal to me no more after I got back from that year in Indiana, so I quit. I'm now living on my farm out near Springtown, Texas. Just doing nothing all [summer] but wait for winter, then when winter gets here, I wait for the good old summer time.

Immigration

Between 1880 and 1900, nine million immigrants entered the United States. Most were from southern and eastern Europe, in particular Italy, the Austrian Empire (including the Balkans), Hungary, Poland, and Russia. Searching for low-paid labor to provide the manpower for mines, steel mills, and other kinds of heavy industry, industries recruited many immigrants. Native-born Americans generally greeted new immigrants with suspicion and scorned their peasant origins, their poverty, their "clannishness," and their inability to speak English. One

Image 2 Medical examination of immigrants at Ellis Island, New York (Library of Congress).

particular group of immigrants, the Chinese, faced open hostility. Chinese laborers had flocked to California during the gold rush of the early 1850s; a number stayed to build the western part of the first transcontinental railroad in the 1860s and to mine in the Rocky Mountain states. A series of laws, culminating with the Chinese Exclusion Act of 1882, strictly limited Chinese immigration. Chinese women in particular were denied entrance, thus making the formation of stable families and communities nearly impossible. Labor unions fueled antagonism toward them by claiming the immigrants undercut wages by working for lower pay. The press heightened general fears of Chinese "strangeness." Although the proportion of Chinese immigrants was always very small compared to migration from Europe, the extreme reaction to them reflected the rigid racial attitudes of the time, as also shown in the segregation of African Americans and the restriction of American Indians to reservations.

Questions to Consider: Because immigration continues to this day to be a major theme in American life, these early oral histories raise issues that are still relevant today. These two narrators, both successful businessmen at the time of their interviews, describe initial periods of job uncertainty and the importance of kin or country connections in finding employment. Both narrators returned to their home countries at least once, making them early examples of the transnationalism that we talk about today. Notice also that as new immigrants both men were targets, in one case of police corruption, in the other of racial violence.

1. Why did these two men immigrate to the United States?
2. How does the historical evidence of transnational ties affect ideas about how immigrants become American? Does becoming American mean that immigrants should cut their ties with their countries of origin?
3. What factors led to the success of these two narrators? What obstacles did they have to overcome? What qualities did they possess that led to success?

A Greek Peddler: Anonymous

Source Note: There are many oral histories of immigration, but most of them date from the twentieth century when tape recorders were easily available. This account dates from a time when mass immigration was new and generally unwelcome. In 1906, Henry Holt, the editor of *The Independent*, a well-known weekly magazine, published sixteen autobiographies of ordinary people, in a book titled *The Life Stories of Undistinguished Americans as Told by Themselves.* Some of the autobiographies were written by the authors, but others were compiled by the interviewer after conversations with the narrator; thus, they are oral histories. Among them was an account by an anonymous Greek immigrant reproduced here.

This anonymous Greek immigrant's account, "The Life Story of a Greek Peddler," from The Life Stories of Undistinguished Americans *describes some difficult early years in the United States in the 1890s:*

I had been hearing from America. An elder brother was there who had found it a fine country and was urging me to join him. Fortunes could easily be made, he said. I got a great desire to see it, and in one way and another I raised the money for fare—250 francs—and set sail from Pireus, the old port of Athens, situated five miles from that city. The ship was a French liner of 6,000 tons, and I was a deck passenger, carrying my own food and sleeping on the boards as long as we were in the Mediterranean Sea, which was four days. As soon as we entered the ocean matters changed for the better. I got a berth and the ship supplied my food. Nothing extraordinary occurred on the voyage and when I reached New York, I got ashore without any trouble.

New York astonished me by its size and magnificence, the buildings shooting up like mountain peaks, the bridge hanging in the sky, the crowds of ships and the elevated railways. I think that the elevated railways astonished me more than anything else.

I got work immediately as a push cart man [a street peddler]. There was six of us in a company. We all lived together in two rooms down on Washington Street and kept the push carts in the cellar. Five of us took out carts every day and one was buyer, whom we called boss. He had no authority over us; we were all free. At the end of our day's work we all divided up our money even, each man getting the same amount out of the common fund—the boss no more than any other. That system prevails among all the push cart men in the City of New York—practical communism, all sharing alike. The buyer is chosen by vote. The buyer goes to the markets and gets the stock for the next day, which is carried to the cellar in a wagon. Sometimes buying takes a long time, if the price of fruit is up, for the buyer has to get things as cheaply as possible. Sometimes when prices are down he buys enough for a week. He gets the fruit home before evening, and then it is ready for the next day.

I found the push cart work not unpleasant, so far as the work itself was concerned. I began at nine o'clock in the morning and quit about six o'clock at night. I could not speak English and did not know enough to pay the police, so I was hunted when I tried to get the good place like Nassau Street, or near the [Brooklyn] Bridge entrance. Once a policeman struck me on the leg with his club so hard that I could not work for two weeks. That is wrong to strike like that a man who could not speak English. Push cart peddlers who pay the police, make $500 to $1,000 a year clear of board and all expenses, and actually save that amount in the bank; but those who don't pay the police make from $200 to $300 a year. All the men in the good places pay the police. Some pay $2 a day each and some $1 a day, and from that down to 25 cents. A policeman collects regularly, and we don't know what he does with the money, but, of course, we suspect. The captain passes by and he must know; the sergeant comes along and he must know.

We don't care. It is better to pay and have the good place; we can afford to pay. One day I made free and clear $10.25 on boxes of cherries. That was the most I ever made in a day. That was after I paid $1 a day for a good place ...

I soon went on to Chicago and got work there from a countryman who kept a fruit store. He gave me $12 a month board, but he wouldn't teach me English. I got so I could say such words as "Cent each, five cents for three, ten cents a quart," but if I asked the boss the names of things he would say never mind, it was not good for me to learn English. I wrote home to my uncle in Athens to send me a Greek-English dictionary, and when it came I studied it all the time and in three months I could speak English quite well. I did not spend a cent and soon found job, getting $17 a month and my board. In a little while I had $106 saved, and I [owned a] little fruit store of my own near the Academy of Music.

One night after ten o'clock my lamp went down very low and I wanted to fill it again. I had a five gallon can of kerosene and a five gallon can of gasoline standing together under the stall, and in the darkness I got out the can of gasoline. I filled the lamp while it was still burning. It exploded over me and I ran out of the place all in flames. The people were just coming out of the Academy of Music when I rushed among them shouting. Men threw their overcoats about me and put out the flames, but I nearly lost my life. I was taken to the hospital, where I lay for four months... I had not had sense to get my store insured, and so had no money when I walked out of the hospital. My landlord stocked it for me with fruits, cigars and candies, and did all he could to put me on my feet, but I had bad luck and gave up.

Then I left Chicago and went roaming, riding about on freight cars looking for work. I had twenty dollars in my pocket when I set out, but it was soon gone. I could get no work. I fell in with a gang of tramps, mostly Irish fellows; we rode generally in the cabooses of freight cars. They used to beg, but I said "No, I'll starve first." I slept at nights in cemeteries for fear of being arrested as a hobo if I slept in the parks, and for seven days I lived on eleven cents. On the eighth day I got a job carrying lumber on my shoulder. I worked two days at this and earned three dollars, but was so weak that I had to give it up.

So I went on, riding on top of a freight car. There were three of us on top of that car, two lying down and one sitting up reading a paper. We came to a tunnel, and when we had passed through the man who was reading the paper was gone. When the train made its next stop I and my companion went back and found the missing man lying dead on the track. That ended my riding on top of freight cars. I never tried it again.

I got a job in a bicycle factory soon after this. It paid me nine dollars a week and I could save seven, so I soon had money again; but when the war with Turkey broke out [1896–1898] I thought I would go back and fight for Greece and I did, but the war was a disappointment. I was in several battles, such as they were, but no sooner were we soldiers ready to fight than we would all be ordered to go back. When the war was over I returned to this good country and became a citizen. I got down to business, worked hard and am worth about $50,000 today. I have fruit stores and confectionery stores.

A Chinese Businessman: Woo Gen

Source Note: This interview with a successful Chinese businessman comes from an obscure source. In the 1920s, a group of scholars at Stanford University began an investigation of the lives of Japanese, Chinese, and (as they said) "other non-European residents" of the West Coast. Directed by the well-known sociologist Robert E. Park, they compiled a large collection of life history questionnaires and hand-transcribed interviews. The "Survey of Race Relations," is now online at Stanford's Hoover Library: http://collections.stanford.edu/srr/. This collection, the first systematic survey of Asian immigrants, has proved to be of great value to scholars of Asian-American history.

Woo Gen was described by his interviewer, C. H. Burnett, as one of Seattle's oldest and wealthiest Chinese immigrants when he was interviewed in 1924. In this excerpt, he describes his early years as an immigrant and his recollections of the Seattle Anti-Chinese Riot of 1886, in which a mob rounded up most Chinese residents and forcibly marched them to a boat that would take them to San Francisco. Woo Gen describes the intervention of members of the Home Guard in this excerpt. The complete interview can be found in the Survey of Race Relations records, Box 27, Folder 183, Hoover Institution Archives, Sanford University.

What was your incentive to come to this country?
Because I 1ike to come get little American idea. I try to get job better than I do in China. The American idea is what I like. When I arrive in San Francisco I don't get much pay, I work in a cigar' factory. I get paid about $4.50 a week and pay my own board and room.

How old were you at the time?
About fifteen years old.

You came over all by yourself'?
No, some relation of mine. He was a baker, and I am one of the smallest boys on that boat. There was about 1800 in the steerage of that boat where I am one, and I am one of the smallest boys in that whole crowd.

[He spent a year in San Francisco and then moved to Seattle]

And you went into the laundry business here?
No, when I first come here I go to a cousin-in-law of mine, Mr. Chin Chon Hock of Wa Chong Co., and stay in that store looking for a job. I cannot get any. After about six or seven months I get a job for dishwasher in Tamada, near Olympia. When he get me, I make him promise to teach me in English. He say. "Sure. I get my sister and wife teach you easy." After I get there, nobody teach me except this man. Every Saturday he come and teach me lessons, but no other. I was there about a year. I went to [a new job] in Olympia. I stay there and I get much advanced in English through this man. Every evening, he come back he teach me...

After I quit Olympia I went to Lycona, time I was about seventeen years old, and I open laundry there. I am first man open that laundry at Lycona. I carried water every night after closing: I put three or four water pails on canoe to get for my laundry. The only water was on the other side. All I stay is about two three years and my father is very anxious to call me back to China. I sold the laundry, get couple hundred dollars, and take trip to China. Oh, I stay about year and half in China. I get married and then I return here again.

Did you bring your wife with you?
No, I couldn't support my wife in that time when wages is awful small. When I come back in about year and half my wife dead in China. Then a friend of mine they get up some money and open a cigar factory in Seattle which is called the Seattle Manufacturing Co. I am manager and the whole works. I had about fifteen men working for me. In that time I was twenty-three years old.

Were all who worked for you Chinese?
All Chinese.

And then when these China riots [the Seattle Anti-Chinese Riots of 1886] come I got to give up my business because I cannot sell my cigars. During that time the China riot ruin every Chinaman, including some of the finest residences in Seattle. They have some good citizens in Seattle. I think the big work is done is by Mr. Dave Kel1og. His brother used to be fire marshal. He get up in the morning he see these China riot and he went to the fire engine house at Columbia Street. He went in and the fire men try to stop him from ringing bell. He say, "I got orders from my brother." He call all these home guard so the home guard is turn out all over in town and protect the Chinese if he can. The only thing I see in the street I see from my window. I see Mr. Wm. H. White. He was United States attorney then. He says to the mob, "As long I am prosecuting attorney in this city you people [the anti-Chinese rioters] have to get back to Tacoma [where there had been an anti-Chinese riot in 1885]." He fight hard. On account of that they didn't drive all the Chinamen out of Seattle. But they did in Tacoma.

What did Judge [Thomas] Burke tell you to do? They didn't disturb you did they?
Oh, Judge Burke and Captain Harris [of the home guard] said, "No, stay in Seattle. We try to protect all you people as we can. If anyone tries to break your door you just kill him." I get my gun ready and my axe ready and if anyone come, I try to kill him. But these mob drove all the other Chinese out from the other Chinese houses, but they didn't come near me. I think I am one of the very few to stay here. The others get out. They go, seventy percent or more of the Chinese people that time they drive out from houses down to Pier A, but the citizens of this town considered it was unlawful to drive the Chinese out of town, so get these home guards to protect all the Chinese who come back, and told them to report and examine every Chinaman willing to go, and protect him to go down to the wharf and take the boat, and those willing to go, 1et him go. Those who are not willing to go they can stay, so then they called for government troops to protect the rest of the Chinese here and turn over to [martial law]. Two men standing on the street together were to be arrested. You wasn't allowed to walk on the street at all. You do, you get arrested. After a while, why this trouble was all settled. I had to open up the laundry again. But Chinese tried to open up their garden again but they were afraid to do, on account Judge Greene have give a decision that anyone

who sells vegetables he got to be a white man and to have license, so the Chinese haven't got any chance to go back to gardener business again...

After the riot, did any more Chinese come to Seattle?

Well, after that riot and there was no more trouble they come from San Francisco, Portland and elsewhere, and settled back again.

Then I suppose you went into another business after the riot?

After about a year I went back to China again. I stay until that big fire at Seattle [1889]. Then I return.

Were you married again?

I was married again. Then I could do no business. I did a little interpreting work in the court. I make a few dollars a day. That is all the money I get but damage I get from the government from China riot, $1000, or something like that. After the fire, I opened a laundry. I make good money in the laundry until I come into this [The Wah Chong Company]. Mr. Chin Chon [Hock] wanted me to help him in this company and after a year or two he give me a share in the business. Then I never changed to any other business from that time on. Now it is about thirty-one years I have remained in this country.

Industrial War

In the years 1865–1900, the nation experienced such rapid economic growth that by 1900 American industry led the world. For workers, however, economic conditions in the half-century following the Civil War were very difficult. Two major depressions (in the 1870s and 1890s) and three minor ones caused 25–30 percent of all workers to be unemployed during part of every year. Workers could no longer expect to "be their own masters," as presidents since Jefferson had claimed as the American ideal. They struggled for decent wages and working conditions in large manufacturing plants, where they had to work at the pace of the machine and adjust to the owner's power to lay them off, cut their wages, or fire them at any time. On the other side, capitalists such as John D. Rockefeller and Andrew Carnegie in heavy manufacturing, railroads, and mining, realized that to dominate the market they had to control their labor force. As a result of this contradiction, workers led frequent strikes and protests, and employers crushed them with the help of the state. In 1877, for example, the President called in the U.S. Army to quell a nationwide railroad strike. Many subsequent labor protests followed the same pattern. The inevitable result was half a century of industrial violence that frightened the general public that benefited from increased productivity but which did not wish to examine too closely the dangerous and exploitative conditions under which much of the new wealth was created.

NEW YORK, JULY 14, 1892. [PRICE, 10 CENTS.

Image 3 A popular news magazine reports the battle between strikers and Pinkertons at Homestead, 1892 (Library of Congress).

One of the most notorious industrial clashes of the nineteenth century was the strike and lockout of 1892 at the giant Homestead steel plant owned by Andrew Carnegie near Pittsburg. The Amalgamated Association of Iron, Steel, and Tin Workers was the strongest union in the American Federation of Labor, but Carnegie's plant manager, Henry Clay Frick, refused to bargain with them and locked union workers out of the plant. To defend the plant and the strikebreakers he planned to employ, Frick hired 300 men from the Pinkerton Detective Agency—creating, in effect, a private army. The battle that ensued between the Pinkertons and the union supporters left 14 men dead and 150 injured. This shocking level of violence prompted a U.S. Senate investigation into the company's reasons, as the report said, for "the employment for private purposes of armed bodies of men." The interview below is an eyewitness account by John Holway given at the Senate hearing.

Questions to Consider: Although testimony at Congressional hearings is frequently biased, John Holway's account seems more honest because he was so disillusioned by his Pinkerton employment.

1. Does his apparent lack of advocacy make his account any more believable than if he had been one of the Pinkerton oldtimers whom he credits for his safety?
2. Given the description presented, how do you explain this episode of industrial violence?

The Homestead Strike: John Holway

Source Note: Testimony given at hearings held by federal or state legislatures and in court cases are major sources of firsthand evidence for the years before recording devices were invented, and because court stenographers took down every word they are more accurate in language than many of the interviews we have seen earlier in this section. But because legal proceedings are adversarial in nature, the words may be accurate, but the testimony itself is often biased, that is, deliberately presented to defend only one side of a disagreement.

John Holway, a young and temporary Pinkerton employee, portrays himself as an innocent victim of the violence that occurred when the Pinkertons attempted to break the Homestead Strike. He was one of approximately twenty five people questioned during the investigation. He was questioned by Senator J.H. Gallinger, chairman of the committee. (Senate Report 1280, 52nd Congress, 2nd session, February 10, 1893).

JOHN W. HOLWAY sworn and examined. By the CHAIRMAN:

Please state your name, age, residence, and occupation.
John W. Holway; 23 years old; 1008 Twelfth Street, Chicago; occupation, chiefly that of student...

Were you a member of the company that was sent by the Pinkertons to Homestead during the recent strike?
Yes, sir.

What kind of a contract did you enter into at that time?
The contract was stated about this way, that in case we were injured we would not sue the company for damages, and that in case we deserted their employ at any time without asking their leave we would forfeit the wages which were then due us.

And on the other hand, what were they to do for you; what rate of wages was to be paid?
We were to be paid $15 a week and expenses.

How many men accompanied you from Chicago to Homestead?
I judge there was 125. I did not count them, but I judge 125.

Did you understand, when you left here, that you were to bear arms when you reached your destination?
No, sir.

Did you anticipate it?
From nothing that they had told us. I read the newspapers, and I formed that private opinion, but we received no such information from them.

Were you given any arms of any kind when you left here?
No, sir.

Were you transported rather quietly and secretly from this point to Homestead?
The trip was rather a quiet one, and very quickly and secretly planned. [He provides a detailed account of the route of the special three-car train from Chicago to Ashtabula (Ohio) where they joined seven other cars of men from the east.] [At Bellview, we] were told to prepare to land—to leave the cars. During our trip we were not allowed to leave the cars at all, we were kind of prisoners. We did not have any rights. That might have been because they were afraid of union men, perhaps spies, who would telegraph ahead to Homestead. They wanted to get inside the works without bloodshed, but we had no rights whatever. Then we entered the boats, some 300 of us. There was two covered barges, like these Mississippi covered boats . . . When we had secured our uniforms we were some distance down the river, and we were told to keep quiet, and the lights were turned out, and everything kept very quiet until we were given orders softly to arise. I was lying down about an hour when the order was sent around the boat for all the men to get ready to land. Then the captain called out for men who could handle rifles. I did not want to handle a rifle, and then he said we want two or three men here to guard the door with clubs, so I said I would do that, and I got over the table and got a club like a policeman's club to guard the side door—that was to prevent men from coming in boats and jumping on to our barge from the river. I stayed there while the men who could handle rifles were

marched down to the open end of the boat, and I did not see anything more of them until the firing commenced.

Tell what further occurred as a matter of knowledge on your part?

I saw what appeared to be a lot of young men and. boys on the bank, swearing and cursing and having large sticks. [These were the strikers and their supporters] I did not see a gun or anything. They were swearing at our men. I did not see any more, but came back and resumed my position at the door. I had not been back more than two minutes when I heard a sharp pistol shot, and then there were 30, 40, or 100 of them, and our men came running and stampeding back as fast as they could and they got in the shelter of the door and then they turned around and blazed away. They fired in rather a professional manner I thought. The men inside the Chicago boat were rather afraid at hearing the rifles, and we all jumped for rifles that were laying on a table ready and some one, I think a sergeant, opened a box of revolvers and said, "all get revolvers," so I had now a Winchester rifle and a revolver.

I called out to see if anybody had been hurt, and I saw a man there apparently strangling. He had been shot through the head and he died sometime afterwards, I think.

I was standing there when [Captain] Nordrum [the Pinkerton officer in charge] came up and he said to follow him, and I crossed over to the New York boat, where there were 40 men with rifles standing on the edge of the boat watching what was going on on shore. Nordrum spoke to the men on shore. He spoke in rather a loud manner—say a commanding manner. He said: "We are coming up that hill anyway, and we don't want any more trouble from you men." The men were in the mill windows. The mill is iron clad. There were a few boys in sight, but the men were under shelter, all of them. I supposed I should have to go up the hill, and I didn't like the idea very well, because it was pretty nearly certain death, as I supposed. While I was standing there, waiting for Nordrum to charge up the hill and we follow him, he went away, and he was gone quite a few minutes...

I judged we were going to have trouble and went back to the end where I had been placed and waited for Nordrum to come, but he did not turn up, and after I stood there about half an hour I concluded, as there was no one there to order us to do anything...I concluded I would look out for my life, and if anything was said about my leaving and not staying there I would say I did not intend to work for them anymore; so I returned to the door I was told to guard, and in that place I stayed for the remainder of the day, during all the shooting and firing...I concluded if the boat was burned I would defend my life with the other men. There is one thing I omitted. Before we started out at all Supt. Murray came downstairs; he is chief of the detectives. Supt. Murray made a little speech. He was the man who had charge of all of us, and who sent us off. He spoke about as follows. He said, "You men are hired to watch the properly of a certain corporation, to protect it from harm. The element of danger which is usually found in such expeditions will be here entirely lacking. You will not be in danger. A few brickbats maybe thrown at you, you may be called names, or sworn at, but that is no reason for you to shoot. You are in charge of experienced men, who have been on expeditions of this sort before, and you need not be afraid at all. If there is any man in this company afraid let him step out and don't go, but there is no danger: there will be nothing required of you which would not be required of any man. All that is required of you is to be and act like men."

Was that speech made to you by Mr. Murray before you embarked?

Yes, sir; in the office. Now I could not tell by looking the men over who was experienced and who was not, but there were 30 or 40 men who had been in previous strikes, always in Pinkerton's employ, so far as I could learn, who had charge of our squad who held the titles of sergeants, just as in a military organization. These men were the chief actors down there at Homestead. They were the men who, after the captain had left us, kept us from being killed. If not for their presence I believe all the men would have jumped overboard. Through the rest of the day there was a second battle when the strikers started the firing...

At about 3 o'clock we heard something; we thought was a cannon, but it was dynamite. It partially wrecked the other boat. A stick of it fell near me. It smashed open the door, and the sharpshooters were firing directly at any man in sight. That was about 3 o'clock. Most of the men were for surrender at this time but the old detectives held out and said, "If you surrender you will be shot down like dogs; the best thing is to stay here." We could not cut our barges loose because there was a fall below, where we would be sunk. We were deserted by our captains and by our tug, and left there to be shot. We felt as though we had been betrayed and we did not understand it...About 4 o'clock someone or other authorized a surrender.

That surrender was effected, and I started up the embankment with the men who went out, and we were glad to get away and did not expect trouble; but I looked up the hill and there were our men being struck as they went up, and it looked rather disheartening. I went about half way down to the mill yards without being hurt, when three fellows sprang at me and knocked me down twice and one said, "You have killed two men this morning; I saw you." I supposed there was not going to be any more crowds, but in front of the miners' cottages there were crowds of miners, women, etc., and as we all went by they commenced to strike at us again, and a man picked up a stone and hit me upon the ear. I got on further toward the depot and there were tremendous crowds on both sides and the men were just hauling and striking our men, and you would see them stumble as they passed by. I tried to get away from the crowd; I had no satchel, so I put my hat on and walked out of the line of Pinkerton men, but someone noticed me, and I started to run and about 100 got after me. I ran down a side street and ran through a yard. I ran about half a mile I suppose, but was rather weak and had had nothing to eat or drink and my legs gave out, could not run any further, and some man got hold of me by the back of my coat, and about 20 or 30 men came up and kicked me and pounded me with stones. I had no control of myself then. I thought I was about going and commenced to scream, and there were 2 or 3 strikers with rifles rushed up then and kept off the crowd and rushed me forward to a theater, and I was put in the theater and found about 150 of the Pinkerton men there, and that was the last violence offered me.

TWO

1900–1920

In reaction to the industrial violence and social inequities described in the previous chapter, political and social reform movements of many kinds dominated the Progressive Era. The scope of reform was ambitious and varied, encompassing voting reforms, labor legislation, industrial regulation, banking reform, environmental protection, prohibition of alcohol, and the introduction of the income tax. The new spirit of reform did not, however, extend to improving conditions for native-born minorities: this period marked the nadir of African-American rights, with a sharp rise in lynching and the consolidation of Jim Crow segregation, and health and living conditions on American Indian reservations declined. Immigration from southern and eastern Europe accelerated, surpassing the record rates of 1880–1900. The era ended on a wave of popular sentiment—at first divided and then vehemently patriotic—in 1917 as the nation entered World War I. Throughout the era reform movements expanded as what began as middle class economic and political reform spread rapidly to other groups, such as women and immigrants, who had their own agendas for social change.

The nine interviews in this section begin with two on *reform*, specifically women's reforms. The next two interviews cover two aspects of *race and work in the South*: child labor in the textile mills and segregation. Then two interviews recall new *migrations*, from Europe to the American West and from the South to the industrial North. This section closes with four interviews concerning *World War I*: a soldier's account, two home front accounts, and one about the fatal coda to the war, the great influenza epidemic of 1918–1919.

Reform Movements

Women were critical to the social reform movements of the Progressive Era. Some of their efforts are spotlighted here to illustrate the overlapping nature of reform causes. A paramount reform was woman suffrage, a classic "rights movement" in which women argued that their exclusion from politics was unfair discrimination. Many suffragists also spearheaded reforms such as the settlement house movement that tried to ease the adjustment of new immigrants. In so doing they created a new public role for women reformers and began the process that over time built the welfare state (federal responsibility for basic wellbeing). Much more controversial was the campaign for birth control, which was illegal because of its alleged "obscene" nature. In the spirit of Frances Willard, who admonished the Women's Christian Temperance Union in the 1880s to "Do Everything," women reformers frequently worked for more than one cause at the same time.

Questions to Consider: The following oral histories highlight the drama of women's reforms, but we can assume that all reformers shared the same kind of dissatisfaction with "business as usual" and a desire for change. Consideration of these interviews can help us to understand the wider reform impulse.

1. What do you think compelled Sylvie Thygeson and Rebecca Reyher to participate in what were, at the time, unpopular movements that were considered unseemly for women? How did they hope to effect change? What weapons did voteless women have to change laws and practices?
2. Considering the activities of these two women, what would you say about the role the individual plays in affecting social change?

Women's Reform: Sylvie Thygeson and Rebecca Reyher

Source Note: Founded in 1954, the Regional Oral History Office at the University of California, Berkeley traces its purpose back to the work of historian Hubert Howe Bancroft (described in Chapter One) who collected the living memories of West Coast pioneers. ROHO conducts oral histories concerning the history of the San Francisco Bay Area, California, and the western United States. The Suffragists Oral History Project consists of interviews conducted in the early 1970s, when women's history was just emerging as a historical specialty. It is one of the nation's largest collections of oral histories with suffrage activists. (http://Bancroft.berkeley.edu/ROHO/projects/suffragist/index.html)

Sylvie Thygeson of St. Paul, MN was interviewed twice in 1972, first by Raida Sullivan (RS) and then by Sherna Gluck (SG), founder of the Feminist History Research Project., Thygeson was 104 at the time of the interviews and was unable to keep focused for long. In the interests of clarity, the two interviews have been edited to form a single account. In the second interview, Thygeson's daughter Mary Shepardson (MS) was also present.

(RS) How did you get interested and get started on woman's suffrage and birth control?

I think always I was interested in that. My mother was always interested in woman's suffrage. Way, way back, when my mother was young there were women working for suffrage...

The part I played in suffrage was, I think, a really good one. You had these little afternoon gatherings of women. You had a cup of tea. A little social gathering. While we were drinking tea I gave a little talk and they asked questions about what was going on. It was a lot better, I thought at the time, than to have a lecture. Because a lot of them wouldn't go to a lecture. I took my own neighborhood when I went out and did that talking.

(RS) Did you have them to your house for tea?

No, I went to their houses. They had a little afternoon tea just to hear me talk.

(RS) How many women would turn out?

Oh, there might be six or eight women in the group.

(RS) What kind of questions [did they ask]?

They asked all kinds of questions, I don't remember exactly. They were usually quite intelligent questions as to what was being done, who was doing it, who was prominent at the time, things like that. I was, of course, enthusiastic, so I answered. I didn't think of putting over anything. I had no feeling that I was important in any way. We just met. It was a very nice, interesting social time for meeting people and enjoying ourselves. I don't remember anything but being very happy about it and feeling that when I went out and spent an afternoon that it was worthwhile. It was what I could do. I couldn't have gone out on the lecture stage.

Then, of course, one of the big things we did was this Woman's Welfare League. a big city organization that I worked with [in St. Paul]. We were prominent...That is the Woman's Welfare League was a very prominent organization. We served a hundred luncheons every week, every Saturday, at 25 cents a piece. We served a hundred luncheons. In order to get the group together. And then we had all the prominent speakers, the different people that came through St. Paul traveling...

(SG) Was this for both suffrage and birth control?

The Woman's Welfare League was identified with suffrage. They couldn't be identified with the birth control movement because that was illegal. But the women who belonged to the Welfare League and were officers in it all supported the birth control movement. So we were closely identified not as an organization, but the people were closely identified with the movement. Yes, we were working constantly for the suffrage movement as well as the birth control movement. They were part of our lives. We were identified with them there in our work; with both movements, the suffrage movement and the birth control movement.

(SG) Can you tell me a little bit about your work in the birth control movement?
We three women—there were two connected with me—organized this birth control clinic that we had; it functuated [sic] in St. Paul. We had one doctor from Minneapolis and one from St. Paul that assisted us in the clinic.

(SG) What did you do exactly?
This was the birth control movement. It had to be secret because it was against the law. It was against the law at that time to buy any contraceptive material; anything that prevented conception. It was against the law at that time. And certainly it was against the law to print anything or to advertise in any way, shape or manner any kind of thing you were doing in the line of birth control. Because, as I say, it was against the law.

(MS) Mother, who was in with you?
There were two women. I wouldn't want to mention their names.

(MS) Why not? They are dead. And they'd be happy to have a place in history.
Well, I don't know that they would want me to be mentioning their names. Of course, associated with me—there were three other women associated very closely with me. I don't need to mention their names, who they were. There were three of [us]. They were very prominent women. One of the husbands—the husband of one of the women was a doctor, a very prominent doctor in St. Paul. And as I say, the work we were doing was strictly illegal...

(SG) Did you just give out information or did you have contraceptives, too?
No. We followed Margaret Sanger [nationally known birth control pioneer]. We advocated and we circulated the birth control contrivance she had invented. We worked very strictly with her, of course, because she was organizing the movement that went all over the country.

(MS) Was she the one who asked you to set this up?
Well, I don't know that anyone asked us to set it up. I think it was needed and she just helped us. She gave us information and advice and help. Mainly, of course, she gave us information which we circulated and gave out.

I was written up because of the prominence of my husband. I wouldn't have been—my two co-partners, they would have been written up as much as I was if their husbands had been as prominent as mine...But my husband was very prominent in the city and so I was written up. I was written up editorially in our principal paper, the Pioneer Press.

(MS) Denounced? Were you denounced, mother?
I wasn't exactly denounced. I wasn't commended. But it was just giving out information and commenting a little about it.

(SG) How was the clinic supported? Where did the money come from?
I don't remember that we had to collect money for it. I don't remember that we ever had any money troubles. I think money was handed out. I don't remember

that we ever had to go out [to get money], or that we were hampered for lack of money. We could just give people who came to us the information, and they had to spend the money. We could get Margaret Sanger's design for limiting family, but it cost a certain amount, but they always paid for it. We didn't have to furnish it to anyone. We had a clinic, but it wasn't designated a birth control clinic. It was just an office, a room where we met and had lectures, and we lectured on the desirability of birth control, tried to educate people to the idea of too many people in the world and things like that. I don't remember that we ever had any difficulties about money...

(RS) Did any of your friends object to what you were doing?

I don't know how many of my social friends knew what I was doing. I wasn't out lecturing to the general public. My name wasn't prominent in that way at all. We were just doing sort of underground work, working with Margaret Sanger principally. She was the great birth control person at that time. It hadn't anything to do with my social life. We didn't make a social affair of it at any time.

We were just working along, just as I would be doing now if I were working among people. I wouldn't be out having a meeting and a place to meet and all that kind of thing. I'd be doing probably the same thing, meeting around at houses, educating women who were either newly married or going to be married, giving them the information. Of course, we did meet many people. I was as active in the suffrage movement as I was in the birth control movement.

Image 4 Suffragist speaking for woman suffrage in New York (Library of Congress).

Rebecca Reyher was a full generation younger than Sylvie Thygeson when she became involved first in settlement house work, and then in the activist wing of the suffrage movement, the National Women's Party. In this interview with Amelia Fry, conducted in 1973 in New York City, Reyher recollects her beginnings as an activist.

How early in your life were you actually involved in the woman suffrage movement? Did you happen to take part in the very first Woman's Party parade in 1913, the day before the inauguration of Woodrow Wilson?

Suppose I tell you about the parade first. I had grown up in Washington [DC]; I had gone to high school there. I told you the kind of background I had, that everyone was expected to do something for the community in which they lived, to help others, to serve mankind. To me this was a goal to be attained when I was grown-up. To be able to find some community service was to be grown-up.

When I was fifteen, I began to work as a volunteer at the Friendship House settlement, to teach basketball, something I knew and could share, as I played basketball at school—to both boys and girls. Friendship House has become one of the best-known community houses in Washington.

Lydia Burklin, the director, was a remarkable woman. She was eager to have me enter into the life of the community, to work not only with the children, but to my shame she sent me, since in those days social work was precariously unprofessional, to be a regular visitor among the neighboring families to urge them to save money. I, who had never saved a penny, and have only in my old age started to save money so that I won't embarrass my immediate family, rather than to uphold the principles of thrift. I was urging these people to put savings stamps in specially prepared little books provided by Friendship House.

I still remember some of the people I went to see about this. I was fascinated by them. One of the women who left an indelible impression on me, beyond just that of regular visiting, was the wife of a former miner in Pennsylvania who had just recovered from having had her eighteenth baby! There they were, these women, with children scrambling all over the place, and there was I coming to ask that miner's wife to save money while nursing her eighteenth child, unable to cope with any of the immediate circumstances of her household.

When I read in the papers that the Woman's Party was aiming to give women freedom, and was going to have a suffrage parade in Washington, here was a group that would have many brave, wonderful women whom I wanted to meet. Jane Addams of Hull House was one of my great heroines (I had read much about her) and her name was among them.

I went downtown to the Woman's Party Headquarters, actually then the Congressional Committee, and simply said, "I would like to be a volunteer to help in the parade." I don't know what they thought, but they immediately arranged for me to do what a little errand girl would do. I ran errands for everybody, hither and yon, and listened avidly to them talking. But no one could have been more obscure or more unknown than I was in that headquarters. I think they were downtown somewhere on "F" Street. I seem to remember walking down two steps to enter.

As they were planning the floats to have in the parade, somebody apparently noticed me, and said I ought to be on the one of southern belles, in costume. This one called for seven young women or nine, two by two on the truck in costume, with one leader. We wore wide hoop skirts, and little bonnets tied under the chin. I don't know whether they were made for us, or whether the Congressional Committee got them from a costumer. The girl in front was one of the La Follettes, a then-famous political family. [Robert La Follette was a Republican Senator from Wisconsin 1906–1925 and a well-known Progressive] I remember her! The *New York Times* carried a photograph of the float they thought was so beautiful, and yet so indicative of the change in the lives and dress of the then-contemporary women.

As the parade got started, and as we moved up Pennsylvania Avenue, I who had never seen dense, surging crowds in Washington before, or a riot in my whole life, saw the crowds begin to close in on the parade. It was really a riotous, menacing crowd. Men on the street were insulting and obscene, and wanted to do injury to the women who were parading on foot. Other men, in some way, wanted to provoke what is today called an "incident." We were wearing wide skirts and, before I realized it, as we passed by, men were trying to lift those skirts. However, there were too many people watching, and ropes to bar onlookers. One grown-up man broke through the barriers and tried to lift one of the girl's skirts and pull her off of the float. At that point a man with a walking stick, a fine stereotype of a gentleman, rushed up indignantly, and waving his stick, threatened if the hoodlum didn't move on immediately, he would break his back. The disturber slunk away.

When the parade was over, and the lines and barriers were down, and the onlookers and paraders intermingled, the rough crowds were terrifying. I had never before, or after, seen any kind of roughhouse on Washington streets. The parade inspired it, no question about it. The parade roused bestial passions and violent opposition. I was afraid to stay in it.

Did you see any real violence?

Well, I saw that a man would have had a stick broken on his back had he moved any further toward us. We weren't supposed to look around. We were supposed to be a pageant, a spectacle, an integral part of the parade, eyes ahead, engrossed, a group apart, representing an idea. Certainly the atmosphere was one of jeering, of shouting—not on the part of women, but yelling and howling of a very hostile male audience. That was my impression. I may have been terrified by the experience. It was the only time I have ever been terrified on the streets of Washington, or anywhere.

Race And Work in the South

The economic recovery of the South following the Civil War was based in part on industrialization in the southern "upcountry," where beginning in the 1880s textile mills attracted poor white farming families. Meanwhile, in other parts of the South, most African Americans continued as segregated sharecroppers (sharecropping is described in Chapter One).

Many children worked in the southern mills, some of whom simply followed other members of their families into the jobs. Progressive reformers sought to abolish child labor, but as the first interview shows, a practice that horrified reformers seemed quite natural to the children involved. In the second interview, Avery Downing, the son of a white landowner, explains how as a child he took the system of segregation for granted.

Question to Consider: These two interviews illustrate the value of retrospection in oral history. Neither Naomi Trammel nor Avery Downing thought to question their childhood experiences at the time, but looking back they draw clear contrasts between the circumstances of their youth and their present-day values. What can we learn from this process of historical contrast?

Child Labor: Naomi Trammel

Source Note: This oral history, along with many others about work in the southern cotton mills, is available online in the Southern Oral History Project collection at the University of North Carolina (http://docsouth.unc.edu/sohp/index.html). The interviews were the raw material for the prizewinning book, *Like a Family: The Making of a Southern Cotton Mill World* (Chapel Hill, NC: University of North Carolina Press, 1987).

Naomi Trammel recalls her experiences as a child worker in a textile mill in the early decades of the century. She was interviewed in 1980 by Allen Tullos.

Your parents [who were farmers] died when you were ten years old. And how did that happen?

Well, that fever went around that summer, and they took a fever and died with the fever. Well, . . . Pa died one week before my mother did. And Maude was really sick, she was down with the fever, that sister of mine had died. Well, and it worried Ma so bad she just died of a heart attack the next week. So they all died in three weeks.

Do you remember much about that time?

Yes, sir, I remember. I'll never forget that. They was a casket come to our house for three Sundays straight. And they all looked just alike. I can remember how, you know, how it worried me, and scared me. I was scared. 'Cause I was just a child, you know, and I'd never known much about anybody dying. That was when we's all separated.

And now, what happened to the children after that?
Well, Uncle Bill Smith, that was Ma's brother, and Aunt Em Marn, Ma's sister, and Aunt Georgia Ann, Ma's sister, well, they divided us children up among our aunts and uncles. But Alma, my oldest sister she was sixteen when they died. Well, she was old enough to come to the mill and work, and take care of me. So she come and got me, and brought me to the mill. The rest of them wasn't big enough to work in a mill. So the others had to stay in the country…

Well, what do you remember about first going into the mill?
Well, I didn't know, hardly, but I just went in and had to learn it. Really, I had to crawl up on the frame, you know. You've seen a spinning frame. Well, I had to crawl up on that to put my—what do you call it?—roping in, you know, because I wasn't tall enough. 'Cause I never was much big, you know. Then I [was] a little old spindly thing, and I couldn't reach up there to put my roping in. And I'd have to crawl up on that frame down there, and put it in. I wasn't the only one, they's a whole place like that. And they had mothers and daddies. They wasn't no better off than I was.

There were lots of other children your age?
Oh, yeah, a lot of them. It's a lot of them. 'Specially in the spinning room, that's where they put the children. You could run a frame, you know, where…a child couldn't run nothing else.

Was there a mill village in Greer [South Carolina] that most of the mill workers lived in?
Yes, sir, they all lived there. You know, it's a mill village.

And you and your sister lived in the same boarding house?
Oh, no, we didn't live in a boarding house, we just boarding with a family. Boarding with a real family. Just like one of the family…

How often would you get paid?
Well, we'd have to work two weeks 'fore we got our pay. And 'bout my highest bill was nine dollars. For two weeks! Worked in the cloth room sixty cents a day. It big money!

How long did you work in the spinning room there, when you first started?
I worked on up till I got grown, and then I went to the cloth room…that's all at Victor Mill. That's where I went, you know, when Pa and Ma died.

Well, when you were on your job in the spinning room when you were just starting out, did someone teach you?
Oh, yeah, they had to show us how, 'cause I'd never been in a mill. They had to learn us. But didn't take me long to learn.

Who taught you?
Just some of them would be a spinner, you know, they'd put us with one of the spinners and they'd show us how. That's all they had to do.

Was it mostly girls or women?
Yeah, they girls, mostly. No, it mostly children. I mean, big enough to spin. It was easy to learn, all we had to do just put that bobbin in there, and put it up.

And what would be your work routine, what would you have to do through the day? Would you have to do so many bobbins, and then did you rest a while, or-?
No. No, we just run the spinning frames. And of course they had to stop them and doff, you know, and take these full ones off, and put them on. All like that, but it wasn't nothing to me, really... the doffers would do that. All I had to do was just—no, they put up all the threads and started it again, they had to do that. Fix it just like it was. But we had to clean our rollers, but that wasn't hard.

So what was the main work that you had to do? What exactly?
Well, you see, some of these threads would break, and if you didn't catch it before they bundled up, why you have a mess there. And all you had to do just watch 'em. And it'd run and run sometime before they even break a thread. And if the thread broke you'd have to tie it up. You'd have to put it back up, you know.

Would you have to tie a knot in it at all?
No, you just had to take it in—they was rollers. Cotton, you know. And all you had to do just put it off and stick it up there, around it'd go. It's easy... Oh, you had to watch it, you know, if you didn't it'd roll around there and make a mess. And you'd have to take your roller out and clean it... sometime I'd run six frames. And the other girls would, too.

How would they pay you, by the number of frames that you run, or by so much a week?
No, they just paid me so much. So much a week, I reckon, so much a day, or some whatever it was. But, anyway, I didn't make much. They none of them make anything. But you could buy things for nothing...

What about going to school, did you get to go to school much?
No, sir, I didn't get to go to school. That's one thing that hurt me, I always wanted to, but I didn't never get to.

So most of the time, during your work day, when you were in the spinning room, would you be sitting down watching things, or walking around?
Oh, be walking around. [laughter] Didn't have nowhere to sit down. But, then, if we'd a-wanted to, we could have, you know, if we'd had anywhere. If we got our sides to run they wouldn't been nothing said to us. But we mostly walked around, because, you see, if a thread was breaking, we couldn't see it, well it'd mess up, you know. So we usually walked around; I didn't see nobody sitting down.

And what did you do when it came lunchtime?
Well, we didn't have no lunch time.

You'd just work right on through?

Just worked on. We'd go to store and get things, if we wanted it. They'd let us go to store. We'd have like one spinner run my side then her side, and me and another girl'd go to store. And when we come back, and got us something to eat, well, we'd run theirs and let them go. So they wouldn't say nothing about it. But we didn't go home where we were boarding, where I boarded. We'd go to store, get us something to eat. And wasn't one thing said about it, they didn't care...

Oh, it was pretty good little piece to the store. Just we'd go up there and get what we wanted, come on back, and eat it. Just so our side was going, they wouldn't say nothing...

So you worked in the spinning room from the time you were about eleven years old until you were twenty-two.

Un-huh. I went to the weave room one time. They let me go to the weave room so I'd make a dollar a day. And I like to took galloping TB. People's dying 'round with it, you know. And that doctor told me, said "Now"—when he'd doctored me about two weeks—he said, "now, young lady" said "you can go back to the cloth room, and live, or you can go back to the weave room and die, whichever you want to do." So I went back to cloth room. [laughter] And the most people died there at Victor Mill... with what you call galloping TB. It'd come out, you know, and it be just wet all over, so hot, you know? And that just give 'em TB. I don't know of the people that didn't die... In the weave room. Just the people that wove. And he said that's what'd happen to me if went back, so I didn't go back.

Image 5 A young girl working in a cotton mill, Roanoke, VA, 1911 (Library of Congress).

Growing Up with Segregation: Avery Downing

Source Note: A transcript for this oral history is available from the Baylor University Institute for Oral History (http://www.baylor.edu/Oral_History/), Waco, Texas, which is devoted to documenting the history of Texas and related regions.

At the same time that Trammel was growing up in the "upcountry" mills, most of the South remained agricultural, and as Avery Downing recalled his East Texas childhood in this 1983 interview, sharecropping and segregation were the rule. Thomas Charlton (TC) and James SoRelle (JS) interviewed Downing, a former superintendent of the Waco Independent School District,for the Baylor University Institute for Oral History in 1983t.

I loved to go with my father to Hallsville and stand around on the little streets and corners and watch—just people watching... that was the big event in those days, was the Saturday afternoon at town. There would be on one side of the main thoroughfare in this little town there would be blacks in great numbers on their Saturday afternoon social event because that's what it was. It's true that everybody bought groceries and some clothes, and so on, on these Saturday afternoons but it was really a social event. And on the other side were these hordes and hordes of white people, great numbers of women included in these things: the mothers and daughters, as well as the fathers and sons in both groups, black and white.

(TC) How large a community was Hallsville then?
Well, I always said in those days that it had about five hundred people... Hallsville was just a crossroad, just a very small place. And I remember that for years the Hallsville school had an enrollment of about three hundred and they came from miles away on buses and every other way.

(JS) Do you recall other things about the racial climate of Hallsville?
Yes, sir. It was very oppressive. I remember—some of the happiest memories I have of working on the farm would be that I would be picking cotton by the side of this black man, I remember this. I don't know why we would be the only ones, but I remember this very much. And, at one time, there was a great scandal in the county about the mistreatment of some blacks by a white landowner who owned a lot of land. And, somehow, the scandal got so out of hand, so to speak, that the man was tried in a court of law in Marshall for this heinous treatment of blacks. And I remember that my family—and, of course, I was young and impressionable and idealistic—I wanted this man punished badly. Ooo, I wanted him punished badly. And I would talk to this black man about this and I was just a little old squirt and I remember talking so authoritatively about it. I wonder how that man put up with me. You know, a kid, not knowing a thing on earth about what blacks tolerate and I know he must have been thinking: What about me and your treatment of me? But, at the end of the row, there would be a jug of water and he'd drink first and I'd drink second right out of that jug of water, you

know, and that—that was not a problem at all. But if we had gone to town, and in a public situation, I wouldn't have—I wouldn't have been allowed to sit next to him or drink with him or eat under any circumstances.

(TC) You mentioned that conditions were in the word—your word—oppressive. Tell us a little more about race relations.

Now, that was—that was very dependent on the individual landowner. Some were extremely kind and thoughtful and helpful. There were a few that did what I would call oppressive—even though I was a product of the times and just as certain of the superiority of the white race as I could be, I guess, still there were limits that me and my family just couldn't conceive of treating anybody.

(TC) You mentioned the social lines being drawn in town. In what other ways were the social lines drawn?

Well, of course, schools were segregated and that causes me to think of this. In those days, the state money was divided in the counties based on school-age population and the common practice in my county was for—the money was sent to the white schools and the blacks were even discouraged from going to school because that meant more money still for the white schools. I remember the black children were discouraged from going to school, if you can say it that way.

(TC) How active was your family in public affairs, locally?

My mother and father were not. My uncle was extremely involved in it. I remember that, I believe, he was in the tenth or eleventh grade in high school and was a debater and the Ku Klux Klan problem was an extremely sensitive and explosive issue in my county, very muchly so. And my family was anti Ku Klux Klan from the word go, absolutely. And you have to understand that that meant considerable criticism from many, many, many others in the community because Ku Klux Klan had quite a following. My uncle and one of his classmates, a man by the name of Merritt Gibson—a lawyer in Longview now—were debaters and they loved to debate the question of Ku Klux Klan. And one night in a small church north of Hallsville, a Ku Klux Klan assembly of some—I was not there; I heard about it later—Ku Klux Klan had some sort of a service or ceremony in this small church, and my uncle and his friend went out there and defrocked one of the leading Ku Klux Klan members and he was the pastor of the Methodist church in Marshall over on Merritt Street and caused quite a furor. And so, yes the Ku Klux Klan thing, and every so often there would be a flogging of a black who was out of line for some reason. I remember that…

(TC) Some communities had lynchings. What about your county area?

Yes. Now, I never knew of one during my boyhood nearby. There was one earlier, before I was born, and the stake stood there until I was a grown man, where this man was burned. And his alleged crime was the raping of a white girl, or a woman. And I remember, when I would see that place or that stake, the feelings I would have: How could this be? But they talked about it constantly and all kinds of threats were made from time to time against blacks that got out of line. I remember seeing a constable beat a black down to his knees on the main street of this little town of Hallsville for something that he had done or said.

(JS) Why do you think your family was anti Klan? I mean, that probably wasn't the norm for the location.

No, it was not. I never thought of that. My father's feelings were largely influenced by my mother and her family. My mother's feelings, I—her side of the family had a large history of participation as a Confederate people—as Confederate supporters and participants. I don't know. I think-I just have to believe that it was her sense of right and wrong.

(TC) The Klan of the twenties—of which we're speaking now—was also anti Jew, anti Catholic, anti immigrant, anti Mexican, what do you recall of that?

Not anything except the black thing. As I said, there were no Catholics or Jews or Mexicans for us to relate to. Blacks, oh, yes. So I can't believe that my mother's family had anything, really, except a gut dislike of the tactics used by the Klan on blacks. That's my feeling inside.

(JS) Do you have any idea what the racial breakdown of Harrison County would have been at that time?

I would say, at that time, 50 or 55 percent black... Oh, there were a lot of blacks everywhere—everywhere-hordes of them, that's right. Well, just take my grandfather's farm, he had five- or six-hundred acres and he had several—just several black tenant farmers—families—and he was not alone. His operation was big enough that he had to have a little commissary to handle staple groceries and supplies for the farm so they wouldn't have to waste so much time going to some town or something for basics, and many of the farms were like that.

Migrations

When we think of migration, we tend to think first of immigration to the United States from other countries. Immigration was certainly a major event in the period 1900–1920, as nearly 15 million people, most of them from Europe, entered the United States at a rate nearly twice that of 1880–1900. Immigration from Japan and China made up less than one percent of the total, but nevertheless created a backlash culminating first in the 1882 Chinese Exclusion Act and then in the 1917 Immigration Act creating the Asiatic Barred Zone that stopped all immigration from Asia to the United States.

Within the United States, migration to the West continued as people were lured by the Homestead Act to settle on marginal lands, often to face failure after 1920, defeated by drought and falling crop prices. Another migration, less noticed outside the South, was just beginning. Conditions such as those Avery

Downing described in the rural South, combined with active labor recruitment by northern factories, led to the beginnings of what has become known as the Great Migration, the exodus of nearly two million African Americans from the South to northern cities by 1940.

Questions to Consider: The first interview with Dora Rosenzweig combines immigration from Europe with her later experience of migration to Montana. The second interview is with M. Kelly Fritz, an early exemplar of the Great Migration in Detroit.

Dora Rosenzweig's story is one that traces the experience of an immigrant who wished to take full advantage of opportunity in America, a sentiment that is echoed by M. Fritz Kelly's desire for freedom within America. Do not, however, see these as easy journeys: notice the violence in both accounts, in Chicago strikes and race riots in Detroit.

Notice also that both of these oral histories first appeared in books, and were probably edited for publication. In that way they are different from most of the other selections in this section, which are actual transcripts of interviews.

1. Based on these interviews, what seem to be the differences between immigration to and migration within the United States? How significant are these differences?
2. Compare these published oral histories with some of the verbatim oral history transcripts in this volume. What seem to be the major differences? How do they affect your understanding of the interview?

From Russia to Chicago and Montana: Dora Rosenzweig

Source Note: The famous and prolific oral historian Studs Terkel began interviewing people in the 1950s, first for his Chicago radio show and later for his many books of oral histories that covered topics such as the Great Depression of the 1930s, World War II, race relations, and aging. When he retired he donated more than 5,000 hours of sound recordings and transcripts of interviews to the Chicago History Museum, which set up a special website in his honor: http://studsterkel.org.

In the 1970s, when Studs Terkel interviewed Dora Rosenzweig at the age of 94, she had a vivid and wide-ranging immigration story to tell. The edited interview with her is included in Studs Terkel, American Dreams Lost and Found *(New York: Pantheon, 1980); the transcript of the interview is in the Studs Terkel papers and book interviews collection, Chicago Historical Society, http://www.chicagohistory.org. Rosenzweig begins with a dramatic story about the difficulties of leaving Europe; we pick up the narrative with her arrival in the United States in 1891:*

We arrived at the depot in Chicago. My father met us there. He brought us a basket of fruit. I remember biting into a banana. I didn't know you had to peel it.

(Laughs) My mother thought it was pork sausages. (Laughs) She said I shouldn't eat it. My father said it's kosher.

We got an apartment near the railroad tracks, a saloon on the corner. Ten of us in four rooms. My mother had never seen a stove. In Russia, we had little brick ovens. The wonder of all wonders: an inside toilet...

I started school, kindergarten. The teacher said something to me and I didn't understand. She must have thought I was stupid. So she slapped me. Well, nobody slaps Dora. I played truant and didn't go back. Luckily, I got sick and didn't go to that semester at all. Playing among children, I learned English.

Evidently, I was fascinated by books. I couldn't read, but I saw the illustrations. I listened to the class and memorized what they read. In the first two years, I made five grades. By that time, I was nine, ten years old. I had some wonderful teachers.

I became very interested in reading. Before Jane Addams, whom I came to know and love, a group of young women started a settlement in the ghetto. My father jumped to the conclusion that they wanted to impose Christianity, proselytize. They'd lure the children by giving 'em candy, and they had a library and music, to get the children to Americanize themselves. My father thought they were going to make gentiles out of us. I had to cross the street to avoid them. My girlfriends didn't have such pious fathers and went in there. I liked the candy, but what I liked best, they'd come out with books. One day I defied my father, was welcomed, and got a book. By stealth I'd go there, and that was really the beginning of my Americanization. That's the first time I met gentile children.

When I was eleven, my father began to talk about me going to work as a seamstress. My mother was interested in my education. She was proud of my learning English and wanted me to be a schoolteacher. That was the heights. In Russia, a woman didn't amount to much. So there was trouble in the house. By the time I was twelve, I got so tired of the arguments that I got a job as a cigar maker. Rather than be a seamstress, which I hated, I'd make cigars like my brother.

It was a garret with a couple of benches. Boys, girls, and men were working. The confinement and the tobacco smell made me sick. The place was called a buckeye, the name for a sleazy shop, filthy, no air. TB was rampant at that time, cigar maker's disease. We had a foreman, Fritz. He could be as mean as the devil. There would be an underground signal: Fritz is coming. We stopped whatever we were doing and shut up. He'd come with a smile. He knew what was going on. But whenever anyone was known to have TB, he was the first to organize relief...

I got into a group of older immigrants interested in social questions, and I began to go to lectures. I met my husband that way. I met people who were interested in the labor movement. Working conditions were terrible, even at the American Tobacco Company where I worked, tops. The toilets were on the same floor where four hundred people worked. Open. That's the beginning of my interest in the union, the Progressive Cigar Makers.

When I was sixteen, my mother died and I left home. I lived with strangers. No Jewish girl lived with strangers, no matter how miserable the house was. It was my key to freedom... Two girls furnished a two-bedroom rear apartment and asked me to live with them. Whoever heard of three girls living together? This was 1905. You know what it is? Prostitution. The sister I moved away from prophesied that I'd have four bastards. Why she took four, I don't know. If ever there was a naive, innocent set of three girls, you can't imagine...

Most of the cigar makers where I worked wanted a better life; they were looking for culture, going to lectures, going to night school. I was the only so-called American because I knew English. I had gone to sixth grade. There was something in the air that affected all of us.

The shop was almost a block long. It had two rooms, a small one and a large one. I preferred to work in the small room, which held about thirty or forty people. They elected me a reader. I used to roll fifty cigars an hour. That was my piecework limit. So if I read for an hour, they would donate the fifty cigars I missed. If I read for two hours, they'd give me a hundred. I'd sit on a chair and read while they worked. I read about current events, a book, or even a play. I would choose the books. Whoever heard of a twelve year-old girl reading Flaubert's *Salammbo*? Whatever struck me, I'd read to the others. Tolstoi, anything.

Most of them were still young and rebellious... We wanted theater, we wanted concerts. Theater was cheap. I saw Mansfield from the most prosaic roles to Peer Gynt. I'll never forget this Peer Gynt. Ibsen's *Ghosts* was played on special matinees. The theater was crowded, mostly with immigrants. I saw Isadora Duncan dancing. We hungered for the better things of life.

There was a terrible depression in 1903, 1904. There were many strikes... In one strike, we saw the police bring out the fire hoses and knock down peaceful marchers who were just protesting. They used to come and raid the houses for [socialist or anarchist] literature. Oh, it happened all the time. I used to go to meetings, but I never joined. I was never active. My name was never signed to any petitions or anything because I was cautious. I was Americanized. (Laughs)...

I was twenty-one and my husband was twenty-four when we married. Jewish girls didn't go to work after they were married. My mother-in-law was scandalized. What will the neighbors say? I said: "To hell with the neighbors." I rebelled against religion, too. I was the hippie of my age. (Laughs)

My husband hated his work and I hated mine. We wanted to get out of the shops, and I wanted a family. We liked the country life and decided to become farmers. We wanted to homestead. In the early 1900s, the railroads wanted settlers in the West, for freight. For thirty-two dollars, you could go from Chicago to the coast. By 1909, it was all: Go west, young man, go west. There was a railroad show at the Coliseum: farm products of the West. Watermelons that big.

They told us of all the wonderful things we could get. Nobody told us there was little rainfall.

The Rosebud Indian Reservation in South Dakota was thrown open for settlers. They took it away from the Indians. They had a lottery. My husband won a ticket, but he didn't want to be separated from his friend Charlie. So they came back to Chicago. On the train they heard about oceans of land in Montana. Whoever comes gets the land. So they came to Scobey, Montana.

You choose your plot of prairie land—three hundred twenty acres—and you didn't stop to ask why. I remained in Chicago to augment our income, to earn my $15.75 a week: a ten-dollar gold piece, a five-dollar gold piece, a quarter, and a half-dollar. We had saved two thousand dollars, a lot of money.

He built a twelve-by-twenty shack. I joined him in August 1910. I got off the train, and there was my brown complected husband, sunburned, with overalls and a red kerchief. Nobody told me there was only nine inches of rainfall a year (laughs) and that the country was subject to prairie fires. In August, there was no grass, it was just yellow. It was blazing hot. I thought: My God, I'm in the Sahara Desert.

I got on a prairie schooner. We started at twelve o'clock. At evening we stopped near a creek. I volunteered to take the horses to water for drink. I'd never been near a horse. Nobody told me there's cactus. It went through my shoe. There was no wood, no trees. He carried a little kindling, took out a rusty pan, and made some coffee. He spread out some blankets and said this is where we sleep tonight.

The air was so clear. I thought I could reach up and take a star. It was beautiful. Everything was new. It took two and a half days to make the trip to Scobey.

The neighbors were simply wonderful. The first morning, a horseman stops near the door, Mr. Larson from three miles away. "Simon, I want you to come for threshing." I said: "Can I come along?" He says: "Come, be our cook." I could make gefilte fish, challah, but cooking for twenty-five Montana farmers... (Laughs)

He tells me the menu: potatoes and ham. I had never cooked it. I asked my husband: "Where are the potatoes?" He said: "You have to dig 'em up." (Laughs) And bake biscuits, too. I had never baked biscuits. Mr. Larson said it was a wonderful meal. The next morning, a sixteen-year-old girl came by and taught me how to cook country style, and I made my first pie.

Our salvation were the neighbors who lived two miles away. Pious Methodists. If not for them, I don't think we could have survived. Mrs. Watts was my mother, my counselor, my everything. When my husband had accidents, they'd come help us. She knew folk medicine. At threshing time, everybody helped.

My husband had to go back and forth for business. I was alone. We were talking about going farther west. Why? I was hungry for people. I was hungry for the family. I wanted my daughter to go to school. By that time, I had another child. The school was six miles away, and I was terrified that my daughters would grow up illiterate. How do you send a little girl in Montana winters to school so far away? We wanted to sell, but there was no one to buy.

The war broke out, but we weren't in it yet. Canada was. One day, as I was doing my chores, two horsemen drove up. Fifteen minutes later, my husband came in and said we sold the farm. There's a Canadian who doesn't believe in the war. He was supposed to join the English army, so he decided to move to the United States. My husband named the first price that came into his head, sixteen thousand dollars. There were two hundred fifty acres under crops that woulda brought in probably sixteen thousand dollars. My husband was not a businessman. (Laughs) We came back to Chicago.

Beginning the Great Migration: M. Kelly Fritz

Source Note: This interview was published in *Untold Tales, Unsung Heroes: An Oral History of Detroit's African-American Community.* As the title suggests, in the 1990s the Detroit Urban League became aware that a piece of local history, the African-American migration to Detroit, needed to be documented. Many oral history projects have begun, as this one did, with just that realization that a piece of history was slipping away without being recorded.

In the early 1990s, Elaine Latzman Moon interviewed M. Kelly Fritz for the Detroit Urban League oral history project that produced her book of oral histories, Untold Tales, Unsung Heroes: An Oral History of Detroit's African-American Community, 1918–1967 *(Detroit: Wayne State University Press, 1994). Fritz was an early participant in the Great Migration, coming to Detroit before 1920, and unlike many migrants, he came alone.*

I came [to Detroit] as a youngster, fourteen years old. I came alone. My parents still in Alabama. They didn't have a damn thing to do with it. By the time I was eleven years old I was on my own. I left my little hometown at eleven and went to Birmingham, which is one hundred miles away. I worked and did what else. I was a good boy. Then I ended up in Sharon, Pennsylvania then Washington, Pennsylvania, finally to Detroit.

In the South they had labor trains bringing people north. They'd come into your town and they would conscript you, follow you and pick you up: "Where you wanna go?" Labor agents would go around town and recruit you, and you got a free ride to this part of the country.

What happened is they would get on those cars; and they were supposed to come to Detroit. And then they'd go on to Flint, because they were building a new General Motors plant then. And some of them would get off other places. So sometimes when they got where they going, they didn't deliver many people. So they got smart and locked the cars, and you couldn't get out until you got where you're going.

Companies were bringing people to supply their labor needs. Sounds gruesome doesn't it? So, myself and two other fellows, older men, came up. But we paid our own way. When we were in Cincinnati a fellow said, "So where'd you come from?" We told him. He said, "Why didn't you come on the labor train?" We didn't want any part of it. I told him we wanted to go when we wanted to go. Police did everything they could to keep you from going, because companies in South were losing their employees.

There were three of us leaving, but the three of us wouldn't go to the window at once because, if three of you went up to buy a ticket they would charge one as being a labor agent, and you'd end up in jail. So you'd go individually and buy your tickets. When we got on the train, it sat quite awhile before it left and finally the whistle blew and at the same time we said, "Wheeee... free at last!" And we worked that day up until five o'clock. The train left about seven. We rushed home and changed clothes. We had our bags packed; and we took a circuitous route. The streetcar went way around the back to go to the depot because we were trying to avoid anyone observing us, because it's a possibility we might have been stopped or arrested.

I was here from 1919 to 1924 the first time. I was almost twenty. When I walked through the dining room at the Detroit Athletic Club, there must have been three hundred people sitting in there. I thought everybody in the world was looking at me. There wasn't a soul seeing me. Who in the hell is going to see a busboy? I was so self-conscious about it.

I had never heard of a cabaret, didn't know what it was. All this singing and dancing, I loved it. I wasn't old enough at that time to be in there, but I was a big boy, so nobody questioned me. I was in there the minute I got off of work at night until they closed. Went home and got a little sleep and back to work the next morning.

There was a place called the Royal Garden which was the most outstanding at that time. The Graystone was just built. It was brand new. It was on Canfield and Woodward. Blacks were only allowed to dance starting at midnight when the whites left. We would crowd in there starting at midnight and dance till morning. St. Antoine was quite a mecca. We'd all proceed down St. Antoine to the restaurants. There were all sorts of cafés and what-not there. If it were a weekend, we'd go on to a morning dance. The Graystone started at about 9:00 A.M. and stayed until 1:00 P.M. It was called a breakfast dance. After having danced the night before you'd think we would have had enough, but it was quite the contrary. I guess you'd consider me a good dancer. I still dance, shake a mean foot, I guess.

When I came to town, the people I lived with went to Bethel A.M.E. Church, which was located on Hastings and Napoleon. It's all torn away now, just expressway. I went there temporarily. I was looking for pretty girls and what we called the "high-yellow" gals. Almost white. Mostly went to St. Matthew's, where the pretty girls were. We had some friends at Second Baptist, so I'd go there occasionally, but I didn't belong. Everybody was looking for pretty girls. They were half-white or mixed and had pretty hair and all that stuff. That was quite the quite.

I came to Detroit because I had a friend here that I knew. He said come on over, and I'll get you a job. That was it. It was a busboy job at the Detroit Athletic Club. Then I stayed here a few years and went back to Pennsylvania.

I finished Eckles College of Mortuary Science in 1925 in Philadelphia, then came back to Detroit. A chap by the name of Samuel W. Franklin, who was one of the outstanding funeral directors in town, gave me an apprenticeship in 1929. In 1931 he made me a partner. I laugh about the partnership now because it didn't mean a darn thing. I was working the hotels and taking the money I made there to pay the rent on the funeral home. In 1937 he died. By that time we had moved up on Garfield and Brush Street. We lived upstairs and had the funeral home downstairs. I carried on there from 1937 to 1947. Then I bought this place and have been here since 1947.

Up until the late 1930s we were laying people out at home. We'd hold funerals in the homes. We'd haul chairs to the house and set them up in the house. Then we would have a green carpet running from the door clear out to the walk. They used to call us and say, "My mother's dead," and they'd want you to embalm her in the home. Didn't want you to take her out. Finally the Health Department ended all that. We'd haul them into the home and lay them out. We had to stand the casket on end and work it up the stairway until we got it into the house. When you look back on it today, it looks very foolish, but we did it because that was what folks wanted.

I took a funeral from Flint to Roseland Park one day. I got to the front gate with a great huge group of cars behind me. The attendant wouldn't open the gate. He said to go around the side. I asked why. He said, "That's where we bury..." In other words, go around to the back gate because you're burying a Negro.

There were two race riots—1943 and 1967. Our first one in 1943 was the worst thing that I've ever seen. People killed like flies. It was all the city. I remember one particular thing. I went down on Alfred Hastings Street, picked up a man down there that the police just took an automatic gun and, he was lying on the ground, cut him in two. You had to pick up one part of him and then pick up the other part. I shipped him back to his home in Mississippi. It was a race riot, and anything could happen. He had an altercation with the police, I guess. That stands out as the most gruesome thing I'd ever seen.

World War I

World War I began in Europe in 1914; the United States entered the war in spring of 1917 and underwent a rapid mobilization of soldiers and unprecedented regulation of home front production. Initially elected as a peace candidate, President Woodrow Wilson put into motion a propaganda campaign that had recruits lining up to enlist for the war effort, as in the case of Homer Nikirk, who describes his war experiences in the first interview. The propaganda campaign also whipped up a virulent dislike of German people, illustrated in the second interview, and the nation's first red scare, which stifled labor and political dissent. On the home front the loss of a young male workforce to the hostilities in Europe created employment opportunities for those who were too young to enlist, and one such experience is related in the third interview.

The influenza pandemic of 1918–1919 formed an ironic coda to the war. Worldwide, more people were killed by the 'flu—between 20 and 40 million—than were killed in World War I. In the United States, more than half a million died, ten times the number of war casualties. The final interview, conducted in a remote part of Alaska, illustrates how far the influenza epidemic reached.

Questions to Consider: These four interviews represent a wide range of interviewer/narrator interactions, and for that reason they provide the reader with an opportunity to think about interview methods. In the first interview, Homer Nikirk at first seems to be an unpromising narrator, but Charles Martin's persistent questions get him to open up. In the second interview, Lola Clyde is an example of a spontaneous narrator who only needs a few prompting questions to get going. In the third interview, folklorist Edward D. "Sandy" Ives is primarily interested in details of bygone logging practices; Adin McKeown's rueful recollection of his father's reaction to his youthful pride emerges as an unexpected bonus. The fourth narrator, Lela Oman, an Alaska Native, uses traditional narrative style to tell her gruesome story of the influenza epidemic. A less experienced interviewer might not have understood her distinctive style and shut her down. These examples serve as a reminder that every oral history is a unique interaction between interviewer and narrator. Based on these examples, consider the ways in which different styles of interviewing elicit different kinds of responses.

At the Front: Homer Nikirk

Source Note: The first interview, with Homer Nikirk, is one of nine interviews with veterans of World War I that were conducted by the Center for the Study of History and Memory, Indiana University in the 1970s. Since then there have been many interviews with veterans of many wars; this project was one of the earliest.

Homer Nikirk, a World War I veteran, was interviewed in November, 1974 and February 1976 by Charles E, Martin of the Center for the Study of History and Memory, which has a transcript (http://www.indiana.edu/~cshm/). Rather taciturn at first, he loosens up in response to the interviewer's eager questions, creating an almost conversational tone. Nikirk was wounded three times in his year on the battlefront. In this excerpt, he describes the trenches, his experience with mustard gas, and his first two war injuries.

Why did you enlist in the Army?
I didn't have nothing else to do. Time was that everybody was going. My older brother went ahead of me. I wanted to follow him.

Do you remember what your pay was then?
A dollar a day. A dollar and a dime over seas...

Did they train you at the front?
Oh, yes. They drilled us every day up there. When they got a chance, they trained us. We all went out, and had a ring around, and they trained you to protect yourself. Stuff like that. And they had a big pole and they would punch you in the back. Then you'd get into the guy and get the thing away from him, and get him if you could. That's the way we went.

Were there trenches there?
No, they didn't have no trenches there. Trenches were up in front. We didn't have no trenches to deal with. We just had a big open field... Well, we sat around for awhile, then we went to one of the front lines. It was over in the north part of France.

Yes. So this was the first time that you would have seen the front? A trench? Seen the enemy? Heard the bombs?
Oh, yes.

And do you remember just the first time you saw that?
Yes. I remember it like it was yesterday... We was just lucky we was safe down and they was just throwing shells. They wasn't throwing anything that exploded. They were throwing shells at us. They put shrapnel over your head, and then the pieces all fall around. They bombarded us for quite a while. That's the trouble. When you first got into it, that's when they wanted to catch you. Before you got settled. They caught us just when we was coming in. But lucky enough a lot of them stayed out of the way, but a lot of them got killed. But we was lucky enough not to get shot down.

Where could you go in a trench? I mean, did you have rooms underneath?
We just had trenches to follow along. When we got in trenches we just dug along the front, see? You go one section to another.

At this time, did you ever entertain the thought, "Boy, I sure wish I was home"?
Boy, I thought that at different times. I never used to worry about that. [laughter] You was in the war then, see? You had to take care of yourself and get the man ahead of you. That's what you had in mind then, mostly. You had nothing else in mind. Get the man ahead of you, before he got you. That's what you thought.

I've often wondered two things. In a trench, what did you do when it rained?
Oh, didn't pay no attention to it. Just had raincoats. Ponchos. Just put them on and forget about the rain.

And where did you sleep?
Well, we just dug out the wall bank. Just dug out the wall. A place to lay down, a place to sleep. That's all we had. Just dug a place to lay outa the bank.

I have this one question to ask. My wife wanted to know this. She has always wondered one thing. Where did you go to the bathroom in a trench?
Just wherever you got a chance.

Didn't make too much difference, did it? Just wherever you got the chance. [laughter] There was no such things as bathrooms and stuff like that around. You didn't have to worry about that.

Did you really have any impression of France after you first got there?
Oh, I never did like France... I don't know. I just had the impression—it seemed like they was out trying to get what you had. They was all trying to get your money or something like that. They'd all come around and try to talk to you, being American and stuff like that. "Voulez-vous cigarette sil vous plait?" [laughter] That's all they'a holler for. Do you want a cigarette? American cigarette, you know. They'd want to know if you'd give them a cigarette, if you please. [Laughter]

I'm backtracking now. I'm just thinking of some other things. After they trained you, and then when they came and gave you orders that you were going to the front, was there lot of anticipation and anxiety knowing that you were going up there?
Oh, yes. You're bound to get a lot of that, you see. We were on the front in Belleau Wood. A fellow I knew was going to the front over there, and his sergeant said "I'm going to get killed today. I want you to take my place." And went and walked back over to his place and he got a direct hit. It just tore him to pieces, you couldn't even see any of him. And I went on up to the front line with him, and I took his place and went on up the road...

Did you ever get that feeling? What he had?
Oh, yes. I had that feeling on July the 18th, when I got hit.

You lost your finger? Let me see. Oh, boy. I'll say.
It went down through here and there and hit these two fingers here. I pretty near lost all three of them. Tiny piece of shell hit the gun—it just went around it, see. Piece of shell—shrapnel—come down and hit the shell. Hit the rifle in the wood and went around and just whipped into that thing. See, it didn't hurt it; just whipped into it. Just as well take it off; it will be stiff anyway. So they sawed it off out there in the field hospital.

They did? What did they give you to kill the pain?
Nothing. [laughter] Wasn't no pain. They just sort of skinned it back and sawed it off. Just like it was a piece of board.

Then did they send you back. or...
Oh, yes. I had to go back [behind the front lines]. Back there for three or four weeks. Let's see—in fact, this happened September 12 and I was back to the outfit November 10.

Are you left-handed?
No.

So that's not your trigger finger?
Oh no...

And then where did you go after that?
That's when I got gassed when I first got up there. I got gassed pretty much. It commenced raining about the same time and everybody got wet. [Mustard gas] soaked through the clothes.

The gas does?
Yes. Mustard gas. Went through the clothes. It really burnt me up.

Is it a bomb, this gas?
The gas was in bombs, yes. They started holding gas in bombs. You can hear—one sounds different from the other. You can tell the difference when one comes over. They make a different noise than the other one. It exploded in the air, and it put that gas all over the place.

Did you have masks then?
Oh yes. We had masks and all that. I wasn't burnt. This is where I had the mask on. They took us to a French hospital and they put glass on my chest, to pull the gas out of my lungs. And they put little things like whiskey glasses ten seconds to stay on and then they would have to pry them loose.

A shot glass?
A shot glass, yes. They would set them all around on my chest. Left ten seconds and they would have to take them off. You'd be surprised. They brought yellow gas out. It was just as yellow as could be.

This gas would actually sink right into the skin, then?
Yes. And then they would turn you over on your back and do the same thing.

Was there a particular smell to it?
Oh, yes.

Mustard gas. They would mix what they'd call a chlorine in it and that gives it a nice odor. Made you smell it. That's what they done. That's where they get the other gas. They mix chlorine and mustard gas together. And that's rough.

What happens to you if you didn't have your mask on?
Well, you wouldn't have been there very long. In fact, I know a sergeant—Sergeant Charles. I waked him up the morning they spilled gas over there. And I went back to check him, he was laying there with his tongue out, gone. Dead.

Just right out?
Yes. He didn't get up to put his mask on, see? And I started waking him up—well, that happened about three o'clock in the morning. He was the first one I woke up. And I got back to him, and he hadn't got up to put his mask on and he was

gone. A lot of them didn't get their masks on, and they wasn't here no more. They inhaled too much of that gas.

And we was down in the low place, the valley. And that made it worse than ever. It wouldn't carry out, so you could just see it in there. We walked back through the gas that morning. After I got gassed we went back to the hospital. That's how they killed the grass—that's how bad it was.

Image 6 Man and dog prepared for mustard gas at the front in World War I (Library of Congress).

What did the grass look like?
Just like it had been frosted.

Really?
It just felt like you was walking through frozen grass.

Just frozen? No kidding?
Yes. Just like frozen grass.

Wow.
Then I went back to the hospital. That's when I saw my old buddy. Left him, and he was in the hospital. Never did see him no more until fifty years later.

On the Homefront: Lola Clyde and Adin McKeown

Source Note: The Latah County (Idaho) Oral History project conducted this interview with Lola Clyde as part of an oral history project with the children of the region's first settlers of thc 1880s. Like many early community history projects, the project was undertaken to honor the nation's centennial in 1976.

The interview with Aiden McKeown is held in the "Ives Collection" at the Maine Folklife Center at the University of Maine, which includes a variety of interviews conducted by the well-known folklorist Edward D. "Sandy" Ives between 1956 and 1999.

The tensions of war were evident on the homefront, as Lola Clyde, a farmer's daughter in rural northern Idaho, remembers. Sam Schraeger interviewed her several times between 1974 and 1982 for the Latah County Oral History Project. Transcripts of the interviews are at the Latah County Historical Society, Moscow, Idaho (www.latah.id.us/historical society/). In this interview, Lola Clyde discusses anti-German and anti-Catholic sentiment during World War I.

In 1916 they ran [Woodrow Wilson] for president on the platform "He kept us out of war." And then he'd hardly been re-elected when we declared war. And here's something interesting—I remember so well the day war was declared in April. I went to school that morning and on the blackboard they had a big sign up, "The United States Enters the War—so many hundred-thousand men are called." And I went into the history class and fine old Reverend Morse was the teacher, and he had the morning *Spokesman Review* [newspaper] there. He held up his hands, and they were kind of shaking, and he said to me, "Lola will you read the president's declaration of war?" And I read it through, and I can remember it just like yesterday, those closing words. He [Wilson] said, "The time has come," I read, '"when America is privileged to spend her blood for those principles that gave her birth. God helping her, she can do no other." That was his declaration of war. And of the boys who sat there and listened that morning, two of them were to die. Holt Cushing died on the Italian front and Jewitt Barnes in the Argonne Forest. And I had entered high school with 110 kids, and I graduated with a class of forty, and there were only twelve boys in the class—all the rest of them were gone to the war. Out of 120, half of them maybe had been boys, and there were twelve boys in the graduating class. The rest of them were all in the war, uh huh. But it just seems like yesterday too...

One thing about World War I: I've heard that there was quite a bit of anti-German sentiment during the war.

Oh, yes, very much. Yes.

What have you heard about that, or seen during that time?

I remember when they smashed out store windows at Uniontown that said Kraut on it. And Kraut on the window. Nobody would eat [sauer] kraut. Throw the Kraut out, they were Germans. And all that was pretty vile, you know. I remember even the great Williamson store, he went in and gathered up everything that was made in Germany, and had a big bonfire in the middle of the street, you know. Although he had many good German friends all over the county that had helped make him rich. And there was all that went on, you know. And some people changed their name. And if it was a German name—we'll just change our name. We don't want anything to do with it. And there was lots of that, just that kind of hysteria going on...

I saw—there were some boys that got draft deferments for this and that other reason, and they rode 'em on a rail and they took off their clothes and tarred and feathered some of them. Some of them as old men dying still resented and remembered those violent episodes.

This deferment business—this was German boys who didn't have to go into the army?

That's right. Some of them said their fathers were sick and dying, and their father had so much land they had to stay home and farm it for them and they got what they called them farm deferments. And a lot of those men felt badly later because they didn't share in the great adventure that the other boys had had. And there was great resentment against them. A lot of them stayed home and married the belle of the town, you know and didn't have to go to war and all the other kids resented that and held it against them even after they all got to be old men they still remembered, you hadn't gone and you chickened out.

But this actual beating up of these fellows? Did that actually happen?

Oh, yes. That happened here, too, yes.

Would it be mostly in the country or Moscow?

In Moscow. I think the Saturday night businesses, you know and like at the dances they'd get a few drinks; and then they were looking for fights, you know.

Can you actually remember hearing of anyone tarred and feathered here?

Yes. I know of one case where they tarred and feathered and rode him on the rail. I knew him later in life too. And he said if he had it to do over again, he would have gone, he would have been glad to have gone but his father—he was the only boy among a big bunch of girls, and the father and mother both cried so and took on so, that he asked for a farm deferment although he was able.

He was German?
Yes. He was of German descent.

Were these people that he knew?
Yes, oh, yes. Boys he'd grown up with. Yes. Yes. Of course there'd been some drinking too you know. And in the heat of it all, you know how those things go. He didn't live to be a very old man, so it was all answered for him then. It was all answered, but I do know that he told me in later life that he was sorry that he hadn't gone. He said, "I missed that wonderful experience. I wouldn't have done it myself but my folks—my father and my mother both were so set"...

It is my impression of it that German people were expected to be superpatriotic, more so than anyone else.
Yes, some of them had to bend over backwards. In fact, when they sold war bonds they'd go out to these German farmers, you know, and just put them right on the spot. They'd made fortunes and "We expect you to buy so many thousand dollars worth of war bonds." And they did. Lots of them went all out, as you say, to prove their patriotism. They didn't want anything to do with this war. But a lot of them were-they'd been brought up, this [Germany] was their home country, this was just a temporary thing here but their home and their loyalty were back in Germany. And there was some of that alright. But they were among the older people.

They were actually—do you think some of them actually hoped to go to Germany some day?
I think maybe they had planned maybe to go back some day. But they had closer ties. They were older people. The old folks that had come maybe half grown from Germany. And they always thought, "We'll make a fortune in America and go back to the homeland." And that was hard on them, I know...

By the way, just one more thing that this reminds me of. The Ku Klux Klan.
Yes, we had a Ku Klux Klan here in Moscow at one time [in the early 1920s]. And they were out burning crosses even and going around in sheets and pillow slips. And it never lasted very long. And of course, it was against the Catholics and not against the Negroes here. The Ku Klux Klan was an anti-Catholic group. And I think that the people who belonged were not very high grade intelligence. Not very highly intelligent. And they did have a Ku Klux Klan going around here for a while.

This anti-Catholic feeling—would they burn crosses at people's homes who were Catholic? Would that be the type of thing they would do?
I think they were going up on Moscow Mountain to burn them as I remember it. Go up on Moscow Mountain so you could see it. And some of them said they wouldn't let 'em go because they'd set the trees on fire. But they were out marching around in white sheets and pillow slips. Crazy!

It was more or less known who belonged?
Oh, it was more or less known, sure, and they hand out these little anti-Catholic books and they were passing them around and just a lot of hocus-pocus, you know. Just ridiculous. And all you had to do was take a look at the kind of people that belonged to it and you knew it wasn't very important.

For young Adin McKeown, the World War I homefront meant opportunity. He got his first job as a Maine woodsman during the war, at the young age of 17. Edward D. "Sandy" Ives interviewed McKeown August, 1979 for the Maine Folklife Center, which has a transcript and videotape (http://www.umaine.edu/folklife/mf027.htm).

In this interview, McKeown relates the beginning of his work experience as a Maine woodsman.

The first winter that I worked in the woods I was seventeen years old. It was during World War I. And I worked at Love Lake, Number 2 camp for the Orono Pulp and Paper Company, I believe they owned the land here at that time.

How big a camp would that have been?
Well I think there were something like 24 or 25 men in that camp.

Would that have been a double camp or a single camp?
The men stayed in one end of the camp. They had the bunks and heater stove in that end of it. Then there was what they called a dingle [shed] between that and the cook camp; cook camp was almost as large. I guess it was fully as large as the men's camp. They had homemade tables made out of boards with what looked like sawbucks for legs under the table... We slept in the part that was called the men's camp.

Would you come out on the weekends?
Yes. I used to come home Saturday night after supper, used to come home and get a bath and clean clothes and go back on Sunday afternoon.

There was a lot of service men you see, in the army. And it sort of left less of a force to work on woods work and log driving and like that. They would hire younger men and try them as they did me at 17. Normally they wouldn't have hired a man—boy 17 years old to work in the woods. But they told me they would give me a try, that's the way I hired. They'd give me a try he said, for a week. And at the end of the week I was so afraid I skipped out; I got my supper and started for home, afraid the boss might say not to come back Monday morning. But my uncle Frank had already told me that the boss said I was as good a man as he had in the crew.

Well. Now, your father was a woodsman too, wasn't he?
He was, yes, a very good woodsman.

Now, did he teach you a good deal about how to use tools?
He did. I worked with him a lot before I was out in the woods. And in these days, a good lot of the lumber was chopped. And I did a lot of chopping and a lot of

sawing with a crosscut saw with my father. And he being a good woodsman, he taught me a lot about it. The customs and the way they worked in the woods. When I did hire out in the woods, I think it was due to his instructions that I did have some success.

I came home on the first Saturday night. And I got a bath and changed my clothes. The next day when my mother got dinner ready we were all sitting around the table and I was telling my father a lot of things which he had already been through. But I felt pretty big, seventeen years old and earning a man's wages in the woods.

So he said, "do they pay you?" I said "They pay me $65.00 a month and room and board." And I said, "That's straight time. If there's a bad rainstorm I get my pay for it just the same." He said, "What?" I said, "$65.00 a month." And me straightening my shoulders. [laughs] He ate for two or three minutes before he replied to that. And he said, "You're not worth it." "I'm not?" I said, "Let me tell you something. My uncle Frank McGoon that was working there told me that the boss told him that I was one of the best men he had."

He said, "They haven't got a man down there that's worth it." He said, "There isn't a man in the crew that's worth it. $65 a month?" And he says, "Mark my words, that's company's gonna go broke."

Did the company go broke?

[Laughs] Of course not. [both laugh] But my father thought the wages unreasonable, see?

The Influenza Epidemic: Lela Oman

Source Note: This interview is in the collection of the Nome Communities of Memory Project produced by the University of Alaska Fairbanks Project Jukebox. This innovative project makes audio, video and transcripts available simultaneously (http://uaf-db.uaf.edu/Jukebox.CommNome/index.html).

Lela Oman, a Native Inupiaq Alaskan, was interviewed by the Nome Communities of Memory Project in 1996. Her audio and transcript are on the Communities of Memory website, #H2007-03-06. Oman uses traditional repetitive storytelling methods to tell the grim tale of the impact of the epidemic on Native villages.

And I would like to talk about our area of Nome, especially old, old stories, our religion and our beliefs and what kind of regards we have towards our animals and birds and all living things on this earth. Down at Cape Nome, what we call Ayak, at one time there were two large villages. The one on this one side, that the Triggs are living on now, was called Ayachigara. And on the other side was Kipiluk. Kipiluk means "steep bank next to the waterway." And James Oksoktaurak's father, Frank Oksoktaurak, was born there. And there were two large villages. David Joe, Robert Joe's father, told me the stories of those two villages. During the big influenza epidemic here in 1918, there were still big villages down there. David Joe and his friend, they were teenagers, but they were working for people that had four hundred dogs at Safety. And they—while they were working there, they had a cook. A large woman. And lots of skipjacks were caught at Safety Lagoon. And with a little laugh he would tell me, that woman was so large she had to eat . . . And skipjacks are fish about so long. She ate twelve for breakfast, twelve for lunch, and twelve for supper. This morning I was just thinking of it and that's 36 of them in one day.

And they heard that their people were very sick and were dying. And those two boys had families right there at Ayachigara, Cape Nome. And they wanted to go and see their people, their relatives. And their boss told them, "When you get there, I'm sure you're going to die. So you give me the money that I had paid you." So, they obeyed him and gave him their money, because they were sure that they were going to die. And they walked from Safety to Ayachigara.

And when they got to that big village, that one on this side, there was only smoke coming out of two smokestacks. And they were David Joe's family's igloo and that boy's family's igloo. David remembered that when he went in, his mother was the only one that was alive. She raised her head and she said, "I am so glad you came." And she laid her head right back on her pillow and she died. And David went out. And he saw that other boy had gone into his family's home and the mother did the same thing. She just raised her head and said, "I am so glad you are here."

And that was in 1918. I was three years old then. What saved us up north was Nome had already put up telephone wire from here to Council and from Council to Dime Creek and from Dime Creek to Candle. Those were big mining places at one time. They'd telephone to—on this telephone was the only thing that saved the North people. In Candle, when they received that message, dogteams went to Deering and to Shishmaref telling everybody up there not to come down this way.

And at Shishmaref, there were guards, sentries, what you would call. With guns. If anybody started coming up this way, shoot to kill. All winter long they were marooned up there. And towards May, it was kind of warm. At that time people walked a lot. A man went to—from Wales went to Shishmaref. And there were two men there with their guns and they said they knew this man. He even kneeled down on the snow and cried. Because that's a long ways to be walking from Shishmaref back to Wales. So they let him in. And after that happened, people started visiting each other.

THREE

1920–1945

The decades following World War I were marked by continuities and disruptions. During the 1920s the nation continued to develop its industrial and consumer economy, and employers and the state were largely successful in preventing workers from unionizing those industries. Legislation restricting immigration from Europe and Asia drew new migrants from the American South and Mexico to the farms and factories of the North and West. The automobile, prohibition, new arts, radio, and movies changed Americans' leisure and culture. The Great Depression of the 1930s led to high unemployment, and then dramatic change with a new government that altered political, cultural, and social relations. The New Deal offered jobs, recognized unions, and supported cultural expression, but it was the economic boom of World War II that stimulated optimism as well as fears. The "Good War" transformed American society in new ways: it offered jobs to women and African Americans, attracted new migrants to cities, created a publicly funded military-industrial complex, and resulted in one of the largest human rights infractions in the country's history, the internment of West Coast Japanese Americans.

The twelve interviews in this section trace these developments from 1920 to 1945. The first three interviews follow the transnational and internal *migrations* of Americans seeking work and home from Mexico to Idaho, Oklahoma to California, California to Mexico, and back to California. Three interviews explore new regional and national cultural creations and *leisure* activities in the 1920s and 1930s: prohibition, the arts in Harlem, and radio. *Work* during the Great Depression is described by three individuals who navigated hard times by organizing a labor union, working for the New Deal program the Civilian Conservation Corps, and moving away from oppressive southern sharecropping labor. Finally, three narrators describe *World War II* as both opportunity and tragedy, in work, military service, and internment camp.

Migrations

Since the 1880s, Americans had primarily associated migration with the massive immigration from Europe. But in the early 1920s, in response to anti-immigrant hysteria, new restrictive laws cut off most of the immigration from southern and eastern Europe and all of it from Asia, shrinking the pool of mobile labor that had driven the economy for five decades. Employers looked south, to Mexico and the American South and Southwest, and to the American possessions of Puerto Rico and the Philippines for workers to fill industrial and agricultural positions. Two internal migrations—one of Mexicans and Mexican Americans and another of white and black southerners—pulled workers north and west.

In one of the era's most abrupt transitions, the depression of the 1930s curtailed economic opportunities for all Americans, including the new migrants. Southwestern states compelled or "repatriated" many Mexican immigrants and their American-born children to Mexico, even as desperate white sharecroppers and tenant farmers from the South headed west to California in search of work. Lumped together with others fleeing the Dust Bowl drought, these "Okies" symbolized the hard times of the depression. The outbreak of World War II revived the US economy and stimulated new migrations north and west to take advantage of the new jobs offered by wartime industries.

Questions to Consider: As the three interview excerpts below reveal, the changing economy, from expansion to depression to wartime boom, uprooted many Americans.

1. What links the migration experiences of the three narrators?
2. What was the impact of migrations on families?
3. How did moving to new places represent new economic and social opportunities, and how did these migrations challenge family, educational, and cultural traditions?
4. How did individuals adjust to their new circumstances?

North to the United States for "a Steady Job": Epigmenio "Manuel" Rosales

Source Note: This interview is part of the Idaho State Historical Society's Hispanic Oral History Project and is available online at the Columbia River Basin Ethnic History Archive http://www.vancouver.wsu.edu/crbeha/ma/index.htm.

In 1918, at age five, Manuel Rosales migrated from Zacatecas, Mexico to Texas with his parents. The family followed seasonal job opportunities in New Mexico and Colorado before moving to Idaho in the 1920s to work beet fields. Rosales' story reveals how many Mexican-American workers in the American West had to endure a life of mobility to find work. Rosales' persistence and family connections helped him land a permanent railroad job in Pocatello during the economic expansion of World War II. Angela Luckey interviewed Rosales in Pocatello on May 23, 1991.

When we first come to this country, that was in around 1918, sometime in April. My dad, he had been here before—a year before. And then he went back and decided to come and live over here—bring the family down this way...We traveled down this way by horseback...And there was another family with us, you know, friends of the family. Because my dad and him had been here before, you know, so they decided to go back and bring the families down here.

So, I don't know how far we traveled by horseback, because from Zacatecas, Sánchez Román, where I was born, that's a long ways to come over here—I don't know how far it was from where we lived, but I remember getting on a train...But then we come down to El Paso...and we stayed there. I don't know how long. And then my dad and this other friend, they got hired on a railroad track working for the extra gang. And they allowed families on these extra gangs, I guess, because they were short of help at that time. There was two families on each side of the box car, living together, and we shared one stove on each side...And then from there, I think my dad decided to come to New Mexico, because we had an uncle on my mother's side living in Santa Rita. And then before we got there...we stopped in Wylie to thin beets.

My dad worked [in Santa Rita] maybe a year, maybe two, and then he decided to go closer to Colorado...And there in Lamar there was *una colonia grande*, a lot of Mexican people used to stay there in the winter time. After the work was done, we moved over there to the *colonia*...There was a lot of snow...it was way up high...And I went to school there, for maybe two months.

There was another family that wanted to go to Pueblo, Colorado, so my dad said, "Well, that's what I want to go." So this man said, "Well I have relations over there, and we'll find a place for you, where you can stay there." We went by train, I guess, to Pueblo...My dad got a job there in the steel works. He was working in the wire mill.

We went to this place—Bessemer School, and the town was also called Bessemer...And I had troubles with the teacher because I couldn't speak English, I was trying to learn. So I didn't learn very much, and besides, the school rooms were crowded. They had to put two classes in one room...I went to school there about five or six years...

I think it was 1927, some of the sugar companies needed people to go to work on the fields on the farms [to] thin the beets and top them. So they needed help at certain places, you know. So they send somebody from the sugar factory to town to advertise it. They would pay everything for transportation...My dad signed for it, because he was not working too steady then...We could go either to Nebraska or to Wyoming. So my dad says, "Send us to Wyoming." [Another family from Zacatecas] and we went on the same train to Riverton, Wyoming. And there we worked on the beets...

Then this other family, they said, "Well I lived in Salt Lake City before I went to Pueblo. There might be more work down there." So we started coming to Salt Lake [in 1927–1928]. [A friend] working there on the railroad told my dad that, "If you join the union, they'll get you a job on the railroad."... So we went over [to the Union Pacific depot]... I was probably about 15... the guy that was collecting the union dues was the road master. So he was the one that got us the job. We gave him $2.00 for me, and $2.00 for my dad. We got a job, and the other people got a job, too.

So they sent us way up—quite a ways from Salt Lake. Nothing was over there, nothing but brush, no trees, no nothing. This place they called Ajax, that's the name of the section where we were... The foreman in this section was a Japanese. And he didn't talk much. He was alright. And when he seen me, he says, "No, you're not old enough to work." I said, "Well, the roadmaster send me here, so I guess it's alright, isn't it?" [He said], "Yes, well I guess so. I'll take a chance on you." So I started working there.

Anyway, we were stamping bars, digging ties out, stamping bars—the little thumb bars, you know, [that they] tamp the ties with. And I stayed about, I don't know how many days, and my joints on my finger and my hands, they hurt, because I was not used to that tamping bars, you know. But that didn't bother me, I just kept at it...

Then in May they was looking for beet thinners. My dad said, "Oh, I think I'll go to Idaho because they need help to work in the beets ..." They send us over there to Shelley, Idaho, where the sugar factory was. The beet field man, he took us around looking for a place for us to work that first year. It was 1929 I guess... So we went down toward Firth, and we crossed the Snake River. He took us to one farmer that needed help over there. He had about 20 acres. And [the recruiter] said, "well I got some beet thinners here. You got a place for them to stay?" [The farmer] said, "Oh, no. Well, I have a chicken coop here. They can clean it up and sleep there." My dad said, "No thank you. You can have your beets!" So we told that field man, "No we're not going to sleep in no chicken coop."... So he took us around, and then he sent us to Shelley. There was a farmer there—between Shelley and Idaho Falls there was a beet dump right there. And the farmer was right there, right next to the railroad tracks. That farmer, he had about 20 acres. So we moved there. He had a nice place for us. So we thinned beets there. He had the biggest beets. You know, if you had 14 tons to an acre, you had a good crop of beets. He had 24 tons to an acre—great big ones. Boy, he made money!... We didn't stay on the farm in the wintertime. We moved to the sugar factory. They had houses there [in Shelley, where I met my future wife in 1935]...

In 1942 [I told my wife, expecting our first child], "Why don't you go stay with your folks, and I'll go to California and see if I can find a job." That's what I was looking for—a steady job. That was my intention all the time—get a steady job.

So I sent her over [to Nyssa, Oregon] and then I took off for California. I worked one week picking lemons and not ever got paid for it, because they were on a strike. I still worked anyway, after the strike, I still picked lemons. And then they had boxing there, too, so I started boxing [fruit] a lot…

Then, at that time, there was a war going on here—overseas, with the Japanese. They started taking all the Japanese away from the coast. They took everything away from them. And this farmer where we worked, he had 25 men working year round, planting seed, vegetables, cabbage, and whatever, you know. He had a big farm. Anyway, they took the farm away from him, and they sent

Image 7 Eighteen-year-old mother from Oklahoma, now a California migrant (Library of Congress).

him to concentration camps. And then that was the end of that job—steady job—that I thought I had...

[My wife's] folks called me and told me [my wife] was really sick, when she was having [our daughter] Rita, and they didn't know what was wrong with her. I was still working there at the Japanese, and so they send me a telegram. So I quit working, because no use staying there. They were going to take all the Japanese away from there. So I went to Nyssa.

And then from there, Rita was born, and I thinned beets over there. You know, they thin beets sooner over [in California], than over here [in southeastern Idaho]. Then I went back to farm over to Larsons [in southeastern Idaho]. This is 1942. And I was working there for the Larsons that summer. I thinned beets there and topped beets there all summer. I had a steady job at Larsons.

But my brother, he was working on the railroad here in the summer time, 'cause he didn't like the farm. He never did want to work on the farm, so he come to Pocatello and got a job on the railroad here...And I thought I was going to stay at the *rancho*, you know, at the farm over there. I like it out there. And my brother, he told me to come here [to Pocatello]. He said, "I have a job for you here, so you better come...You don't get no benefits over there. You have better wages here and everything." So because of him, I come over here to Pocatello. And ever since I was a railroader—worked in the roundhouse there—held different jobs, and moved around. I moved around, from one job to another, because the diesels started coming in.

From Oklahoma Dust Bowl to California: Mildred Lenora Morris Ward

Source Note: The interview is part of the California State University Bakersfield project, "California Odyssey: the 1930s Migration to the Southern San Joaquin Valley," which collected reminiscences from 57 residents who migrated to the Valley from Oklahoma, Arkansas, Missouri, and Kansas between 1924 and 1939. The full transcription is available from the Dust Bowl Migration Digital Archives maintained by the Walter W. Stiern Library at CSU Bakersfield. (http://www.csub.edu/library/special/dustbowl/interviews/Ward101.pdf).

Mildred Ward was born and grew up in rural Oklahoma, where her family farmed and she taught school. During the depression, Ward and her husband struggled to make a living; they decided to migrate to California for a new start. She describes below her expectations, experiences, and adjustments associated with the move to California. Judith Gannon interviewed Ward on January 19, 1981.

For years [my father] rented land [in Oklahoma]. I guess I was about twelve when he bought a little 80-acre farm, but we were still just about as poor as we were before. There were nine kids in the family. It was hard to make a living for us and pay for the farm. I remember the summer that I was sixteen and my younger sister was fourteen, we worked in the fields all summer barefooted. We even shocked grain and if you know what it is to walk in a stubble field barefoot you know that it hurts your feet. That summer my sister and I shared one good pair of slippers. One Sunday Gertrude got the shoes and went to church and visiting or wherever and the next Sunday I got them.

When I was fifteen I dropped out of school. I went to high school one year but I had to live away from home and work for my board. I'd get up at four o'clock every morning and work before I went to school. The next year the folks tried to get me to go back, but I thought if that's what it's gonna take to get an education to heck with it! So I stayed home. I thought I would work in the fields or do housework or something, but before I was seventeen the teacher said, "Mildred, why don't you take a teacher's examination and teach school?" At that time only ninth grade education was required to teach school. So I borrowed some books and stayed at home and studied by myself...

When I was seventeen I passed the examination and started teaching school [in 1925] and things began to look up. [But] the Depression came and times were really rough. We didn't have any money. Of course, we'd always been poor before and most everybody else in the country was poor, too, so we didn't feel any stigma or anything because we were just like everybody else...

Yes, we would have dust storms there till we couldn't see. It would be as bad as the fog is here in the Valley when it's at its worst, only the dust is a little different color and it's difficult to breathe. We had to hang sheets over our doors and windows to help to keep out the dust. When we'd go out we'd put something over our mouth and nose to keep from breathing the dust. It was a kind of a yellowish color. It was as dense as this fog now only a yellowish color and it would completely hide the sun. You couldn't even tell where the sun was...

I married a boy that lived just next door to the school. He tried to farm. We borrowed money to buy a team and seed and a plow and a cultivator. One year the drought killed everything. We made $100—just enough money to pay the rent. And the next year the flood did the same thing exactly, and that's what decided us to come to California. Of course I could have stayed there and continued to teach, but my husband didn't want that. Being a young man he wanted to work. We were reading articles in papers about how many hundreds of workers were wanted out here in this crop and how many hundreds of workers were wanted in another crop some place—all over California. We just knew that there was work in California because of what we'd been told and what we'd read in the papers. So we decided to come to California.

We came to Dinuba [in 1938] because I had a brother who had come here a year or two before. We drove an old Chevrolet with our belongings in a little two-wheel trailer pulled behind the car. We even brought our dog along. We had a highchair tied on top of the trailer, and we had a flat [tire] every day I think. We stayed in motels on the way—motels that had a kitchen where we could cook our supper and our breakfast. My brother and another young man came along with us. They came to get work, too... Oh, the road was just full of people like us coming out here. People with all their belongings tied onto old cars—all over their runningboard and even on tops of their cars. Cars full of kids—most of them had big families of kids... Many people slept out on the way to California. We'd see them fixing the breakfast out or see them asleep yet...

When we came out here we found that the work wasn't to be had—like we'd been led to believe that it would be, and my husband worked at just anything he could get to do...

Jim worked in packing houses and in the fields. Several summers he went to Bakersfield and worked in the potatoes. He worked in any of the harvest that there were here, anything there was to do, packing houses, anything. I didn't work then. I had a baby right after I came out here, and a few years later I had another baby. I wanted to stay and be a mother. I did go back to teaching when our youngest daughter was about four or five years old. We came to the realization that we would never be able to educate the children just on what Jim could earn. We decided then that I would go back to teaching. That was after the war and then they would just hire anybody to teach, there was such a shortage of teachers. First I started out substituting. I thought I can do that for a little while. I substituted one place and I was asked if I would like to come back next year so I told him yes I would like to come back and stayed there 24 years.

How did you manage when that first year jobs were so few and far between?
We just managed. We ate beans and oatmeal... and lots of time that would be all we would have. Biscuits and oatmeal for breakfast or beans and potatoes for supper and dinner. It was rough. It was rough for everybody then. It really was.

During this time, what kind of reception did you get from local California people? What was it like to be a migrant during that time?
Wasn't too pleasant, sometimes. A lot of people were kind and good as they could be, but some of them weren't. I even had a minister whose sermon one Sunday morning was about the migrants. During the course of his speech he said that we just find it virtually impossible to integrate these people into our western culture.

My son was about three when we came out here and after he started to school he was six, seven, eight years old, he'd come home and tell me that kids called him a dumb Okie. Well now, the kids didn't know what they were saying. I'm not blaming the children at all but they'd heard it somewhere. No it just wasn't very good sometimes...

At home [in Oklahoma] we were some of the leading or outstanding people in the community. In our community everybody looked to my father for things for advice and help and so forth, and in Jim's community everybody looked to Mr. Ward for the same thing. They were both outstanding men and we had been of those families. We were kinda looked up to and at least respected, and come out here to this where we were nothing.

Involuntary Migration to Mexico: Emilia Castañeda de Valenciana

Source Note: The interview comes from the Center for Oral and Public History, California State University, Fullerton, which houses close to 4,000 tape-recorded interviews that pertain to the personal, regional, ethnic, political, and international histories that link Southern California to a globalized world.

The disrespect that white migrants experienced did not match the actual loss of country for a half million Mexicans and Mexican Americans compelled to "repatriate," or move to Mexico, between 1929 and 1937. Once in demand for their labor, now Mexican Americans were believed to take "American" jobs, even though most of those persuaded to leave by county and city governments were U.S. citizens, the children of immigrants. Emilia Castañeda de Valenciana was born in Los Angeles in 1926, where her parents had lived and worked for over a decade. During the depression, because her father could not find work, her family had to give up their home and move to Mexico. Mrs. Castañeda de Valenciana was interviewed by Christine Valenciana, her daughter, on September 8, 1971. Since she was a young girl when she left for Mexico, Mrs. Castañeda sometimes does not recall details requested by the interviewer.

Tell me about the house of your parents; what happened to that?
Well, during the Depression, we lost it, since my dad had no employment. I heard from a friend not too long ago that her mother-in-law told her that a lot of the Mexicans weren't hired because the Anglos came first when there were jobs. Also, my dad wasn't a very young man, because according to my birth certificate, he was 50 years old when I was born...

Tell me how you originally got to Mexico.
After my mother died, I guess my dad was pretty sad. Here he was left with a family, a couple of children to raise, no wife, no work and living off of welfare. He had a trade and could work if the work was available. Maybe he thought that he should go back to his country. I'm sure he was looking forward to going back to his country at some time.

Why do you say that?
Because I guess some people had asked him or told him to become an American citizen, and he said that he would never become an American citizen. He wasn't going to step on his flag..."Yo nunca voy a pisar mi bandera." So he always wanted to be a Mexican until the day he died. I don't know what brought him to this country; I don't know if it was the revolution or what. Anyway, we went to Mexico because my dad asked [Los Angeles] county to send him back to Mexico. He told me that he asked to be sent... He knew he could get work there and that he wouldn't be living off welfare. So he asked us if we wanted to go with him, and

we told him, "Yes, our place is with you ..." We had a father so why should we be made wards of the state? That's for someone who's an orphan...So anyway, we left with my father.

I guess the county paid for our fare, Christine, and we must have sold our things for money. I don't remember that we had too much when we left. I don't remember us taking any furniture. You know how men are. They don't worry about anything like us women do. They aren't like us who say, "We want this and we want that, and let's save this and let's save that." A man, well, he probably just packs up his sleeping bag and throws it over his back and that's good enough for him. Now a woman, she'll think about whether she wants her sewing machine, her bed, and her dishes. I don't remember if we took all that, maybe we took some dishes. I remember we had our blankets. I remember we had a big trunk; it was one of these big trunks that they used years ago. So my dad must've packed as much as he could in that trunk...

First we went to Gómez Palacio, Durango to live with some relatives of my father. When we arrived there, I'll never forget it. I can still picture that man at the train station to this day. He was what you call a "porter" here in the United States. It's a *cargador* in Mexico. I guess it was funny to me because I was used to seeing the porters with those dollies that are used for carrying the suitcases. In Mexico, the poor man had a big white belt. It was sort of like a canvas belt that he put on his head. Underneath that, right on top of his head he put a padding and that was hooked on to the trunk. He carried that thing on his back for blocks from the train station...I'll never forget that poor man; that thing looked so heavy on him. I wasn't used to seeing such things. I'd come from the United States, and we were going to an entirely different kind of life...

So we arrived at the home of these relatives of my dad. She was an aunt of my dad's named Santitos. I think his mother and this aunt of his were sisters because her maiden name was Ochoa. I call her aunt because this is the way you're brought up. The Mexican people are brought up where you respect your elders, and if someone is your father's aunt, then she's also your aunt, too. First cousins are called *primos hermanos* and *primas hermanas*. They're just like brothers and sisters...Anyway, we arrived at my *Tía* Santitos' house. It wasn't really her house because she lived there with her married son. His name was Salvador...I'm sure my dad was paying them rent after he got started with a job...This family that we lived with had six children, three girls, then three boys. The oldest boy used to call me *repatriada*. I don't think I felt that I was a *repatriada* because I was an American citizen. Maybe we were *repatriados*...

You were telling me that you and your brother were a novelty.

Yes, we were a novelty, because, I guess, we spoke mostly English. We used to go to the store and we used to refer to the money as pennies, not centavos. So you know, the people used to laugh at us. They didn't really laugh at us, but, they used to get a kick out of it. So I think we spoke more English than Spanish…

Did you get the general feeling that you didn't belong there [in Mexico]?
Yes, I guess that I was putting it in the back of my mind. A lot of people did discriminate against us because we were Americans. We didn't belong there. Isn't it strange? Here, the Anglos discriminate against us because we're Mexicans. So, really, where do we belong? Tell me, where do the Anglos belong? They belong in Europe, don't they? They look down on us, but I think they should look down on themselves because their parents came from Europe and our parents came from Mexico. We're all foreigners. Their parents and our parents were foreigners in this country when they first arrived here. People used to discriminate against us because we were American citizens and didn't belong in that country…

I'll just say they didn't want us there. Maybe a lot of American citizens who went to Mexico during the Depression were kicked out of the country to get rid of us because we were a burden to the state and to the country. They went through the same things. Something should have been done to keep the American citizens from being thrown out of the country…

[After I returned to the United States] my godmother thought that it was good for me not to look for a job right away. She thought that I would go to school first to brush up on my English. I don't know how long I went to school. I don't remember how long it took before my English was good enough for me to go job hunting. And after I got a job, I paid Nina the money back that she had loaned me to come back into the country. I also started paying her for my room and board.

Before you were going to leave Mexico, what did people in Mexico say about you coming back to the United States?
In a way they were happy, but they did tell me that I was coming to a rat race, and asked me if I really wanted to come here. They told me that life in the United States was hurried. So I told them, "Well yes, you know, I belong there." I didn't know what a rat race was. But I'm finding out now what a rat race is, especially after having children. It seems that we are always in a rat race, going here and there…

Once you got over here in the United States, did you ever think of going back to Mexico?
To visit my dad, yes. As long as my dad was there, I had something to return to Mexico for. My only reason for going back was to visit my dad and my brother, but not for anything else. I have relatives there now and I'll visit them as long as I have the opportunity to go, because they are my relatives. I don't feel that I should forget about them. But I don't go back because I liked the life in Mexico. I mean, I wouldn't live as comfortably as I'm living here. Maybe someday, in old age, I may decide to retire in Mexico, but not really!

Leisure and Culture in the 1920s and 1930s

Even if the "roaring" twenties did not create economic prosperity for most people, Americans embraced new forms of leisure, entertainment, and mass media. Prohibition—the period from 1920 to 1933 when the sale, manufacture, and transportation of liquor for consumption were banned in the Eighteenth Amendment—pushed many leisure activities, such as social drinking, underground. Movies, mass-circulation magazines, and radio spread a national and commercial culture and found large audiences, even when the depression curtailed spending. The Great Migration of African Americans to the urban North also transformed American culture. New York City's neighborhood of Harlem became a magnet for ambitious, creative, and talented African Americans who infused new life into black literature, art, and journalism. The three excerpted interviews below reveal the myriad of ways that these new forms of American culture affected the lives of citizens on a personal level.

Questions to Consider: The interviews in this section reflect three very different communities—Butte, Montana; Harlem, New York; and Louisville, Kentucky—but they speak to the cultural tastes and creations of Americans during this period.

1. How did these narrators' views of Prohibition, the Harlem Renaissance, and the birth of radio shape their telling of their stories? Why do all three narrators share enthusiasm for their subjects?
2. What can the passage of the Volstead Act and the apparent lack of enforcement, at least in one city, tell us about this "noble experiment"?
3. Based on the information presented here about the development of the Harlem Renaissance and local radio stations, to what extent did ethnic and regional preferences shape new cultural forms, and to what extent did a larger, commercial culture bend these expressions in certain directions?

Drinking and Leisure during Prohibition: Helen Raymond

Source Note: The interview comes from the Montanans at Work Oral History Project, which collected reminiscences from people working in the state's major industries of logging, mining, and agriculture between 1900 and 1950. Deposited at the Montana Historical Society, the project's 200 interviews were collected between 1981–1983.

Temperance activists struggled for decades to ban the manufacture and sale of liquor, and their efforts paid off in 1919, when Congress passed the Volstead Act, which provided for enforcement of the Eighteenth Amendment (or prohibition). However, Prohibition did not end drinking, and as illegal sales of liquor generated more crime and vice it became increasingly unpopular. President Franklin Roosevelt promised a loosening of restrictions, and in December 1933, the Twenty-first Amendment was ratified, repealing the Eighteenth Amendment. Helen Raymond recalled her youth in Butte and its wide-open atmosphere during Prohibition before she married in 1924 and moved to another mining town, Sheridan, Montana, where she and her husband operated a hot springs or "plunge," hotel and tavern. Laurie Mercier interviewed Raymond in Butte on October 9, 1981.

Of course I lived in Kansas and we had prohibition always, it was never lawful to buy or sell liquor in Kansas. They had what was called the Blue Law and so I had never seen a saloon, or a little [road] house...

But prohibition as everyone knows was an unpopular law and it was badly abused and not recognized. I think that it was a shame that they ever had it because I think it broke down the morals of the people that would never have happened if they didn't have it, because once you think you can break a law, why you're in worse shape than if you never had it. As a citizen, you know. And they found out that they could, and it brought about an awful lot of grafts, you know, pay-offs. But Butte was rather notorious for being a happy-go-lucky town, mining town, and they had lots of violations of the prohibition and they had rules that were set up that were a little bit peculiar to their own town, more so than in some places...

I also understand that it was very easy to acquire liquor in Butte. Would one go to a speakeasy [place that illegally sold alcoholic beverages]?

Oh yes, and they served it kind of in the open. But they paid off... officers, there was [the] head of the Prohibition Act and he was supposed to keep it down and he would take money... Or he'd take—somebody squeal, there were all these people that would talk and tell on others, well if they didn't want to pay money, then they would have to tell on one of their cohorts that was making whiskey...

So it made people not very nice, it spoiled their character, and I think it was an awful mistake all the way around. But it wasn't quite as rough as Chicago and [prohibition-era smuggler and gangster Al] Capone and all them, but it probably would have gotten that bad if times had kept on. I don't approve of making the law and then not enforcing it, but I sure didn't think it was the right kind of a law. You cannot enforce morals, you just got to have other ways of education to teach them how to handle it, I think. Maybe it's just a dream, but I believe it could be done, I think better education on what liquor is and how to handle it is far better than saying you can't have it because when you do that people want it.

Was there money to be made off of bootlegging?

Yes, you could make money in the whiskey business, but the people that did make it, usually drank too much themselves. But there was quite a few people that operated and made whiskey and then all the business that never took a drink at all, and then there were people that ran bars that never drank a drop and they got ahead pretty good. I've known operations that made whiskey, they had thousand gallon vats. And they made it just like they did in real times, you know, but it was harder to put money into something and then get knocked over as the saying was. And you'd lose it all, cause they were rather foolish, they used to take and fine maybe, I remember one place they had eight hundred gallons of nice whiskey made and [enforcement officials] took axes and broke kegs and let it run down the street...

Lots of times [stills] were in the basement of your home, or they could be out in the hills [surrounding Butte]. I think that most of them were out. And you know, today you couldn't do it because the hills are so overpopulated that there'd be streams of people go by, you know and you'd be reported right away. But I have seen outfits that were in the hills that... up where the mountains are and the trees are and they'd just operated and run the still at night. Nobody walked up there... well people weren't as curious and there wasn't as many of them and the few people that would go by on a hunting trip and see a still, ninety percent of them wouldn't report them because they were more or less in sympathy with the operation anyway. So they didn't make it their business to turn them in... But today, I think anyone would go by and see you breaking the law, I think they would. That's why they had it out in the hills... it takes a lot of space to run a big outfit, you couldn't do it in your house. There were an awful lot of people made whiskey on the small scale.

For their own consumption?

Yes, and maybe they'd sell a little to their friends. I know people like that. And of course the bars had to buy it, and there were lots of bars.

How did they operate?

Well, they'd operate almost in the open. Sometimes they'd have soda pop and near beer in the front bar, and then in the back bar which wasn't right in front of the door would be a place where they'd sell liquor... Oh, and they'd get notice if they was hooked up to the protection agency with the head guy, they'd be notified to get your liquor out of the place. But if they weren't why somebody would just walk in and say, 'I'm so and so of the U.S. Marshall' or something and they'd walk back and behind your bar and if they found anything, you were put under arrest. But they would know that those other places, they'd go in and look behind the bar and there'd be nothing but soda pop and the glasses were rinsed and they couldn't find any liquor well then they'd just say, 'Okay, be careful not to be handling any' and go out.

American Renaissance: Marvel Cooke

Source Note: The interview is part of the Washington Press Club Foundation Women in Journalism oral history project and deposited with the Columbia University's Oral History Research Office. This nationwide oral history project collected about 60 interviews with women journalists who made significant contributions to society through careers in journalism since the 1920s. A full transcript is available by the Washington Press Club Foundation at http://wpcf.org/oralhistory/cook.html.

In the 1920s Harlem became the intellectual, political, and creative center of the "New Negro." Artists, writers, musicians, and others congregated here to develop a distinctive black culture that was rooted in the history, traditions, and experiences of the African-American people. Marvel Cooke was one of thousands of African Americans who migrated to Harlem to be a part of the excitement. She had grown up in Minneapolis, and her father, an acquaintance of the famous civil rights activist and intellectual W.E.B. DuBois, helped her land a job with the Crisis, *the publication of the NAACP that DuBois edited. In her interview, Cooke describes how she met many of the leading lights of the Harlem Renaissance, including writers Jessie Fauset, Eric Walrond, Jean Toomer, and Richard Wright, among others. Cooke was interviewed by Kathleen Currie in October and November of 1989.*

Can you talk a little bit about how you came back to Harlem to stay?
I came at a very low salary. There was a problem about where I was going to live. I had a cousin who lived in Brooklyn, and she insisted that I come and stay with her. I had no intention of living in Brooklyn. I didn't want to live in Brooklyn, I'll put it that way. Because it wasn't where the life was. The life was really in Harlem. Most of the people I wanted to know lived in Harlem...

I worked with an artist in Dr. Du Bois' office. He was trying to make a living as an artist, but he couldn't. I don't know if you've ever heard of him. He's one of the artists in that particular period—Aaron Douglas. He became the head of the Art Department at Fisk University afterwards. But he knew me and he lived here in 409 Edgecombe. He and his wife, who was a schoolteacher, encouraged me to come live with them. So I lived with them, and my husband [Cecil Cooke], who was not my husband at the time, spent many lovely hours in that apartment...

I didn't have any trouble at all getting that job [with WEB DuBois]. He was in Africa when I got there, and the business manager of the *Crisis* showed me the ropes. I was quite comfortable by the time Dr. Du Bois got back. Jessie Fauset had been his editorial assistant, and she had left...I had met her only once on a visit to New York. She was a very literate woman who had ambitions to be a novelist. She had written a novel that was published...So he put me in that place. She was an older woman, and I felt very inadequate.

What were your duties?
I learned how to make up a magazine. He assigned me a column, "The Browsing Reader" and I would go through the black magazines and newspapers and pick out interesting things and capsulize them and put them in this column called "The Browsing Reader." I think it's the first time I ever had a byline—Marvel Jackson. Then he taught me how to physically make up the *Crisis*. I worked with

him once a month on make-up...Anyway, we would take the different articles. He had written his editorial. There was a spot for that. He taught me how to paste up. After the articles that we were going to use were put in type, we would take them and just paste up the magazine...

Aaron Douglas was the artist on staff. There wasn't another writer on the staff—just Dr. Du Bois and the little bit of writing I did. But there was the business manager, Augustus Granville Dill. He had two secretaries. That was the staff...

I kind of came in at the tail end of [the Harlem Renaissance]. It was a fascinating period. Jean Toomer was around...I had a boyfriend named Eric Walrond. He just took me around every place, that's all. I was star-struck. I was lucky to meet all these people...He had met me before I actually came back here to live, and if I examined it, I wouldn't be surprised if he weren't one of the reasons I really wanted to come to New York. But anyway, it was a very thrilling experience for a little gal from Minnesota. I went to a lot of very interesting affairs with him, and I remember the shock I got one night when we went to a party. It was in some white person's home down in the [Greenwich] Village. I don't remember who it was. Someone said to him, "So Eric, you've got a Rosenwald Fellowship" [established in 1928 by the Julius Rosenwald Fund to provide graduate education for African Americans]. He hadn't told me. When he took me home, he said, "I'm going to have to leave you for about six months. I'm going to Jamaica to do some work on my book."

So Eric left, and I was just devastated because all my social life was built around him—he used to meet me from work. I was working with Dr. Du Bois on Fifth Avenue and Fourteenth Street. We spent every evening after work at the Forty-second Street Library, where I wrote and he wrote. We'd go across to the Automat and he would go over the stuff I wrote, and he expressed himself that he thought I had a lot of ability. I was really emotionally involved—it wasn't just for the writing, it was just that I liked Eric...

I know there was a club called the Civic Club, which used to have programs and dinners and stuff, and [artists and writers] would be around...You were invited. I was very lucky...I remember about Richard Wright. A few of us had started a writers' group, and Ben Davis, of whom I've spoken, was very interested in that. He was a very cultured person himself, a graduate of Harvard and a lawyer. He was very interested in the writers' group...One day, Ben came to our meeting...and he said, "There is a very talented young writer that is coming to New York from Chicago, and I'd like very much for him to be a member of this group." It turned out to be Richard Wright. He met with us for maybe six months or so, and then he asked for a leave, because he was writing a novel and he wanted to spend his time on that. It was *Native Son*...

How did you meet Langston Hughes?

I don't know. For instance, the Douglas home was a meeting place for all of these people, and there used to be terrific parties there. I remember Wally

Thurman...He was a writer...But they used to congregate around the house, and white people were fascinated by this group of young black artists. They used to come in droves into this area. I remember one time Aaron—I was married and living here at this time—Aaron called and said, "I want you and Cecil to get dressed up and come to my house." We were like on a show. A very wealthy white woman, I've forgotten her name, but she was a millionaire, used to love to come to Harlem to meet these strange black people who were writers, artists, etc. He said, "Be on your best behavior." That's what Aaron said to us. I remember being interrogated. They asked you: "What do you do for a living?" We told the truth, but we dressed it up.

In what way? Give me an example.

For instance, I worked for Du Bois. I did a lot of secretarial work for him, but I also wrote a column called "The Browsing Reader." I was editor of the column. I didn't talk about the endless filing and typing I did daily. Instead, I dwelt on the more creative part of my work...

Who read the Crisis? What was the audience for the Crisis?

I would judge from my own experience that most literate black people in the country took that magazine. I was very familiar with it, because it came to my home when I was a little girl. Every month we got the *Crisis*. As I say, during World War I, it was considered the number-one magazine in the country, black or white. Had great prestige...The *Crisis* went into homes all over the country, and the black press usually is centered in whatever city it's in. Therefore, I would say that the *Crisis* had more clout than any of the black newspapers at that time...

Dr. Du Bois was surrounded by all of those young people who were in the Renaissance...They were to write or to paint or, you know, to be involved in creative activities. Some of them, afterwards, did really do a lot of good things...

Coming from where I came from in Minnesota, to this very vibrant and alive group of young people was wonderful. Here I felt a freedom I had not known in Minnesota where I didn't realize that I was growing up in a racist society. I didn't realize it until I was sixteen or seventeen, and my best girlfriend, we used to sleep over with each other and all, I met her downtown and she refused to speak to me. She was probably with her very first boyfriend, and I guess she didn't know how to explain me to him. I never discussed it with her. I discussed it with my parents. They pointed out to me, "She probably didn't know how to explain you." That's when I first became aware of racism, that it was in the North, as well as in the South, and it was more difficult to handle in the North. You get hit straight in the South and you know how to fight it, but being hit at a tangent, you don't...

In 1928, late in the year, Dr. Du Bois came to me and told me that he was going to leave [to teach at Atlanta University]. He had some political dispute with the NAACP. I never knew what it was. But he wasn't getting along [with the leadership who he believed increasingly conservative]. He said, "I want to tell you that I'm leaving. I don't want you to be left hanging. If you want to stay, you can." But I decided I didn't want to stay if he was not going to be there. I started looking for a job. I found one in 1928...a job at the *Amsterdam News* [one of the largest African-American newspapers in the United States] as secretary to the women's editor...

I hated that job. But I wanted to stay in New York. I had made some very good friends, you know, in the Negro Renaissance, and I wanted to stay here...One day they needed a little filler for a spot in the paper, and the editor asked me if I could write it. He couldn't find [the woman's editor]. There was an empty spot on the women's page. I wrote this filler. He said, "You wrote that?" I said, "Yes." He said, "You shouldn't be here as secretary. You should be writing."

Turn Your Radio On: John Koch

Source Note: The interview comes from the History of Broadcasting collection of the Louie B. Nunn Center for Oral History, University of Kentucky Libraries, Lexington. The collection contains 19 interviews documenting the history of radio and television broadcasting in Kentucky.

Beginning in the 1920s, Americans could tune in other worlds via a new medium, the radio. Hundreds of radio stations sprouted across the country, reaching into urban and rural homes and public spaces like neighborhood stores, spreading regional music such as country and a national culture based on popular comedy and drama programs. In 1922 the Courier-Journal *and the* Louisville Times *launched WHAS, the first radio station in Kentucky. John Koch, a veteran employee of WHAS, recalled the heyday of radio in the late 1930s and 1940s and its programming that showcased local talent before national network broadcasting came to dominate the airwaves. Terry L. Birdwhistell interviewed Koch on October 18, 1979.*

Well, that summer in '37, I was planning to go to work for "State Circulation" [at the *Courier-Journal*] and a job opened at the radio station. They needed someone as a mail clerk and I went down to see them and they hired me...At that time they had a staff orchestra. A fellow named Harry Currie was the leader of the orchestra. Later he was replaced by a fellow named Bob Hutsell. It was pretty good size. They had around twenty, I'd say, on the staff. And they made a lot of use of them.

And then, in addition to that, they were doing all this live programming in the morning. I suppose now they'd call them "Country and Western," but we called them "Hillbilly" in those days. At that time they had...a fellow named Bob Drake who did a one-man show called "The Jackson Family." He did all the characters. I used to watch him. He'd write his script out. He'd just make notes on the back of an envelope, and he'd go and do this fifteen-minute show. They had a group called "Uncle Henry and the Kentucky Mountaineers," "Sunshine Sue and Her Rock Creek Rangers," "Cousin Emmy and Her Kin Folks." A man and wife team called "Salt and Peanuts." They would do these early morning shows and, although I guess you'd call them staff, I don't think they were on the payroll. They would do a show five days or six days a week, early mornings, in order to be able to plug their personal appearances. Then they'd get in their cars and run out to Frankfort or sometimes they might drive 150–200 miles to a town, do a show that night... and then come back the next morning. Oh, they had a group called "The Texas Rangers." See, before I'd gotten there, just a few years before that, I guess maybe '30, in that area, Gene Autry was singing at the station...

At that same time I can remember when I started working at HAS the girl staff vocalist was Dale Evans. And she was married at that time to a fellow named [Robert] Dale Butts, who was a piano player in the orchestra. And they had decided to leave 'HAS and go to the West Coast. In fact, as I understand, [how] she got her [stage] name [was] she took his first name, and there was a woman named Madge Evans who was a popular movie actress of the day, and she took her last name and became Dale Evans. Then, of course, eventually they were divorced, and later she married Roy Rogers...

Well, after you came to WHAS then, what did you do during the years that you were there?

I started out in the mailroom there. In '39 I moved into sales... Now, of course, they were with CBS then and radio was going big in those days. You had in your prime time, oh, "Lux Radio Theater" was a big show Monday nights eight to nine, as I remember. "Amos 'n' Andy" was tremendously popular then. I think it was on fifteen minutes every night around nine o'clock or so... it seemed like the whole country stopped when they went on the air. And they had a soap opera on then, real popular, by the name of "Mert and Marge." It was on at night, fifteen minutes, five nights a week. Eventually all the soap operas then moved to daytime. The networks didn't have so terribly many. They had some in the morning. But I remember WHAS used to carry about seven or eight. Procter and Gamble in Cincinnati would buy maybe four 15-minute periods back to back. Kroger in Cincinnati was buying about three soap opera shows... At that time sports wasn't too big. But then in the late '30s, I think, they began doing the Louisville Colonels baseball games. At that time General Mills was a big sponsor of baseball around the country for Wheaties...

One of the things that I find interesting about radio is that it sort of changed Kentucky in a sense that Kentuckians could turn on a radio and hear a UK [University of Kentucky] broadcast, they could hear [former Senator and Vice-president from Kentucky] Alben Barkley or [former Governor and Senator Albert] "Happy" Chandler or somebody giving a political speech, this type of thing. What type of effect do you think it had on the state?

Well, I think people depend on it for news a great deal. But really, until television came along, it was a tremendous entertainment medium for people. There were people who wouldn't miss the Lux Radio Theater and you know, Jack Benny was popular in those days, [George] Burns and [Gracie] Allen. The prime time hours from 6:00 or 7:00 until... of course in those days we were on Central Time, so at 10:00, people wouldn't miss the ten o'clock news at night...

That was the heyday—the '30s and the '40s... Yeah, you had Bing Crosby... [Grats] Colombo, all the Big Band era, they were on every night, you know. Here in Louisville, they did remotes from... oh, the Madrid had big name bands, and then across the river in Jeffersonville they had, I think they called it Log Cabin, and they had gambling over there. But they brought in the big name bands, and 'HAS would do remotes from over there every night... I think they got more into it right after the war... Well, see one of the big names there in radio was Asher Sizemore and Little Jimmy... But Asher Sizemore, he sold his song books for fifty cents or something like that, I guess. And it was before my time, but they told me about it, and he'd have people opening his mail and he'd have buckets of half dollars he'd be carrying out of there. He'd go around to these neighborhood theaters and play, you know, and just jammed-packed the place... well, some of them that were live were there selling things on the air, and they ran contests on radio, gave away prizes. And you'd be amazed at the number of entries they'd get in those things. I mean in the *thousands*...

And in those days they did a half hour show at 11:30 till midnight called "Dream Serenade." Herbie Koch played the organ and Jim Walton read poetry and they called it "Dream Serenade."... And I imagine it was real popular with the young people. And they had some of these mystery shows on radio that were extremely popular, where the people would get together... whole groups of them to listen. Turn out all the lights and they'd put them on around, I don't know, 11:00–11:30 at night, somewhere in there, and I can't even remember them all. "Inner Sanctum" was the one I know, and they had a creaking door on the opening... and it was amazing how popular people got who were on radio, and the listener had no idea what they looked like. They'd visualize them... and so many of them would just fall in love with a voice.

Work and Labor during the Great Depression

The Great Depression that lasted from 1929 until 1940 was the most severe depression in U.S. history. At times 25 percent of Americans were unemployed. Upon assuming office in 1933, President Franklin Roosevelt and Democrats in Congress instituted a series of reform and relief measures, called the "New Deal." These programs sought to steady financial markets and banks, rescue struggling industries and agriculture, and provide work relief for the unemployed.

Although facing insecure employment, millions of workers joined unions and went on strike between 1934 and 1937 to gain recognition and improve

Image 8 Striking seamen picket Commerce Department, Washington, DC, Jan. 18, 1937 (Library of Congress).

wages. Across the country, truckers, longshoremen, autoworkers, and miners won strikes and gained new rights for working people. Pressured by this labor militancy, on July 5, 1935, Congress passed the National Labor Relations Act, or the Wagner Act, which for the first time in U.S. history granted labor unions the right to organize and bargain collectively. Still, many employers, including the nation's powerful steel industry, attempted to hinder union organization.

Questions to Consider:

1. What do you learn about the nature of the depression from the three narratives presented? How did race, age, and region determine choices and actions of the three men?
2. How did the New Deal affect the lives of working people and families?
3. What explains the determination of Thomas White, and many others, to organize a union? Why did "Little Steel," and other employers, resist? Towards the end of the interview, White claims a supposed incident never occurred. How do you evaluate his version of events?

The New CIO and the 1937 Steel Strike: Thomas White

Source Note: The next two interviews are from the Youngstown State University Oral History Program. The oral history collection, begun in 1974, collects and preserves first-person narratives of northeastern Ohioans who have participated in or closely observed events which have significantly affected both the state and nation. The full transcripts of the interviews are available through the Youngstown State University Archives & Special Collections digital collection: http://www.maag.ysu.edu/oralhistory/oral_hist.html.

In June of 1936, the Committee for Industrial Organization (CIO), under the leadership of United Mine Workers' president, John L. Lewis, set up the Steel Workers Organizing Committee (SWOC) in Pittsburgh, Pennsylvania to organize steelworkers to bargain as one united group. To the surprise of many, by March 1937, the largest steel corporation, U.S. Steel, agreed to recognize SWOC as the bargaining agent for its members. But the "Little Steel" companies, including Republic Steel Corporation, resisted. On May 26, 1937, 85,000 workers of Little Steel went on strike. Aided by local police and National Guardsmen, Republic Steel mounted an aggressive defense, and sixteen strikers were killed on picket lines in Chicago and Ohio. Although the strike failed, by 1941 lucrative wartime contracts compelled Republic and other Little Steel Companies to halt unfair labor practices and allow secret ballot elections which later established bargaining rights for the new United Steelworkers of America. Thomas White, the first president of Local 1331 at the Republic plant in Youngstown, Ohio, was interviewed by Emmet C. Shaffer, on July 9, 1974. White recalls the struggles and intimidation endured by workers during the 1930s to establish the first local steel unions.

How did you get started in the labor movement?
My father was a member of the executive board of the steelworkers union in the old country, in Scotland. It was from him that I got my education and I was in the labor movement in Scotland and that's where I received my education. I started working for Republic Steel in 1930. I joined the Steelworkers Organizing Committee in November, 1936. I was, as I was in the old world, actively engaged in trying to bring a union into the Republic Steel. We had the assistance of organizers who were employed by the national office and they were very helpful in assisting us, too, in our efforts for organization. We, later on, were successful in organizing a majority of the workers in the Republic Steel.

We, then, held our first meeting in the Romanian Hall in Youngstown in the middle of May. I was elected president on the Friday of that month and when I went to work the following day, which was Saturday, I was told that I was discharged and no longer employed at Republic Steel for three years and two months. That was the penalty I had to pay. At the meeting of the executive officers, we also elected a guy by the name of Ira Alberts. Shortly after he was in office, we began to have suspicions that someone was supplying the Republic Steel with the names of the members we had signed up. This went on for some time and... we were able to find out that Ira Alberts was a professional scab and he had been a scab during a taxi drivers' strike in New York. At the following meeting... I asked him to resign...

The strike took place in June... However, when the strike was called, we had almost one hundred percent cooperation from the members who had signed up. During the strike, there were many incidents that took place... At Stop Five, on Poland Avenue, two steelworkers were killed and as a result, there was a riot that was instigated by the security forces of the Republic Steel. One of the picketers had a camera and he was taking pictures with the camera towards the entrance gate at Stop Five, when a policeman assaulted him. When the striker's wife, who was also on the picket line, started to interfere, she was assaulted too. This ended up in a riot. The security forces called the sheriff, Sheriff Elser, and the sheriff's deputies came up to Stop Five and were surrounded by the strikers. For some reason or other, the deputies felt that they had no right there in the first place, so then they left the car in which they were riding. The strikers upset the car and the gasoline started to flow on the ground. Someone threw a match, which lit the gasoline and lighted up the whole place. During that time, shots were coming from the security forces at the Stop Five entrance, and two men were killed. They were rushed to the hospital, but both were dead on arrival. It was shortly after that that Governor Davey sent in the National Guard, which was done at the request of the Republic Steel Corporation, and had an effect, no doubt, on some of the strikers...

Gradually, the workers began to go back to the Sheet and Tube. Republic was still holding fast. The Sheet and Tube opened an office in the Dollar Bank building and anyone that wanted to go back to work, could sign up there. Before too long, streetcars by the loads were headed towards the Sheet and Tube. Shortly after that, the strike was broken. And the workers at Republic Steel went back to work, except some who were kept out for six months, some for eighteen months, and as I said, for myself, I was out for thirty-eight months.

Anywhere I tried to get a job, the "Republic Steel" was there. I went to look for a job [at the Valley Mold in Hubbard] after the strike was broken. I was told to come out the next morning. Well, when I went out the next morning, the boss told me that the rush was over. No doubt the Republic Steel was there before me... I went out to Columbiana and was hired there and after a few days of employment, the Republic Steel sent an emissary out to Columbiana and endeavored to see that I was discharged...

To which group did the outside organizers belong? Did they belong to another union... these outside organizers, such as John Mayo?

Well, John Mayo belonged to the United Mine Workers. When John L. Lewis was approached by individuals from this district, to organize the steelworkers, he appointed Phil Murray as head of the steelworkers organizing committee. He then sent John Mayo into Youngstown as the district director. This effort to organize the steelworkers was possible because of the fact that the United Mine Workers of America paid into the organizing fund every month. Only because of the finance given by the United Mine Workers were we able to organize the steelworkers. I don't think that most of those who took the responsibility of each local in order to organize the people in their plant were too well acquainted with the labor movement as a whole. The result was that not only did we get a self-education, but certainly we were given a full education by the efforts of [Bobby] Burke, [Shorty] Stevens and Gus Hall. No two ways about it...

Did the Amalgamated Steel Workers do anything for the workers prior to the formation of the CIO?

Oh, yes. Sure. To those who have been active in the labor movement, it is a well-known fact that someone lays the groundwork before you go there. That certainly was the case here. Not only that, but I must give credit to the mine workers who were working at Republic Steel at that time. Also I should give credit to those who were on the WPA. These men, while they received a handsome sum of sixty-two or sixty-four dollars a month, most of them paid their dues every month...

Then, from 1937 on, could you describe the union activities up until you got the maintenance agreement contract in 1942?

Well, it was mainly a matter of survival. The only people that were paid at that time were the organizers. As far as the president of the local union or any other officer of the local union, this service was gratis. We were, I think, inspired with the idea that here we were, fighting back, after the strike was broken. I think it gave us more encouragement to know that someday the contract was possible and from there on in, the road would be a bit easier...

Most of the [organizing] work had to be done inside [the plant] after we went back. Most of the work had been done both inside and outside. After work, you'd see people at their homes and try to get them to sign up. That was the trouble in the first place. You know, Bobby Burke, regardless of what his political affiliation was, could persuade you that what he was saying was correct, without too much effort...On pay day, he would go to a beer garden and tell the guy to shut off the drinks. He would give a speech and I'd go out and sign them up. He was rambunctious, boy, I'm telling you...

One day there was supposed to have been a bunch of women and men and everybody else going down Poland Avenue with crowbars and pitchforks and clubs. Do you recall this?

That's a goddamn lie. I was there all the time. I ought to know. I never left Poland Avenue six weeks [during the strike]. Who the hell told you that? Boy, that's strange. Any demonstration was organized, believe me, because I helped

Image 9 Civilian Conservation Corps boys at work, Prince George's County, MD (Library of Congress).

organize them and I know what the hell I'm talking about. There was no disruption or anything else. They were told to be there at so and so because we're meeting at Stop Five. They were there, men, women, and children, and they would try to get across their ideas to women because we knew that we had to satisfy the women, too. After all, they were the ones that were suffering the most. They had a family and no money coming in. That was pretty goddamn tough.

Working for the Civilian Conservation Corps: Marvin Whaley

One of the first New Deal measures established the Civilian Conservation Corps (CCC), which provided work for unemployed young men in national and state forests and parks. It was one of the most popular national relief programs and lasted until 1942. Marvin Whaley, interviewed by Bridgett Williams on March 10, 1990, for the Youngstown State University Oral History Program, describes his brief stint with the CCC.

So, I graduated [from high school] in 1939. There was no work... I graduated from Leetonia, which is down in the Salem, Lisbon, Columbiana [Ohio] triangle. The work available was chopping weeds for the farmers at 50 cents a day or whatever. It was terrible. I tried to convince my mom to let me sign up in the Army. This was in 1939. Wouldn't it have been marvelous if I could have gotten in the service in 1939 before the draft hit. Who knows? Anyway, she came all apart like a volcano. She would rather kill me and bury me in the backyard than see me go to the Army. We survived that.

Then I heard about the CCC camp. A buddy of mine from school went over to Youngstown to find out about it. I was afraid of the fact that if it was similar to the Army, I wouldn't have a chance because I wasn't old enough to go on my own yet. Anyway, I went home and told my mom about it. The deal was that they would pay me $30 a month, but I only got $5. Twenty-five dollars had to be sent home to my family. That was part of the deal. She liked that part of it, it made sense. She could see the advantages there. [Since] I only had to sign up for six months instead of two years or longer, she finally agreed she'd sign the papers for me to find out what the CCC was all about.

Here's a high school graduate, 165 pounds, not a muscle on me anywhere—I was not a sports addict, and I didn't get into weight lifting or any of that stuff. [I] signed up. It's so vague, I can't remember how they got me there. I was on a train headed west. Where I enlisted and where they processed me, I can't remember that.

How far away from home had you ever been on your own?
Thirty miles, at my grandma's house. Here they are, sending me 2,000 miles away. Who ever heard of Wyoming and Utah and places like that? I can remember going through Denver. I got off the train there to get a candy or to just look around, and I got the devil because they ran it like the Army. They had sergeants and guards and so forth. You had to do what the rules said. There wasn't any room for individuality.

They were taking a bunch of people off the street. Some of them like me with no problems, but some of them were juvenile delinquents. Some of them were so bad that the judges said, "We'll suspend your sentence if you sign up in the CCC camp." We got quite a few people that way. What a mish-mash of people.

We finally got to a place in Manila, Utah. Now, as I got better acquainted out there, Manila was a town with about four houses, one store, a gas station/post office combination. It wasn't even a crossroads, it was a T-intersection. That was seven miles from camp. I got a toothache while I was in camp, and they sent me 57 miles to Green River, Wyoming, which was our nearest civilized community with amenities and so forth.

I was homesick, thrown in with a bunch of people that I didn't know. But I was big enough and strong enough that they put me on the jackhammer crew. I ran a jackhammer for four months. Then I graduated to the powder crew and set off explosions. We were blasting a highway through Ashley National Forest. We set off 55 cases of black powder. Now, that's a big truck load of black powder . . . The bulldozers moved in and shoved the rubble over in the valley. So instead of coming around this hill and back up this gully and out here, now the cars could go straight across. We felt we were really doing something. [Laughter]...

We had a group that was building fence to corral the animals—sheep on one side, I think, and deer on the other, or whatever. We had the road crew besides our jackhammer/blasting crew. We had another crew that cleaned ditches and fixed signs and stuff like that. I really think the boys did a lot of good...

They gave us two dress uniforms. These were probably left over from World War I, I don't know where they got them. Anyhow, they were olive drab, wool...Then, of course, we had our work clothes...blue denim and they might even have been used, I don't know. [Laughter] But I was so proud of this fancy uniform, I never had anything like that in my life. I kept one set down in the bottom of my foot locker underneath everything, nice and neat to wear home to get that conquering hero sort of feeling...but on weekends you'd have to kind of clean up, you couldn't wear your dirty old work clothes. I was down at the educational center, movie center...I was down there reading one night and I smelled something. Here I'd walked up too close to the pot belly stove and burned the knee out of my pants. Oh boy. Now they had to go to the laundry and repair it and I had to wear my others. I remember how terribly disappointed I was that I couldn't have a brand new outfit to wear home.

What was a typical day for you like?

We had a set length of time to dash over and wash up, shave, whatever. I don't think I was shaving yet. So, it was easy to run over, wash up, comb your hair, brush your teeth, get back, get dressed, and hit the mess hall at the right time. On the way out of the mess hall you cleaned your gear and put it over here and picked up a boxed lunch or bag lunch. You'd go out and get on the truck to go to the work site...This might take a half hour some mornings. [It might be] cold and snowy. We'd blow the snow off of [the compressors] and get them fired up. [We'd] get all the hoses blown out, get the jackhammers out and get them oiled and going and drill holes. All day long. Of course, it wasn't hard like commercial work would be with an employer driving you every minute. It was pretty sensible because we were kids. Of course, we'd have to stop early enough in the evening to put everything away because we didn't know how much it was going to snow that night.

One of the advantages I had on the jackhammer crew, I did not have to stand night guard and I did not have to serve KP. So, in a sense, I had earned myself a slot just above the ordinary...They rotated that around so no one person had to do it all the time. About four times while I was there, this one fellow worked night guard on Saturday night. I wish I could remember his name. He played a trumpet, I think. He blew reveille on Sunday morning and you could hear it echo off those hills. I tell you it was beautiful. And the beautiful part of it was that you didn't have to get up and go to work. That was real music and entertainment. I wish I could meet that guy today and tell him how much I enjoyed him doing that. He should have done it every morning. I suppose we would have got sick of it if we heard it every morning.

What was the biggest complaint in the camps? I know you didn't like getting up early in the morning.

That was the very first adjustment. I suppose most of the guys talked most about things back home. I mean, the gripes were, "If I were home I could do this," and "My girlfriend misses me, my mom misses me, I'd like to see my grandma," that sort of thing. This was the usual and generally what you would hear going on was the complaints that they didn't want to be where they were...

Was there stealing in your camp?

Yeah. I remember one time I really almost got psychologically destroyed. I had been very careful with my money. My mom had bought me a camera my second month out there. With the proceeds that I sent her, she bought me a camera. I'd been wanting a camera, so this was to be my Christmas present. I had to have money for film and stamps and developing and processing to get my pictures made. So, I was extremely careful with my money. I did not buy candy, I did not buy cigarettes, I did not buy beer, and so forth. I made the mistake one night down at the canteen of opening my wallet. I had five dollars tucked in that back slot back there that I'd saved up. Somebody saw it. I have no idea who saw it and I have no idea how it happened, but somebody got my five dollars. That was heart breaking...

I was there about five months and then it was time to re-sign or come back home. I didn't want to re-sign; I wanted to come back home. I was homesick. They offered me an assistant leader job, which was a six dollar a month raise and a little prestige. I didn't need the prestige, I needed to come home. So, I didn't re-sign up and came home. I realized when I got home that 165-pound high school kid that went to camp, came back a 191 of massive muscle from that jack-hammer and the work that I'd done. [It was] extremely good for me and helpful I'd say. That was the end of it, that was all I was taught, just a job.

Things began to perk up. When I got back in 1940, the war had started overseas and business was beginning to pick up, and jobs were beginning to bloom...

Discrimination and the Depression: Rev Walter M. Cavers

Source Note: The interview comes from the "Behind the Veil: Remembering Jim Crow" oral history project produced by the Center for Documentary Studies at Duke University. In the early 1990s a team of interviewers collected over 1,200 interviews that document African-American life in the segregated Jim Crow

South, from the 1890s to the 1950s. The collection is housed at the Rare Book, Manuscript, and Special Collections Library at Duke. Excerpts from the interviews appear in the co-edited volume, *Remembering Jim Crow: African Americans Tell about Life in the Segregated South* (The New Press, 2001), the 2001 American RadioWorks documentary *Remembering Jim Crow* (http://americanradioworks.publicradio.org/features/remembering/), and http://cds.aas.duke.edu/btv/menupagered.html.

With high unemployment during the depression, African Americans found it even more difficult to make a living, since entrenched racism privileged white workers over black. In the Jim Crow South, where President Roosevelt feared offending powerful white Democratic politicians and even refused to support an anti-lynching law, New Deal programs often operated on a double standard, paying black workers less than white. Because of extreme hardships and the constant threat of white violence, Rev. Walter M. Cavers had to leave his family in Alabama in the late 1930s and "hoboed" to Charlotte, North Carolina. Karen Ferguson interviewed Cavers on June 17, 1993, in Charlotte.

One of my ambitions, the biggest one, was to go to college. See, we didn't have no public schools back then. I attended public school three months in a year. Then that's all we got until the next year. The white [children] would be going to school up to May or June, but we only had our school open in November and it closed the last of February.

[One day] we were picking velvet beans. It was the kind of bean that would eat you up, scratch and sting you. I told my boss that I wanted to go to school. He asked me where I wanted to go. I told him Tuskegee. He turned around and hit me in the mouth and told me George Washington Carver should have been killed a long time ago.

I used to work for the gentleman [whose] place we stayed at. He asked me to turn a big log, and I couldn't turn it, and I walked off and came home. I told [my mother] what happened. She said, "Well, you better move on somewhere else and not let them find you here tonight." Sure enough they came. Just because I said I couldn't turn the log. Part of it did dawn on me before I left, that I wasn't a man, and I wasn't respected [by] the other race...

[In Alabama] I used to work on the WPA [Works Progress Administration]. I couldn't get nothing to eat. There wasn't no jobs. When [you] worked for the WPA, you saw no money. They gave you a slip, a little piece of blue paper and you could take it up there where you buy your coal; they specify how much coal to give you. Then you got your meal. They put it in there and you put it in a croaker sack and throw it over your shoulder and come on home. We cleaned out ditches. You didn't get no money. You only got food. I was scheduled to work two days a week. That's all I could work...They came around to all the employees and give them a green slip. That was to buy coal, food, and then they would give you a supplement which was dried beans, hog jaws, hog head, butter, meal, and I think it was five pounds of flour, five pounds of loose sugar. It depended on how many you had in the family.

I worked for 10 cents an hour in Alabama. If I was picking cotton—I never was a good picker—I would get 50 cents for that day's work. On a Sunday when they got ready to go [my sisters] would wrap their hair in plaits out of a cotton stocking. My shoes, brogans, I'd take lard and soot and make up the shoe polish. A car was out of the question. I had worked all year and didn't get anything, didn't have anything, and I couldn't see where I was getting no more. So a gentleman came down. I saw him coming down across the field on his horse. He said to me, "Walter, let the mules cool off a little bit." I said, "OK." I let them cool off and I got to thinking while I was out there and I just kept walking. Just kept walking. They looked for me and I was gone. What prompted me to leave there, it was spring and we were breaking land. I didn't even get a pair of shoes for the winter. I didn't get nothing. [The landlord] gave us an acre. My brothers and sisters, we worked hard on it and [made] a bale and a half of cotton. He took the cotton and gave us the seed. It wasn't nothing that my father could do about it. So that was in the back of my mind. I said, "Well, I'm going to leave here. Don't know where I'm going, but I'm going to leave here." I had nothing to look forward to. He had taken everything I'd made. So I'm going to go through another year and come up with the same thing, not even shoes. Uh uh, couldn't do that. So I just wandered off.

I didn't go back there no more. That was back in the thirties. I just had to get out from down there and I walked until I got to Calera. Then from Calera I went on to Saginaw, and I'd go around to the back door of some white residence and ask for food. They'd always hand me something...

So I went on to Saginaw, later made my way to Anniston and the train. [It was a] steam engine, and they had what you called the mail car. I got between there and stood there until we got in Atlanta. When I got in Atlanta, the sheriff discovered me. I mean the conductor or somebody discovered I was on there. I ran through the yard, and finally they turned around and left. I was talking with a colored person who was there in the yard, and he said... "I'll show you where to stand." So I went with him up there. After awhile, two locomotives came up with a string of cars [and] I climbed up between the mail car and the engine. That's where I stood all night long. So when I got in Charlotte somebody said to the conductor, "We got company back there." He came around there looking for me, and I went out on the right side and jumped off and went up Trade Street and then turned and went to Swatts Junkyard. Went over in there where they couldn't find me... Then I said, "Let me go and see if I can find something to eat and a place to stay." I never did that day, never did. So I slept at Martin's Shop up here on Statesville Avenue that night. The next night I didn't find anything. I was walking with no money and nowhere to live, and I was just sick [with pneumonia]. Those two Christian gentlemen [Bailey Young and Dr. Moore found me]... They took me to a widow lady's house on Palmer's Street... They put me to bed... [and Miss Butler] put tar, what they get out of pine, and covered my chest with that tar...

The gentlemen told her that they would pay her. I had nothing to pay her with. She was an elderly lady, and she liked the home remedies... The next morning... the Sunday school department [of] First Baptist Church, that I am now a member of, sent me thirteen dollars. The pastor there saw to it that I got food. I didn't know nobody, and I've been here ever since. Up and down, I just didn't know all of this could happen to a person in their lifetime.

World War II: Opportunities and Tragedies

The U.S. entry into World War II in 1941 presented opportunities for many Americans at the same time it brought tragedies to others. As the nation geared up for war, its industries demanded more labor. Pumped by government war spending, the economy bounced out of the depression and workers found plenty of jobs. As enlistments of men into the military increased, industries opened up formerly segregated jobs to women and minorities.

Images of "Rosie the Riveter" were designed to inspire patriotism, but higher wages moved most women to apply for war jobs—whether married, single, new to the wage work force, underemployed or experienced workers. Yet while three million women secured traditionally "male" jobs in war plants, fifteen million other women worked in traditionally "female" occupations in the service sector.

Following Japan's bombing of Pearl Harbor, a coalition of politicians, business and agricultural leaders, and military officials on the West Coast called for the removal of all Americans of Japanese descent from coastal areas. In this climate of racial prejudice and war hysteria, in February 1942 President Roosevelt signed Executive Order 9066, which forcibly evacuated and interned 120,000 Japanese Americans, two-thirds of whom were U.S. citizens.

Questions to Consider:

1. In what ways did World War II reorganize American society and alter gender roles?
2. How did the three women featured here experience the war differently from one another? Why? How did they face opportunities, challenges, and adversities as they entered the workforce, military service, and internment camp?

Women at Work: LueRayne Culbertson

Source Note: Like many community oral history projects, the Northwest Women's History Project (NWHP) began as a grass-roots effort to collect the stories of women who worked in the Portland, Oregon shipyards during World War II. Beginning in 1978 volunteers in Portland located and briefly interviewed 200 women workers on the phone and conducted in depth interviews with 30 women thought to represent a cross section of the shipbuilding experience. The NWHP produced a video and DVD, *Good Work Sister!*, available for order (http://www.goodworksister.org/), about the women workers. Interviews are deposited with the Oregon Historical Society.

LueRayne Culbertson's family lost their Wisconsin dairy farm during the depression and moved to Portland, Oregon, in 1936 to find work. LueRayne worked as a domestic servant and waitress to earn her way through high school. In 1941 she enrolled in a welding course and after graduation became one of the thousands of women who found work in the Kaiser shipyards in Portland. Welding was one of the few skilled jobs available to women; a few women became crane operators and pipe fitters, and others worked as cleaners, helpers, or in other lower-wage jobs in the shipyards. Despite earning higher wages during the war, Culbertson also experienced tragedy: her only brother died from head injuries when his Navy ship was attacked. Sandy Polishuk interviewed Culbertson in Portland in 1981. Culbertson's descriptions of dangers and accidents on the job challenge myths about women having "soft" positions in wartime shipbuilding.

My brother was in the service long before the war. He wrote and said that it would be a good idea if I got over there [to Hawaii], and the waitress work was good. But he said, "If you don't want to, take a welding course, because it won't be long before the women will be doing the welding." And that sounded like a good idea to me…

But I sure didn't know what I was getting into when I got into it. It sure wasn't anything like school. I mean, you go to school and they give you this nice little booth where you have everything, your machine is perfect, your rods are perfect, everything's lovely; and you go out to the shipyards and you get a bunch of green rods…and you'd get soaked to the quick [from rain], you'd take your first rod and put it in the stinger, and wham! You'd get a 240-degree volt shock…

I think I cried myself to sleep the first week I was in the shipyards. "What have I done? How did I ever get into this mess?"…That was tough, for complete greenhorns to go out on large construction and not know what on earth you're getting into. I mean, sure, you're going to be a welder. You get a little plate like this and you weld it, and then all of the sudden you go out there and see a big ship with all these cranes and operations and whatnot, and noise…You just weren't expecting that…

[As a waitress] we were making twenty-five cents an hour, but the tips were good. So I worked the day shift in the shipyards and then went nights to Nendels [restaurant] and worked…When we went out to the shipyards, we didn't know whether we would be staying, or whether it would be temporary or permanent, or what the score was. And you took a while to get adjusted…I must have been in the shipyards a good year before I gave up the waitress work. And just welded. We had fun! It was hard work, but it was interesting work. I think what made me decide to give up waitress work was one day I went out there, I had my hair all braided, and one of my braids came out of my bandana and burned off, and I had one long braid and one short braid, and I had to go to work. I thought I smelled something, and here my hair was on fire. It just was burned completely off... and [I]was supposed to go to work and look like a human [laughs]. Of course, we were always burned up, you know. No matter what precautions you took, those sparks would get in the gloves, in those suits. My boss promised me an asbestos bra from the day I started, and I never did get one.

I've got [a scar] on my face that slagged during the hot weather. I was welding a big three-eighths rod up on the main deck and put my foot up, and that slag hit right on my face. It just took the hide right off. But it wouldn't cool as fast as normal during that real hot weather. [During the summer] I bet those decks were a hundred and thirty out there. And you'd weld with that real hot metal, and then it would slowly cool, and when it would cool the slag would crack off and just shoot...

But I have yet to complain about the heat, because I said, "If I ever get thawed out, I will *never* complain again about the heat." You'd get chilled, wet and chilled, going into that yard, and you'd freeze to death the entire time you were there. That was so miserable! You'd just get cold to the bone and couldn't get thawed out... You dressed for it, but your leathers weren't waterproof. And they'd just soak the water up going in... And you'd look kind of funny trying to weld with an umbrella. You'd just get soaked to the quick...

One time I thought I'd be real clever. I was going to keep my hands beautiful because I was going out that night. I put on a pair of black gloves under my welding gloves, and I got a spark down in there. I can't even remember which hand. But the spark burned through, and I got that black dye in there in the burn. Some of those welding burns just wouldn't heal. You'd get a scab over them and they'd fester underneath. Of course, it wasn't the cleanest place in town [laughs]...

In 1941 I paid 120 dollars for my first suit of leathers, custom-made, from Oregon Welding. But that was expensive! Every week it was a new pair of welding gloves, and at that time they were [$] 7.95. And you'd get a month's wear out of a suit of leathers. Just burn right through them, if you were serious about your welding. I was on the outside shell specialty crew for at least seven months. That was premium pay... something like $1.36 an hour or something. But you'd sit there and these sparks would keep going down on your suit, and it didn't take any time till it burned through. You'd just, all day long, sit there and weld the shell, or else you'd be welding the roll steel to the cast steel on the end of the boat. And that really shocked, because it was a tough weld to make. The two metals just didn't want to adhere, and the sparks would just burn up your suit, burn up your gloves... A lot of times we'd have those [dark glasses for the hood] so spotted in one shift that you couldn't see out of them. You just had to send over your lead man or they'd bring you a new one…

And then I used to burn up so many welding boots and wear them out. They were expensive. And I put cleats on this one pair, boy, I was smart. I was going to save those boots. Put cleats on them, and the first thing I knew I was welded to the deck. Some smarty came along and just welded my cleats right down to the deck. I go to move and wham! [laughs] So I didn't cleat any more of my boots…

There were jobs all over. In fact, I got restless and I went to Willamette [Iron and Steel] and worked on those PT boats for a couple weeks…I quit without a clearance. And when they found out I didn't have a clearance, I went right back to Oregon [Shipbuilding Corp.]…A kid's got to change around and see what's going on. There might be something greener over there. Same wages; it was all standard wages…

I used to weld the thrust foundation where the actual molder sat for the ships. They had an eighteen-inch hold that you crawled through. And you'd have to put your hood in first, you had to take all your rods out of your pocket and strip down to get through the hole so you could get in there and weld, and it had to be absolutely perfect. But most of the time…you welded without ventilation [because] you couldn't get your sucker or your blower in there because there wasn't room…I had pneumonia twice while I was in the shipyards. You get down there without air, and hot or cold…It had to be done. Those boats were moving fast. You were putting out one every other day there towards the last…

I worked for [my future husband] for about six months. And then we got married, and then I got pregnant and had my first little one in '43. I went back to work when she was seventeen days old and worked up until three weeks before she was born. And that was rough, climbing around on those yards [laughs]. But those leathers concealed it; nobody knew.

What did you do for child care?

I guess I must have been fortunate, because one of the women—her husband worked with us—took care of her until she was six months old. And then I got in the Fruit and Flower Mission…I'd walk over to the Fruit and Flower Mission and catch my ride to the shipyards…[The Mission] charged according to what you made, and when my husband and I were both working we paid the highest rate. And our apartment was $45.00 a month…Food seemed to be awfully high then…and of course you had to have your ration stamps…the red stamps were for meat, and the blue stamps were for sugar and coffee. And then you got one bottle of liquor a week…

The only thing I had trouble with was, in the apartment, you washed once a week. That was it. And there weren't any laundromats then, so you washed by hand every night diapers…My husband wasn't a washer. He'd wash dishes, he'd take care of the babies, he'd do everything, but washing diapers was not his speed…[I'd] hang them out anyplace I could hang them, because if I got caught washing more than once a week, I got chastised and I could lose the apartment...

You worked so hard that... A lot of them would stop at the tavern and have a beer, but I never had much time to actually linger with any of the people that I worked with... You didn't have too much time, because you always tried to prepare for when [your husband] would get drafted and have to leave, and you always tried to get ahead just three or four steps so that in case the worst came to worst you'd be prepared for it. Because they were even talking about drafting women there for awhile. Rumors get around, and you think, "Boy, I'm going to make it now while I can." Do it right now!

Was it a lonely kind of thing?

Oh, heavens, how could you be lonely with a chipper over here, and a welder over here, and somebody else over here, and somebody else tapping you on the shoulder to see what's going on? No, it wasn't lonely under those hoods. And it was such a pretty sight under those hoods. Really, welding is a beautiful art. It's much more fun than stained glass or something. But you could sew the prettiest seams, especially those verticals. You could just make the prettiest seams. And when you'd chip that slag off and see that gorgeous weld underneath, no undercuts, no nothing, just a beautiful weld... It was a real satisfying job.

Women at War: Violet Hill Gordon

Source Note: Created by the United States Congress in 2000, the Veterans History Project of the American Folklife Center, Library of Congress (LOC), collects, preserves, and makes accessible the personal accounts of Americans who served in World War I, World War II, and the Korean, Vietnam, Persian Gulf, Afghanistan and Iraq wars. Over two thousand interviews have been digitized and are available on the LOC website: http://www.loc.gov/vets.

In addition to industrial jobs, women found other new opportunities in the nation's armed services during the war. More than 350,000 women served in the military, most of them in the Women's Army Corps (WAC) and Women Accepted for Volunteer Emergency Services (WAVES), a branch of the naval reserve. Barred from combat, many of the women still faced dangers as pilots, photographers, and nurses near battlefronts. However, most were stationed in the United States.

Violet Hill Gordon joined the Women's Army Corps in 1942. She received Officer Candidate Training in Ft. Des Moines, Iowa, and then was sent to Ft. Huachuca, Arizona with the first detachment of black women. She then moved with a detachment to Ft. Lewis, Washington, and then reported to Ft. Oglethorpe, Georgia for an overseas assignment to the European Theater where she served as an officer in the 6888th Postal Battalion. Judith Kent interviewed Gordon in her Florida home on March 25, 2002. Gordon describes her historic experiences as a WAC and how they shaped her life on return to the States.

Well, I joined because my best friend, Mildred Osby, appeared at my house one day, all excited because she had either received information or had learned that there was going to be an organized Women's Army Corps. She wanted very much to be part of it; and, as we were very close friends she thought it would be wonderful if I also was interested and would do so.

At that time I was working in State Civil Service; I was supervising a stenographic pool. I was not bored, but restless, kind of stuck, I guess. But I wasn't that excited about entering into anything that sounded as regimented as the Army. So I didn't pick up on it initially. She kept after me and after me and I finally said, "Well, OK." That OK involved filling out a detailed application, and then taking a series of examinations which included physical, aptitude, psychological tests...

Those steps determined whether or not you were considered material for Officer Candidate Training. This was such a bold step in a way. One has to remember that at that time the Army was segregated and number two there were nurses but there were no enlisted or women officers as an official part of the Army. Of course, this would not be officially a part of the Army; it would be an Auxiliary branch of the Army...

Then having applied I was sure that I would never pass all of this business. At that time I had completed two years of college. Their goal was forty Negro women who would then form the officer corps that would train the subsequent enlisted women who came into the service. Their expectations and their hopes were high. They wanted forty professional women. I think that the minimum age was eighteen, and of course they preferred women who had not only the education background but also some maturity and work experience, which would be an asset in embarking on an endeavor that was experimental and had a lot riding on it. I really didn't expect to be selected, but in the end I was, along with my friend...

So then you were inducted.

Yes, I didn't know at that time, but there were four of us who were inducted from the Chicago area...when I say four I am referring to four Negro women who were selected. I knew of one and she is the one that I trained with; my first assignment was as Second Officer under her...

I remember I had never been at an Army camp; I don't think that any of us had. Ft. Des Moines is an old, established camp. Of course, there had not been women there before so they had to set up and establish housing and facilities for women. I do remember writing a letter home because officially we were dubbed "The Third Platoon" referring to the platoon of women who were being trained as officers. We were housed in a separate barracks, one long building...

These are all African-American women?

Right. You have to remember that this was all before Truman truly desegregated the services...

What helped you get through that period?
It helped that we were young! [laughs] I think that the thing that really sustained and enabled all of us was that underneath the adventurous aspect of it was a sense of duty; it was our country, that we were at war and that there was a purpose to all of this. So, that there was excitement and fatigue. In the beginning it was mostly fatigue because it was: up at the crack of dawn and a day that just continued at such a pace until taps at night you were just exhausted... It was the feeling, the sustaining feeling was that we were doing something purposeful and had value to it...

There were two Companies that were sent out to Ft. Huachuca [Arizona], the Thirty Second and the Thirty-Third with a commanding officer and two additional officers... As the troop train took us to the boundaries of the camp, of course the male units that were already there knew that we were coming. There was a lot of controversy about women in the Service, a lot of rumors, most of them not really very complimentary. The curiosity, of course, impelled as many of the enlisted men that were available and free to view this arrival, to come out and meet this so called "Women's Army." It was a little frightening in one sense in that we were like engulfed and surrounded by all these men. But fortunately, the Army is usually prepared for most things, so the enlisted male units were not there without officers who made sure that some kind of decorum and order was maintained. As we embarked from the train and the companies were formed, we then marched the units into our quarters. They had set up a whole area for the women so that we had our own headquarters building, our own barracks, officer quarters, mess hall, and the whole shebang. We were really a self-sustained unit and that is the way we operated for the period of time that we were there.

A certain portion of the women [were] being assigned for training. You had to have cooks, you had to have pastry chefs, and you had to have motor pool people and all of that. So the initial phase was to see that our women were trained to take over. The basic idea in all of this is that women were to replace and release the male soldiers so that they could be sent overseas or dispatched someplace else. Our initial stay at Huachuca really involved a training period for the women in the various areas that were needed to function properly...

What would you say was the most stressful aspect of [the experience]?
Two things. One in Ft. Huachuca, when we realized (or when it was brought to our attention by one of the sergeants) that there was lesbian activity in one of the barracks. We had not been given any special directive in terms of how to handle something like this. So, it was a question of trying this and trying that. Basically, as I recall the Commanding Officer did not ignore it, talked directly with the women who had been singled out (or whose names had been given) and there was some reshuffling in terms of the barrack assignments. No one was discharged or given any negative marks...

The second had to do with the assignment overseas. First we were in England, then we moved from England to Rouen, France . . . the area in which we were housed was an old, not a castle, it was more like a fort. It was a larger area surrounded by an eight-foot wall. The German prisoners of war were housed in one part and they were the ones who worked on the grounds and all of that. The part that was difficult was that it was cold! . . . We were working like around the clock, three shifts, because we were handling mail that had been piled up waiting for this Postal Unit to come and handle this mail. It was like a factory, which was all right except that if we could have been more comfortable. I can almost feel that dampness and dankness of the whole thing. There it was a physical thing.

Were there entertainers that came?

Yes there were, but I guess that the only one that stands out in my mind really is Cab Calloway, for some reason. He must have been with the USO and sent overseas. That is the one name person that I remember. Both in Birmingham, England, that is where we were for the first part of the ETO [European Theater of Operations] for the first part of the assignment overseas. This has nothing to do with entertainers, but the townspeople in Birmingham particularly were so warm and receiving, when we had free time and went into town. One of the things that I remember is that, I love music, and the churches would have twelve o'clock or one o'clock concerts. If you had free time on that particular day you could go into town to the concerts. That was just like a wonderful reward. And of course we had free time to travel . . . And the townspeople were really very supportive. Then of course in Rouen, the damage was more prevalent and visible . . . I think also that the prisoners of war made you constantly aware of the war; it was ever present . . .

Then after the act was passed to make this a full part of the Army we had an option at that point to leave or to stay, and I had a conflict. I remember that I wrote not only home but also to very close friends saying that I wasn't sure that I wanted to stay in. All of the advice that I got was, "Stay.". [laughs] So I thought, "Well, maybe they know something that I don't know" . . . They were so right because on discharge I finished my college and graduate school on my G.I. Bill . . .

Do you think that would have happened without the G.I. Bill?

I don't know. I was floundering at the point that I went into the Army. It was like . . . certain things became resolved and I became focused and knew what I wanted, what I wanted to do. I wasn't sure about the occupation, but my Company Commander was a graduate social worker; many of course were teachers . . . I doubt that I would have gone into social work if I had not had the interpersonal experience with Irma and a couple of other people who were also in the service and were moving in that direction. It drew my attention to a profession

Image 10 Japanese American evacuees in Pinedale (CA) Assembly Center dining hall, 1942 (U.S. Army Signal Corps).

that I had really not considered up until that time. So, once having decided on that, I knew where I was headed...

So that I went from having gone to elementary and high school in Batavia, Illinois, which is a suburb of Chicago, a town of five thousand people. So that I was really in development from there to the experiences that followed with the labor union movement, followed by movement into the WAC, which moved me then into both an administrative as well as a command level. It kind of enabled me to move away from a bucolic, somewhat shy, introspective person. So that I would say that the Army influence was like the final push in a very positive direction, if that answers what you asked.

Negotiating Internment: Amy Uno Ishii

Following Executive Order 9066, Japanese-American families in California, Oregon, and Washington had short notice to close up businesses and homes and pack what they could carry, and they were transported to one of ten internment camps established by the War Relocation Authority. This action represented the worst violation of American civil liberties during the war: families were broken up, lost millions of dollars in hard-earned assets, and faced psychological anguish as they spent up to four years behind barbed wire. Amy Uno Ishii was interviewed by Betty E. Mitson and Kristin Mitchell for the Center for Oral and Public History, California State University, Fullerton, in July 1979. Ishii describes the impact of the war and the internment on her family.

Do you recall the day of the Pearl Harbor attack? Do you recall any special feelings you had?

Well, of course. I think we all went through a terrible shock. On that Sunday morning I was living as a domestic away from home, and so I was not with my own family. By that time I was almost twenty-one. I was working as a domestic out in San Marino, and I had just served breakfast to the family when the news came on the radio that Japan had attacked Pearl Harbor. It's hard to describe the shock. I know that the American people were in great shock at the time of Pearl Harbor. And they were angry; they were very, very angry at the Japanese for having been so daring as this...

We had mixed emotions about the bombing. We were thinking, "Japan is committing suicide," because it is such a small country. All of Japan could be laid right across the whole of California, and it would be all over with...And at the same time we were very upset because the general public...even the people that I worked for treated me and talked to me as though it was my own father who was piloting those planes out there at Pearl Harbor...I remember they told me that I could go home and how I had better stay at home until the FBI could clear me of any suspicion. I said, "Why should I be suspected of anything? I've lived in your home for many years now, nursed you when you were sick and fed you. And I never poisoned you once, and I'm not about to do it now." But they said, "You had better stay at home until we can get the FBI to clear you." And I thought, "Wow!"

I felt like an ant. I wanted to shrivel up into nothing, and my mind was going a mile a minute, thinking, "What am I supposed to do, what am I supposed to say? All I know is that I am an American, and yet now, at a time like this, people are going to say, 'You are a Jap,' and that turns the whole picture around." I had never been called a "Jap" in my life. All of these things were going through my mind. By the time I got home the FBI was at our house...They were tearing out the floorboards, taking bricks out of the fireplace, and looking through the attic.

How was your family reacting to this invasion?

Well, we just stood there—blah! What could we say with military police standing out in front with guns pointing at the house, and telling us to stay right there in a particular room while they went through the whole house? They tore part of the siding out on the side of our house to see if we were hiding things in between the walls. And all we could think was, "How ridiculous!" It was so nonsensical. They didn't have a search warrant. They didn't have any reason to be coming in like this and tearing up our house. And when they left, they took my father with them...We didn't hear from him for a long, long time...

How much time did you have between the announcement of Executive Order 9066 and the actual evacuation?
Well, we knew in February that we would eventually be evacuated. We didn't know just when, but there was a deadline. They offered us a chance to leave the West Coast voluntarily. Japanese people who had money, or businesses, and could liquidate all of their property and businesses could take their families and move voluntarily inland... But our family was not able to voluntarily evacuate so we were at the mercy of the military police...

First, we had to dispose of all our belongings, and this is a thing that really, really hurt. We stood by so helplessly when people, who we thought were our friends and neighbors, came by and said to my mother, "I'll give you two dollars for your stove, a dollar and a half for your refrigerator, a dollar for your washing machine, and fifty cents for each bed in the house, including the mattress and all the linens." That really hurt because we knew—I was old enough to realize—it took my mother and father twenty-five years of hard work to put together a few things. And then to have this kind of a thing happen!

We finally got rid of everything except we had an old fashioned upright piano that we were very fond of, and there was no way that my mother was going to let that piano go for two dollars. She just refused; she said she would take that piano out in the backyard and take an axe to it before she'd let anyone take it away for two dollars. On evacuation day, we were all told to assemble with our belongings. We were allowed to take approximately a hundred pounds per person or as much as each individual could carry, and they told you what kind of things you should bring...

Depending on where you lived you were told to be at a particular place by 9 a.m. on a particular day. Then the trucks and the buses would roll up and take all your belongings. They tagged everything with your name. Then you got on these trucks and buses. From the minute we left our home to the time we arrived at Santa Anita Racetrack, we had no idea where we were going...

What were these barracks like at Santa Anita?
They were just temporary housing... People were living in Seabiscuit's stable. The horses were not there, but the straw was, along with the smell. The Terminal Island people and the San Pedro people were the people that really had it the worst because they had to live in the stables. We called it Dogpatch, but it was actually the stables area. It was a terribly dusty, dirty, smelly area. We were lucky; we lived in the parking lot area where they had constructed these new prefabricated barracks. Each barrack was broken into six units, and each family took one unit, so there were six families living in one barrack... we had approximately twenty-two thousand in the Santa Anita Assembly Center... we were there the first week in April, 1942. I left Santa Anita the first of September to go to Heart Mountain, Wyoming. My mother, sisters and brothers... were sent to Amache, Colorado... When we were in Santa Anita, I decided I was going to get

married . . . The man that I married didn't register at the same church where my family had registered . . .

What was your first impression of Heart Mountain when you got there?

Well, we knew that America was huge, but we didn't know it was this huge, to have so much barren, open space the way they had up there. For miles and miles around—you could look as far as your eye could see and you couldn't see the first tree. No trees, nothing green, it was all brown and there was this mountain just sitting behind us. We thought, "Well, maybe the mountain will act as protection for us." By the time we arrived there, which was approximately the tenth or the twelfth of September, they were in the middle of a dust storm . . .

For the first three days, we didn't even know where our baggage was. We couldn't find our things, and trucks were going up and down between the barracks yelling out family numbers to see who would claim certain things. They said, "Don't go looking for your things, they will bring them to you." So all we could do was to sit on the stoop of our barrack and wait and wait and wait. Life became a waiting game, the whole time that we spent in camp. You waited in line to go to the latrines, to eat in the mess halls, to do your laundry and to take your showers. It was just a total waiting game. The fellows complain about doing this in the Army, but it was no different in our concentration camp—the same thing.

Did you and your husband have jobs? Were you assigned jobs to do?

Yes, I worked in the camp hospital as a nurse's aide. My husband, a musician, was on what they called the educational program, and he was assigned to either teach or to play music. He chose to play music. So he organized the Hawaiian Band and they called themselves Alfred Tanaka and His Singing Surfriders. We got a bunch of Japanese girls that were from Hawaii, and we taught them to dance the hula, some of them already knew how. I used to do a lot of singing, so I was the vocalist for the group, and I learned to sing all these Hawaiian songs. We used to go from block to block. Each block had recreation halls, and in order to keep the morale of the people up, we'd have what we'd call talent night. We would do the entertaining, and he got paid nineteen dollars a month for that and I got nineteen dollars a month for being a nurse's aide.

You mentioned you had four brothers serving in the Army. What units were they in?

Well, my brothers all volunteered at the same time to go into the service. They were in Amache, Colorado. There were bad feelings among the Japanese people in the camps, because all the Nisei, the American citizens that were eighteen years of age and over, were made to sign a [US War Dept. loyalty] questionnaire, to state whether they would be faithful to this country or not [and whether they would serve in the armed services if ordered] . . . Many, many Japanese people said, "Don't sign it. By golly, they've got us here. If they want us to be loyal Americans, turn us loose, put us back where we were, send us home, and then draft our boys into the service. Then our boys would be justified to go and fight for this country and prove their loyalty to this country." So there were a lot of hard feelings.

My mother, brothers and sisters all agreed that if the boys volunteered to go into the service in spite of the fact that their father was interned in a so-called "hard core enemy alien camp." My mother—who had done nothing against this country except raise ten children—was behind barbed wire. In spite of all that, my mother felt, "If you boys go and serve this country and prove your loyalty, maybe they will turn Daddy loose, and at least give a chance for Dad to join Mother and the children and bring back the family unit" ... So the boys decided that they would go ... They entered what you call Military Intelligence. They called them G-2s. They went as interpreters ... to the Pacific theater of war. Two of my brothers went with Merrill's Marauders to the Philippines and then on to China, Burma, and India ... In the meantime, Ernie ... thought he was going to go where his brothers had gone; instead they sent him to the 442nd ... So he went along with his brother-in-law to Italy and France, and fortunately, both of them came back to America after serving in Italy and France. So it was a very interesting thing to see the boys go to the various parts of the service in the United States.

FOUR

1945–1965

World War II changed work, gender relations, and American culture, and it also elevated the role of the military, government, and industry in society. Optimistic about peace at the end of the war, Americans were soon faced with a "Cold War"—the tense relations and military competition between the powerful United States and Soviet Union—that lasted 45 years. The Cold War led to military actions abroad and growing tensions at home, as politicians exploited fears, instituted loyalty oaths, and restricted free speech.

Despite these Cold War anxieties, Americans embraced new possibilities in their social relations and educational and economic opportunities. The labor movement gained new members and influence in spite of Cold War attacks, and its wage gains contributed to a growing middle class. African Americans organized after the war to challenge systemic discrimination and segregation. The civil rights movement of the 1950s spawned new social movements addressing a host of concerns in the 1960s. Migrations of Americans from city to suburb, and from rural Indian reservations and the South to urban areas, changed the spatial as well as demographic nature of communities. These migrations, encouraged by government policies, created social change as Americans reorganized family, work, cultural, and social life around the automobile, suburb, and consumption, and new ethnic identities.

The eight interviews in this section explore these dramatic changes in the postwar period. The first two oral histories reveal the *Cold War* strains among leftists and labor unions, two groups under attack by those who insisted that the United States and its capitalist economy deserved only praise. The next section expands the discussion of *migration* by probing how African Americans and Native Americans adapted their cultures to new homes in the urban North and Southwest. Two more interviews describe individual and collective efforts to gain *civil rights* in the 1950s and early 1960s. The final oral history excerpts illuminate how women negotiated *gender roles* at work, home and neighborhood prior to the revival of the feminist movement of the late 1960s.

The Cold War at Home

At the end of World War II and the emergence of the United States and the Soviet Union as the world's most powerful nations, Americans became increasingly fearful of communism abroad and at home. McCarthyism, named for the Wisconsin senator Joseph McCarthy who held sensational hearings of "reds" in the government in the 1950s, actually began earlier with the creation of the House Committee on Un-American Activities (HUAC) in 1938. Initially chaired by Martin Dies Jr., the committee investigated the charges of communism in several New Deal programs. After it became a permanent committee in 1945, HUAC targeted Hollywood, academics, and the labor movement to ferret out suspected communists but in the process chilled dissent. Yet for all the hysteria about domestic communists, few Americans actually belonged to the Communist Party USA. Its heyday had been in an earlier period, in the 1930s, when the country suffered a tremendous economic crisis and left-leaning movements found appeal for their attacks on the capitalist economic system that had failed many Americans.

Because of their intermittent challenges to corporate power, labor unions not surprisingly came under attack in the hostile Cold War political climate. Unions had attracted communists and other leftists in the 1930s and 1940s, and many labor leaders welcomed dedicated and talented organizers regardless of their ideological stripes. But faced with rising anticommunism and penalties under the Taft-Hartley Act, passed in 1947 to limit labor's ability to strike and harbor radicals, the American labor movement adopted anticommunist measures to retain its respectability. In 1949–1950, the CIO expelled eleven left-leaning unions, exposing them to jurisdictional raids by other unions and weakening the labor movement. The political alliances and machinations among opposing forces preoccupied many unions for over a decade because of Cold War anticommunism.

Questions to Consider: In the following two interviews we read about opposing perspectives concerning the role of and supposed threat of communists in American life.

1. How do the narrators characterize American communists? Why did they or did they not represent a threat?
2. Are the narrators different in their sympathies towards workers? If so, how?
3. How might a controversial subject such as domestic communism shape the way a narrator frames a story about the topic?

The Left during the Cold War: Rose Leopold

Source Note: Portions of the interview were first published in the February 1996 issue of the *Portland Alliance*, and the interview is deposited with the Oral History of the American Left project at the Tamiment Library and Robert F. Wagner Labor Archives in New York City.

Rose Leopold, born in 1918 into a left-wing, immigrant, Jewish family in New York, joined the Young Communist League in 1935 while enrolled in Hunter College as a night student. She later joined the Communist Party USA (CP). She moved to Portland, Oregon, in 1951 and remained a political and cultural activist, despite the postwar repressive atmosphere. Sandy Polishuk interviewed Leopold in November 1995 in Portland. Leopold describes why many were attracted to the CP in the 1930s and how the Left became marginalized and more fearful of openly criticizing the United States during the Cold War.

[When I was in college in the 1930s] there was a lot of activity. We're talking about a tumultuous New York, full of activists of all kinds. Oh, they had all kinds of demonstrations in Times Square and... thousands upon thousands of people...

But, like a fool, I took a year off from going to school and I became politically very, very active. All kinds of meetings. You can go crazy with all the committee meetings and this kind of meeting, that kind. Go to the picket line for this strike or that strike. And then I decided that was a mistake and that I was going back to school and graduate...

I led a very busy social life because New York was such a big city, there were so many things going on there. The [CP] *Daily Worker*... had a column called "What's On" and all of these social activities were listed. That included performances of one kind or another... All kinds of dances went on, all interracial dances.

It was a marvelous time to be young, to be involved in every aspect of what was going on in the world. To be involved up to the hilt and to really feel very positive about it... It seemed like everybody in New York was politicized. Everyone had a political idea, political notion. Might not agree with yours, but they were very political. They understood what the score was...

I was in the midst of everything. I was discovering dance and theater and concerts... You had all the wonderful WPA projects, Living Newspaper, theater arts... So I was in sort of that maelstrom of all kinds of intellectual and cultural activity at the same time that I was busy with my politics and it was a real fermenting of processes. I sort of see it in a... jumping for joy kind of era. Even though there was [World War II] and so on, but you were in it and you were contributing to anything political there and you were doing. You know, you were not passive... It was a marvelous place to grow up in and I think I was very lucky...

[By the 1950s] it began to slow down. It was post war and the living was high. You know, there were lots of jobs for everyone and a different era and attitude. And we won the war, right? We moved out [to Portland] and I got in touch with people who were in the Party, but it petered out here and I was happy to see it go...

I was beginning not to believe in what the Soviet Union was doing toward socialism. It took a long time. You didn't just wake up one morning and say, "Hey, they're terrible." It didn't operate that way. It was over a period of years...Things began to leak out. I think a lot of Communists held back because we expected all these lies and all these deceptions on the part of this government to try to discredit the Soviet Union. So we thought, "Oh, sure they're gonna put out this false information about labor camps and what's happening there," never believing that it was true...

But that's not the way it turned out. As time went on these things emerged and the [communist] clubs just dissolved. No great surprise to me when Khrushchev was busy confessing and explaining [and delivered his famous speech denouncing Stalin in 1956], being a brave man, actually.

Why did you join the party?

Well, I read Marx and I read Lenin. I took courses at the [CP] Worker's School downtown Manhattan and various places. And I believed in it. I believed that socialism was the answer in order to get a brave new world. And the Soviet Union was there and here was a chance to see if it was working out. For a period of time the feeling was that they were struggling, but they were surrounded by a capitalist conspiracy—which they were...I came to realize that the Soviet Union did it in absolutely the wrong way and the Russians, who were brought up on the Czar's authoritarianism, never learned to change themselves, you know...I still consider myself a radical socialist, but I'm not sure anymore about people and governments.

Did you feel victimized by anti-Communism?

Sure. Especially here, that time with the [Republican Congressman Harold] Velde [HUAC] committee coming here [and holding hearings in Portland in June 1954]. I wrote a letter [to the *Oregonian*] about the Velde committee, [a] very carefully worded letter and a daring letter, when I think about it. I was of two minds about sending it because I thought, "How can I send it and they publish it? What's going to happen?" I sent it and it was published...

I think when I wrote about the Velde committee I was still a Party member. So I was quite frightened about that. I thought they're gonna put me in jail. Who's gonna take care of my children? That kind of stuff. And it could have very well been possible if they wanted to do more frame-ups, you know. I don't remember any repercussions to that letter specifically... It was such a dead silence about the Velde committee and it was so fearful. It was just terrible here.

One weekend, I think it was Decoration Day weekend, everybody went to the beach, every progressive that I knew of and some who thought they might be called by the Velde committee. But if they're out of town they can't be found. That was a perfect place to hide and that's what some of them did...You didn't have to be Communist. A lot of people were caught in that web. They were not Party members, but they sympathized with left-wing causes. It was a nightmare time. A lot of fear...

And then I was head of the [Ethel and Julius] Rosenberg-[Morton] Sobell committee [after their arrest in 1950 on charges of espionage], so that was a real step into the limelight, I'm sure. Once I formed it here, there was nobody in the Jewish community to talk to...The only one who had any response to me was the mother of one of the dentists here in Portland. She said, [whispering] "I'll send you a little money." Something like that. Afraid to talk about it. It was like dead silence...

You got the left-wingers to form a committee, that's who you got. The Jewish community was silent all over. They were scared shitless...You had two Jews who were national spies? We never had anything like that before, ever.

It was a terrible, dreadful time. Really, we were very brave here to stick our necks out when I think back on it. I didn't think one way or another, you just do it. Right? It came to be me because I think I was on the mailing list of the *National Guardian* and they called me would I put up William Reuben who had written the first articles on the Rosenbergs, which took a lot of guts, would I put him up at my house. He was coming here to speak. So I said yes and that's what began because once he was here then a committee began to be formed and then other speakers came. Some very nice people.

My house became the center for it and we had a lot of affairs, raised a lot of money or tried to raise a lot of money. People going in and out with literature. So step by step I got involved. I felt worried from time to time, but the thought never entered my mind that...you're gonna stop what you're doing. It just never occurred to me.

Did the FBI ever come?

We all expected the FBI. I knew that my phone was tapped. You could hear those click-clicks all the time. In fact, we'd joke about it over the phone. I was prepared for what I would say. We all tried to be prepared. You knew that eventually they'd come.

They came to the door and they wanted to talk to me. I said, "I'm not interested in talking to you..." and I closed the door. I don't even remember what they said...I was a little scared, but not terribly much. They never came again. I think that they knew what the answer would be...in the process, see, of denying them...very often people would start a little speech and...they would latch onto something...and something would leak in some way and they'd put all of these little leaks together in this big enormous crossway puzzle. That's why they came.

We never got any publicity on the Rosenbergs except adverse publicity... But mostly we raised money. We had big dinner parties and charged for it. We had a lot of fun. Raised money and sent it to the committee. That was the function. There was nothing else you really could do in those times. The speakers spoke mostly at homes; I don't think we even rented places.

Then [the Rosenbergs were executed June 19, 1953] and that settled it. I'll never forget the day they executed them. I can see myself where the radio was in a hallway of that little house that we rented and [my son and husband] Jaime and Bernie were out in the back yard and I must have screeched, "They electrocuted them, they electrocuted them!" Jaime came running in from the backyard. He knew just what I was talking about and he started to console me. It was really a day of mourning.

But then we went on because of [the case of codefendant Morton] Sobell. And the Rosenbergs' name had to be cleared, you know. Sobell's wife came a number of times and stayed at my house and we raised money for Sobell. He was in jail [sentenced to thirty years for alleged non-atomic espionage] and she was trying to get him out in the worst way. She tried everything. She saw the queen of Holland. She saw just about everybody you could think of. Then by the time he got out, of course, the marriage was gone...

I was busy. Rockwell Kent came out. There were a number of celebrities within the left-wing circle that came out and stayed, now that you are reminding me. A number of literary people. And then somebody from the *Worker* came out. Very good writer, an editorial writer. It was very exciting. It was a very intellectually stimulating cause, I had a lot of very interesting people come, you know.

The Cold War and Labor: Frank Fiorello

Source Note: The interview is part of a larger collection, the Schenectady General Electric in the Twentieth Century / General Electric Oral History Project, at the University at Albany (UA), State University of New York. Since 1991 the project has focused on the history of one of the nation's premier electrical industry pioneers. Many UA oral history interviews are also featured on the U.S. Labor and Industrial History World Wide Web Audio Archive, and in the "Talking History" radio series, which can be heard at http://www.talkinghistory.org/.

Frank Fiorello was a second-generation General Electric worker in Schenectady, New York and an important player in the local struggles within the United Electrical, Radio and Machine Workers of America (UE) in the late 1940s and early 1950s. Like many of the left-leaning unions expelled from the CIO, UE had organized workers regardless of craft, gender, region, and race. But many of its white ethnic members, some influenced by the Catholic Church, worked to disaffiliate and join avowed anticommunist unions, contributing to disunity within the labor movement. Gerald Zahavi recorded the interview with Fiorello on November 22, 1991, in Schenectady. In the excerpt below, Fiorello provides details of his growing opposition to left-wing leaders in the UE.

You said you joined the union very soon after you got the job—when you came into the plant. Did you participate at all in the union?
I didn't really start participating [in the union] until after the [1946] strike... I got a call one day from my cousin [Frankie Sibitello]. He was a shop steward. They were having a meeting; he called me up, and he says, "Frank, there's a bunch of guys here, they want to get rid of the communist control of the union." So I says, "It's about time." They were shop stewards and I can't remember all their names, but there was about twenty—thirty of them there. They talked about the commies that were in the Local... That's how I got active, started to decide then I had to do something about it.

You mentioned that it wasn't until after the strike that you got involved with the union. Was that because of the strike? I mean the union—it had always had communists.
There was no difference between the *UE News* and the [Communist Party's] *Daily Worker* [on]... foreign policy and everything. As a matter of fact, during the '46 strike, there was a pledge amongst all the CIO unions, the Auto Workers, the Steel Workers, and so on, that no union would... settle before there was a joint settlement of all the companies together. The UE broke that pledge. That's how it started. That fight went on until 1949, when they finally were expelled from the CIO... [I was] doing all I can [laughs] to get rid of those guys, yep, oh God.

And what did "doing all you can" involve?
Well, I never missed a membership meeting and raised my voice every time—and many times I was there all by myself. You know, people didn't want to go to meetings in those days, except the real die-hards. The only time they showed up at meetings was when there was a big issue at hand. And so many times, Marty [Stanton], Carmen [DiGirolamo] and myself were the only three of our group at the meetings, and just a handful of others. But this went on for, you know, '46, '47, '48, well that's a few years to carry on that torch all by ourselves, just to let 'em know we were there and they weren't going to intimidate us, or push us out, by any means, and quiet us. It was just loose knit... As a matter of fact, I and Marty and Carmen were expelled from the union in 1947. They made a big mistake, doing that...

There was a trial [by the Executive Board]. I never received notice of the charges... never got 'em even at the membership meeting... By that time I had an attorney, John Vaughn, who... came and helped represent us to make sure that we had our rights. He volunteered his help. Nothing came of that. They brought the recommendations out to the membership meeting to expel us from the union. At that time, we had a maintenance-of-membership clause in the contract, which meant that the company had to fire us. It was a way of firing us from the plant, to get rid of us! That's why we had to go to court and defend our rights. There was supposed to be a membership meeting scheduled in the latter part of November, where there was to be nomination of officers. And that was the urgency of going to court, so that we'd get our membership reinstated so we could participate in that meeting to elect and nominate the people that we wanted to run for office. That happened in the latter part of '47. By virtue of the injunction that the court gave us to reinstate our membership, we went to the meetings—not without much ado.

OK, so you won in court. What happened at the meetings when you came [back] in?
They kind of harassed us. We didn't take it serious. I mean, there was no violence or anything like that. They'd follow us around and half of the meetings that we had—well they had their spies there, and I knew who they were...

What were the issues that split the left wing and the right wing? What were the things that most bothered you about what they were doing in the union?
Well what they were doing in their dealings with the company. They were in the company's back pocket. And we put it that way. And there wasn't much redress for grievances and things like that from their representatives... I had one specific example that I can recall. I was working in Building 37 at the time. And one of my guys that I work with was complaining about his rate. He wasn't getting paid enough for the job that he was doing. So I said, "Look, put in a grievance, call the shop steward;" and he did. So they tried to talk him out of it. I said, "Look, you stay with that, and you insist that you get full process on that grievance." They wound up meeting on his case... So they told him after the thing, "No way." They says, "This is it." You know, and, it was the union that backed off on that case.

And there were other cases that I heard of too, especially down there in Building 69. It was a piecework place—milling machines—and Marty Stanton was their shop steward down there. He had to protect himself against the Local, because they were consistently trying to come in and find out why his rates were higher than any other milling machine operator in the whole plant. And what they did was they policed their work—the shop stewards did themselves—because they didn't want the guys to turn in too much so that the company would come down and cut their prices. They did that very effectively. But in the other areas, the guys went hog wild and the first thing you know the company came and slashed their prices and the union never did anything about it. They did try to get on Marty and his crew down there and different things like that.

Was that after he began opposing the leadership?
Oh yeah, yeah. Even before I knew him. I met Marty in 1946 or '7. But even before that there was that kind of strange relationship going on between his

group and [the other group that opposed the left wing] were from the shops, too. I knew a lot of the boys who were in that group, and we knew that we couldn't stand a chance if we had three groups running—two groups opposing the incumbent... I didn't hear too much talk about being anti-communists so much from that group as from our group. We had several meetings together, you know. We had to wrangle it out and we finally did. Some of the people we had on our slate we had to take off, and intermingle who they had. We had socialists... Dave Fisher was chairman of the Liberal Party. He was the first president of the union when it was organized, back in 1936 or '37, and he was in our group. Charlie Campbell [was] another one. I don't know if he was a socialist or not, but he was certainly not a Catholic. It was a mixed group. We sorted out our slate of officers and [in 1948 we won]. [I was elected] Recording Secretary...

Were [pastors] actively involved in local debates over [union] politics or other things? I understand there was a labor school run by one of them...

[Father Edward LaRoe ran the labor school]. Most of the things it covered, like, you know, what was going on in the unions, the Communist Party, and the history of the Communist Party, and what they were doing and what they were up to. That's about it; [he took] no other active role other than conducting the school, and once in a while he'd have a speaker talk. They were democratic unionists. They were told how to do that, but most of it was about the Communist Party. There was nothing formal. It was just open discussion. It was just a group of guys getting together, no materials, just listening to everybody talk. [Father Charles Owen Rice, noted pro-labor and anticommunist priest] came up here a couple of times. One time he came up here when we were electing delegates to the UE convention—in 1948, I think it was or '49. He was a very effective speaker—fiery...

In these fights that were held locally, did the company ever get involved on one side versus the other?

[The Company] always claimed that they were neutral... Yeah, they got involved... The fight we had with the commies was nothing compared with the fight we had with the company. Jeez, it was fierce.

Migrations

The migrations within the United States set in motion by 1920s immigration restrictions and industrial expansion continued after World War II. Many people moved from rural places to cities. African Americans and whites from the South, Puerto Ricans, and Mexican Americans continued to be pulled to the North and the West. The Great Migration altered the racial makeup of cities, as many whites began leaving central cities for new suburbs. The Sunbelt region—stretching from Florida to California—and its sprawling new cities and suburbs, also attracted new industries and migrants. With all of these different movements of people, the postwar era became characterized by geographic as well as economic and social mobility.

Native Americans made up another internal migration in the United States. After conquest in the nineteenth century, the U.S. government had sought to assimilate Native Americans into the dominant culture through a variety of policies, including land allotments and boarding schools. In the 1950s, the federal government initiated a "termination" policy to end its relationship with Indian tribes and make them assume all responsibilities of full citizenship. During this period the government terminated over 100 tribes, including the wealthy Menominee of Wisconsin and Klamath of Oregon. It also encouraged American Indians to leave their reservation homelands for jobs and new lives in urban areas. The lack of economic opportunities on reservations also compelled many Native peoples to migrate. However, instead of ending their tribal identification as Sioux or Navajo or Shoshone, a new urban pan-Indianism developed, which fostered the development of an Indian rights movement that in the 1960s and 1970s demanded a return to tribal sovereignty, re-recognition of terminated tribes, and support for Indian education.

Image 11 People sitting on front porches in an African-American neighborhood in Chicago, IL, 1941 (Library of Congress).

Questions to Consider: In the following two interviews, narrators recall opportunities obtained by moving but also report some ambivalence about their transitions to a new home in the postwar era.

1. What was gained, and what was lost by uprooting families from the rural South and a southwestern Indian reservation to move to an urban area?
2. What aspects of their traditional cultures did narrators retain in their new communities, and why?

Opportunities in the Industrial North: Joe Farmer

Source Note: The interview comes from the Hudson River Museum (Yonkers, NY) project: The Great Migration: Stories from the South to the North. Additional interview excerpts are available at http://www.hrm.org/Migration/MigrationThumbnails.htm.

Joe Farmer left North Carolina at age 12 to join family who had migrated north to Newark and New York City for wartime job opportunities. He attended high school in Long Island, graduated from SUNY Oswego, and became the first black teacher at Bay Shore High School on Long Island. He later came to Yonkers as a principal and retired in 1995 as Assistant Superintendent of the Yonkers Public Schools. Here he recalls his migration experience, the impact on his family, and the challenges and opportunities presented by both city and suburb. Roger Panetta of Marymount College interviewed Farmer in November 2001.

Joe, we have been talking about why people left the South and what went into that decision. Do you recall that experience?
I recall that experience very well... Shortly after World War II when they stopped making war machines they came back and started industrializing this country. And they also started making farm machines. And as a sharecropper [in Wilson County, North Carolina], part of a sharecropping family, the need for all of those hands picking cotton and tobacco and all of those crops, it just dried up. Because I remember one season, we were picking cotton on this side of the road and on the other side of the road, I as a little boy, I saw this big machine picking cotton. I said, "Wow, why are we doing this if that machine can do it?" Guess what. The next year, the machine was on this side of the road and we were on our way north to try to make a living in the industrial North...

When you decided, because of the industrialization of agriculture, to move to the North, did you have images of what the North would be like in your head?
Well, I did have images. I thought it would be, you know, just a municipal place and I thought everybody was doing well because some of my older siblings, they had already left before. They had established themselves, and they would come back to visit. I had a brother with an automobile. In those days, that was the biggest thing happening.

But something happened that wasn't so nice... I'm from a family of eleven, and I was the last of eleven. And my father and mother, we were a very nice family on this farm, but when we migrated north there was no apartment that could accommodate, at that time there was still about five of us... My father, who was in agriculture, he was a great farmer, wasn't prepared for the industrial North. And he took a job in sanitation but there was no way he could support his family. There was no way that we could help. Like on the farm, everybody participated. But when we came North, and I remember it so clearly, one day I woke up and my father was gone. And I think, and as I look back, I think it was the pride that he had, you know, always being the head of his family and then he did not have the ability to support his family... Because I remember he had a job at the sanitation department and every now and then I would see him cleaning the streets or something, but meantime, we had all of these children in the house trying to go to school and all, whereas when we was on the farm, we all had chores, we participated, we did this, we raised our own food, we had our vegetable garden, pigs, cows, chickens, and we raised everything that we used to eat.

So it was a total culture shock in many ways. When I was in the South, I remember that it was totally segregated and my whole society was black. And when we came to the North, there was a strange kind of integration... I was in Newark, New Jersey... First thing I noticed, all of the teachers were white. Then I noticed the little grocery store on the corner in my neighborhood, an all-black neighborhood, the owner was white. And I became very aware of the... racial difference here... Because I lived in a black society in the South. I mean my teachers, the principals, my doctor, the storekeeper, the undertaker; they all looked like me and I had no question about my future in terms of what I could be...

See, I was denied school, because when it was time to do the harvesting in the South, you just didn't go to school. You just put in tobacco, shucked the corn or picked the cotton. So I found myself, in the eighth grade, the teacher had me stand up to read one day, and I couldn't read too well. And I was embarrassed... But when I told my mother, she thought we should learn how to read. We learned how to read. And that's when I think education... was always the one thing that we said was the liberating force. It was always preached in my house: if you get an education, boy, you can determine your future. And I kind of believe that...

You know, as a kid, I remember in the South, your whole environment was family, your neighbor, and relatives. And I remember these family occasions where we would get together to celebrate, and cooking, eating, and music and all. I came north; there was none of that. And the families were dispersed. I remember I had to live with sisters and brothers where because my mother was working in a hospital over here... so we kids kind of had to move all around. And that secure family tie and the family reunions which happened often in the South, was absent in the North. So you were like on your own. You were an island. No one seemed to have any expectations for the young people in our community and they didn't seem to have any expectations for themselves.

I remember... what saved me, in the ninth grade I was in Manhattan staying with a brother and I quit school. And my mother was working in this hospital in Long Island, rented a house and brought us out there; that's kind of what put me on track educationally because now I'm out in the suburbs where my skills and my ambition really kicked in. You could play sports, you could do all these things and I participated... I had a strange record until I was in the tenth grade. I never started... and finished in the same school, because we were kind of transient in the South. We moved a lot. We'd be on this farm this year, another farm the next year, back in the city, and that happened to me once we came north. Living with different relatives. But when we moved to Bay Shore when I was in the tenth grade... then I spent my last three years in one high school. And that's basically when I got an education and helped to educate myself...

The migration aspect of it was very similar. It was like two different countries, being the North and the South. And then being, you know, like most blacks from the South, we ended up in these industrial, metropolitan areas, and then for me to go from there to the suburbs was another big transformation... So it was difficult but there was nothing that could stop me, because I always felt this mission. It wasn't just me; I'm representing my family, I'm representing my race, I'm representing a major part of this country, and I always just thought if I can't do it, it can't be done. So I always had this absolute drive that nothing could get in my way... I think one of the things that always helped me was that my family was able to give me a philosophy in dealing with myself as a black man in this society, and it was simply to understand, as my father put it once when I was a very young kid. He said, "Boy, you gotta pay the colored tax. You're colored. You're not going to be treated like everybody else. Don't think it's you. You're gonna have to work harder. You're gonna have to get up earlier. If you're going to have the same job as a white man, you're going to have to be better than he is." And he was right, and I understood that.

And then you have these incidents where all kinds of stuff that you have to deal with, you know that it is happening to this black man, but it's not happening to me, the person, because, you know, I'm bigger than the skin that I'm wrapped in. And I learned that early. In this society, you deal with incidents. I was a principal here in this city when I moved here; I had to go into a federal court to be able to move into that house. And I was the principal of the area where the house was located in. So that's an example of these things happening. I could have just gone to another house, but I always fight these kinds of things, you know; it's just a matter of principle. It always happens, a continuous process. And that's what I say to young people. You have to kind of accept that. Don't let it become part of your psyche; it's not you, it's a whole concept and you are part of that. And so I feel very strongly about those issues and that's what I instilled in my children, I think as they grew up and had measures of success, it was that philosophy...

What has been the role of the church in your family sustaining itself?

Oh, that's a major part. Because we really believe that religion is the seat of all of it, so much of it is the answer, that's the part of you that you're in touch with when you're not in touch with anything else. It's a retreat; it's your solace. So it's been very, very important to us. We've always, as a matter of fact, my mother, in her later years, was the minister for a short time of a Pentecostal church, but we're all basically Baptists now. And that was just automatic that you believe strongly, your faith, you share, and you just pass on your knowledge.

Is the black church in Yonkers or in the North different from the black church experiences you had or recall in the South?

I find them very similar. I find that is the one thread that's consistent. It's like if I went to the New Bethel Church in North Carolina or Mount Carmel Baptist Church where I'm a member of now. It's that culture. It's the same rhythm, it's the warmth, it's the feeling, it's the caring, and... that's why church is so important, I think, in the North. It's about the only institution that we have a linkage with that's been consistent. And that is truly yours. And I think a lot of that is what you get from the church, you know? It's that remembrance. My kids always tease me that there's not a hymn that could be sang in church that I don't know. I've been to church all my life; I know all of the songs. You know? That sort of thing, which I didn't realize until they pointed it out to me. So they'd take the hymnal and read this... I don't have to take it out... I've sung that song a thousand times. That sort of thing. So yeah, it's very consistent, the church.

Urban Indians: Gertrude Chapoose Willie

Source Note: The interview is a part of the American Indian Oral History Project, deposited by the University of Utah American West Center at the J. Willard Marriott Library Special Collections in the Floyd O'Neil American Indian Archive. The American West Center has collected thousands of oral interviews in the past four decades. Information about those interviews and the Utah American Indian Digital Archive, which provides access to many of the Center's American Indian interviews, can be found at: http://www.awc.utah.edu.

Gertrude Chapoose Willie was born in 1936 at Ft. Duchesne, Utah, to Connor Chapoose and Lula Wash on the Uintah Ouray Ute Indian reservation. She was a member of the Uncompahgre Band. She married David Willie who was a member of the Navajo (Dine) Nation. Employment opportunities attracted the Willies to move to the Salt Lake City area. Willie represented many urban Indians as she struggled to retain her culture, teach her children, and adapt to the demands of suburban life. She was deeply involved in education programs that tried to maintain the Ute language and culture and worked in the Ute lab at Ft. Duchesne for several years. She died in April 1985 and is buried at Randlett, a village on the reservation. Norma Denver interviewed Willie in Fort Duchesne in 1970.

My dad used to tell me, never take a back seat to anybody. Always be proud of your heritage and who you are. Speak up for yourself 'cause nobody will do it for you. And this is the same thing I have told my kids over and over again. If you get knocked down get back up and defend who you are. If you are labeled as something, say that "I am an American." That's the only thing that will, you know, kind of help out... We've walked down through streets... or we went to a cafe and they didn't serve us, they told us, "We don't serve to Indians"... Many people have come to us and said, "Well, what's it like living off the reservation?" And I tell them how would you feel if you went over to England and lived? I said that's the same experience we Indians have living among you white people... A lot of people say, "what do you eat?" Come to my home, I say. Eat dinner with us and see if we eat anything else different. And my aunt sent some frozen blueberries out with us and we had some little kids that come around and play with our kids and they eat it by the handfuls. And the little white kids want to eat some. Before you know it, it's all eaten by the little white kids because they don't know what it is and we tell them. They ask us where we were growing it. I say on my reservation where I lived and they want to know if my mommy or my daddy and my sisters all live in tepees. And I tell them, "Well, if that's the way they are then I guess you speak funny too, don't you. What language you speak?" And then they just start laughing...

We used to live in Bingham. See my husband works up at the copper mine in Bingham Canyon... He works on these big machines that dig out the ore from the dirt there... He's been there for nineteen years now. He left his reservation at the age of fourteen. His mother died when he was six years old and his father he never knew. His grandmother raised him. At the time of his mother's death, he was going to a day school in Ganado, Arizona, and then his grandmother thought that it was very foolish of him to go to school. And so she took him out of there. He claims he had to ride a mail truck in order to get down to Ganado about five o'clock in the morning and get home about five. His mother when she was alive would stand in the road and wait for him in the evening with an apple or an orange for him, trying to reward him for going to school, because that is what she wanted. Then after she died then his grandmother just raised him and took him out. But he'd always heard of the outside world and how much money the boys make 'cause they were going out. So his brother told him to come to Gallup and they'd catch a train to someplace and work on the railroad. And this sounded real good to him so he went out to work. He has never had no education at all. But he is trying to go back to school with this adult program that the community action program has put out in the Granger area. And that's where he's going. He feels very lucky to have this chance of trying to learn something. He's a wonderful worker and he really puts all his effort out because he knows what a struggle it is. And he knows what it means to be without money and to live on a reservation. He's always claimed that he is an adopted Ute now because he thinks he'll never be able to go back to his reservation. That life is so hard there.

But the only thing, the problems that they have, I've heard it from a lot of them young guys that go out or come out of school from the different Indian schools. Their problem is that they cannot cope with the white people. That it's just, they're labeled just like if they were wearing a label across their backs or their fronts. But they're labeled Indians and no good workers and they can't do anything right. They always say the only good Indian is a dead Indian. And that isn't the way it is. If you put your effort up and do the best you can and show them you can do it then that's the way you'll get your reputation. It's hard, but once they get that respect for you then anybody's willing to stick up for you then. A lot of kids have come up to my kids with their long hair and they yank on their hair. They think they're wearing wigs and stuff. Just cause we live in the city, they don't think it's possible for them to have long hair. Even elderly men will come up and stroke their hair and say, "Is this real?" And we say, "Yes, it's real." They don't believe us. Then they yank on it a little bit too hard and the kids start crying. And then that takes them by surprise. "Oh, I thought all the Indians cut off their hair," they say. "Well, this Indian didn't," and that's the way it's been. It's just, you have to find yourself out in this world... you just have to make up your mind. And once you get there then you've got it made.

But we're all labeled alike. It don't matter what tribe we are, we're all, we're the same label. I'm sure [these kids] would have the same problems when they go out into a city. They don't know what to say or... some people act like they never seen you. They walk right past you, bump into you. You say you're sorry and they turn around. Some other white person that's behind you sees what you're trying to do and turns around and say, "Now, that is the true American." And boy my heart just swells when I hear someone say that. They say, "Well, just let them be," that's just many of their people that treat the Indians like that. And then it makes me feel good to think well, I didn't start an argument on the street, or start shoving back. So I just take it what they do, but somebody else notices it and then compliments us on this.

Gertrude, how do you see the Indian people and the white people, how do you see them, are their ways different? Do you think the Indian people think different than the white people?

Well like I say, you're brought up by old people and you're around these oldsters like our grandparents and they tell us do this, do that and then you live like that and it's pretty hard to forget when you've been brought up these old ways. And you go out among the white people and things are done differently. I remember being told to get out of bed before the sun come up. And you do that. It's just a habit you have. You go to bed early and try to get up early. And then when you get out in the white world, you know, nobody comes alive until after eight o'clock.

And our neighborhoods will be still sleeping and there we are trying to mow the lawn, and they tell us, "Turn that thing off, it's waking us up." So we have to wait until about ten o'clock to mow our lawn and that's when everybody comes alive.

But it really is hard but you know, you never forget some of these things that the old people tell you. You just can't forget it. Then you try to pass it on to your kids and then the little white kids they hang around, "Why do you do that, Mrs. Willie?" And I say, "Well, I just don't think that they should be doing this or that." But it's challenging both ways. You come back and try to be an Indian and find yourself, you can't speak very good and by the time you get the hang of it and go back to city life, you can't speak English very good either. So when anybody asks me...like this one Navajo kid says, when he went into the Air Force they asked him, you know on a paper, on a questionnaire, it says, "Do you speak a foreign language." And he says, "Do you know, they don't even know that we speak a foreign language and that's English."

The only thing that I can really strongly remember that [my father] hashed over and over with us kids was, some day you're going to lose your identity as Indians. You're going to forget your language. You're going to forget your culture, your tradition. That's just where you're going right now, by not teaching your kids how to speak Ute, he'd tell us. And he told us be sure to teach the kids, your kids, my grandchildren he says, teach 'em to speak Ute. And don't let them ever forget how we're supposed to live, who we are, where we come from...But when President Lincoln set the slaves free he set the red man free, too. He said, "Some day it's going to be asked...who's an Indian now. Who's got their right heritage to claim this land. And you know what we're going to do? We're going to say, 'I am, I am.'" And that person is going to say, "Okay prove to me that you're an Indian." And what are we going to say? You guys gonna to stand up and you're going to speak in English, "Well, I'm so and so's daughter, my grandparents are this," and he's gonna say, "Nope, that's not what I'm looking for." And some day somebody, it's got to be somebody that'll say [in Ute], and that's the one that that man's gonna say, "Right, you're the Indian, the only Indian that's left." The only Indian that's gonna get all this reward or whatever is going to be at the end of that time.

Race and Civil Rights

African Americans had long struggled against the historic injustices of slavery, segregation, and racism, but in the postwar period a combination of factors led to sustained and successful challenges to systemic discrimination through social movements, the courts, legislation, and popular culture. In 1947 Jackie Robinson broke the race barrier in major league baseball; in 1954 the US Supreme Court unanimously ruled against segregated schools in *Brown v. Board of Education*; African-American residents in Montgomery boycotted the local bus system through 1956 until it was desegregated; and in 1957 nine black students in Little Rock forced the federal government to enforce the school desegregation statute.

Young people were often at the forefront of organizing movements and actions across the South in the 1960s. In 1960 black and some white students staged sit-ins at white-only lunch counters in southern cities, and in 1961 joined the Freedom Riders—interracial groups of bus riders that sought to force compliance of court orders banning segregated interstate travel. Young people formed their own civil rights organization, the Student Nonviolent Coordinating Committee (SNCC), which developed the nonhierarchical and militant style emulated by subsequent youth movements of the 1960s. White resistance in the South was fierce and often violent, demanding great courage, stamina, and creativity on the part of African-American activists and citizens.

Questions to Consider: As the two oral history excerpts below illustrate, African Americans employed a variety of strategies to advance civil rights in the 1950s and 1960s. Some were engaged in quiet struggles to integrate the workplace or schools; others participated in mass social movements and civil disobedience to bring change.

1. How did McCreary and Blackwell contest the racism and discrimination they encountered?
2. In their interviews, how did each address the other forces, individuals, and movements that changed the climate of the times or assisted them in their efforts?

Desegregating the Nation's Capital: Christine Stewart McCreary

Source Note: The interview was produced by the Senate Historical Office in Washington, D.C. Senate historians interview individuals who can offer a unique perspective on Senate history but may otherwise be missed by biographers, historians, and other scholars. Since 1976 they have interviewed parliamentarians, clerks, chiefs of staff, reporters, and Senate pages, as well as senators. Transcripts of the interviews are deposited in the Library of Congress, the National Archives, and the appropriate presidential libraries and senatorial manuscript collections. Some interviews are now available on the U.S. Senate Web site, including this interview with Mrs. McCreary: http://www.senate.gov/artandhistory/history/oral_history/Christine_ McCreary.htm

Born in New York City in 1926, Christine Stewart McCreary went south to become a student at Bethune-Cookman College in Daytona Beach, Florida. But when the United States entered World War II, McCreary left school for a government typing job in Washington, D.C. By chance, she took dictation for Stuart Symington, who was impressed with her work and hired her to accompany him when he became chairman of the National Security Board, director of the Reconstruction Finance Corporation, and United States Senator from Missouri. Very few African Americans held professional positions in the Senate when McCreary started in 1953. Illinois Senator Paul Douglas had hired the first black secretary in 1949. McCreary remained on Senator Symington's staff until his retirement in 1977, and then worked for Ohio Senator John Glenn until he retired in 1998. Here she describes how she navigated lingering racism and segregation in the halls of Congress. Donald A. Ritchie, associate historian of the Senate Historical Office and a former president of the Oral History Association, interviewed McCreary on May 19, 1998.

When you came to Washington, where did you work initially?
I worked at the War Production Board, where I met Stuart Symington... It was a big government agency, and they had a big secretarial pool. The work would come down from upstairs and you'd do it. So Symington needed someone to come up and take shorthand. Nobody in the pool could take shorthand except me. The head secretary indicated that Mr. Symington's secretary was ill and that he needed someone who could take shorthand. So I went up to his office. He looked at me and said: "How old are you?" [laughs] I must have been 17 or 18 at that particular time. It was a long time ago. He said, "Well, can you take dictation?" I said, "Yes, sir." And then he started dictating his letters. I ended up with about thirty letters... Right place at the right time. I took the letters back and he looked at each letter and he said, "Well, I'll be darned. That's fine. You did an *excellent* job. How would you like to just stay here with me until my secretary comes back?" I said, "I would like it"... So I worked with him for quite a while. And then he decided he was going to the Reconstruction Finance Corporation and he took me with him. I had my own office and a messenger. It was really very nice...

What kind of a person was Stuart Symington?
Oh, he was one of the nicest persons you'd ever meet. He didn't think about you being black or anything like that, he just treated you as a human being. He was just that type of person. Tall and good looking and very nice, and so was his wife. She was a Wadsworth, and she was lovely. In fact, I had dinner over there three times. They lived in Georgetown. And you'd walk in and he would have a big table where some would sit with him and another table where some would sit with her. He always wanted me to sit with him. He'd say, "Now, you sit right there." [chuckles] It was just a whole new world. I just never dreamed I'd be in something like that. And you learned things from things like that. I enjoyed it. But I always made sure that I did my work and did it well, I thought...

In 1952 he ran for the U.S. Senate. When he won did he ask you to come to work for him?
Yes, I was so excited. But see, by that time my husband and I were expecting our second child. Mr. Symington said, "Well, I'll hold your job." So after the baby was born I finally came to the Senate...

What was it like coming to work in the Senate in those days?
Well, it was different. I'll be frank, it was different. I didn't know what to expect. I didn't know if I could eat there, because you see Washington was segregated and you had to deal with that. I mean, I wasn't pushing myself, but I asked the senator, "Where do I eat?" I think he was taken aback by my question. He called [New York] Senator [Herbert] Lehman. Senator Lehman called the cafeteria hostess to let her know that I worked with Senator Symington and that I would be eating my meals there.

Lehman didn't tell the lady that I was black. So Symington said, "It's taken care of, you just go over there and eat your breakfast." I thought everything was fine. When I went over there and I got to the door, the hostess came rushing over to the door where I was and asked if she could help me. I told her I'd come for breakfast. She said, "Oh, no, this is only for people who work in the Senate." I said, "Well, I work in the Senate with Senator Stuart Symington." [gasps] "Oh, oh, okay, come on in, have a seat." Well, everybody was stopped and looking and it was like a big to-do. I felt stupid. I wasn't used to this.

She said, "You just take a seat anyplace you can find. You just go through [the cafeteria line] and get your food." So I saw what they had. The cooks would put it on the plate and pass it to you. I was very uncomfortable, nervous. You could hear a pin drop. There appeared to be resentment. The cafeteria workers who I thought would be supportive were also very cold. As a matter of fact, my plate was shoved at me and I stepped back because I didn't want it on my clothes, and it all went on the floor. Well they were looking at me, but I had to deal with it. So anyway I got another plate. And then I went back the next day, and the next day, until finally they got used to seeing me coming in there and then there was no more problems with that.

. . . I'd come out of the restaurant and all of the black people that worked in the Senate were people who worked on the custodial staff and were mail carriers. They were all lined up in the hall out there just to see me. Well, I felt like two cents, because I wasn't used to that. I didn't know what to say or do. And then of course there were some snide remarks, and all that kind of foolishness. I would just keep on going. I wouldn't even bother to stop and answer that. But you get through that too. It was just a lonesome time.

Well, after the initial problems, did you go to the cafeteria regularly? And were there no more problems?
There were no problems. I'd just go in there and eat whenever I wanted to. But they knew me then, knew who I was. Then sometimes the girls in the office, they wanted to meet with me, so we just made a little pact, we'd just bring our lunch and we'd go to the park and sit and eat. And if we wanted to eat together we'd just bring our lunch and sit there and eat in the cafeteria. And then in the Russell [Senate Office] Building there was a little opening where you could

get your food and take it back to your desk... That's where I met all the secretaries and other office staff who worked in the Senate... Yes, and especially on a Monday because they would tell you about all the fun they'd had on the weekend. I'd always be with them, and it was nice, because they weren't prejudiced. Those who worked in Symington's office weren't prejudiced, either. There were one or two but they didn't bother me. But Symington was open. He'd tell anybody, "You can't get along with Chris, you can't get along with anybody."

Did you work on Saturdays in those days?

Sometimes. It all depended. If you had something going, you had to work Saturdays. And when the Army-McCarthy hearings were going on, now that was a mess! I couldn't go out of the office because that black lady [Annie Lee Moss, an African-American Pentagon employee who denied Senator Joseph McCarthy's charges that she had been a member of the Communist Party] they said had done something... [Symington] didn't want me out in the hall because he didn't want people to think I was she. Well, I didn't look nothing like that lady! She was older. But I couldn't go out of the office. He'd say, "Chris, I don't want you out in the hall. Now you never know, some of these crazy people might shoot you." [laughs] But I didn't go out in the halls, you never know.

Senator Symington was really on the opposite side from McCarthy and was fighting McCarthy.

Oh, yes, that's why he didn't want me to go outside, because he didn't want anybody to mistake me for Annie Lee Moss. He didn't want anything to happen to me.

Image 12 Civil rights march on Washington, DC, Aug. 28, 1963 (Library of Congress).

I was wondering about Senator Symington being from Missouri. Did you ever have any dealings with his constituents showing up from Missouri? Were they surprised that he had a black woman secretary?
They were surprised, but they handled it. It was amazing the way they handled it, and I think it was amazing with me because I didn't know what to expect. But I was going to be prepared for whatever. But I would say hello and let them go ahead and say what they were going to say. I liked them and they would like me. I never said much, unless they started a conversation . . .

Did the atmosphere in the Senate change much in the 1960s? You came in the '50s, but in the '60s lots of things were happening: segregation ended in Washington.
Yes. That's when they started changing, and more blacks began to come and work for senators . . .

How different is working for the Senate today than when you first got started?
There's just no way in the world you could compare the two. The way it was, it was segregated. The way it is today, you wouldn't even think there had been segregation. Then your biggest problem was not the senators per se, it was the people who worked for them. But if you hadn't been taught how to deal with people you couldn't do it. I think my father was good for me on that. He didn't like any foolishness. If you are going to do something, do it right. I was taught this as I grew up, so I know this.

Black Freedom Struggle in Mississippi: Unita Blackwell

Source Note: The entire transcript is available at the University of Southern Mississippi (USM), Center for Oral History and Cultural Heritage, Civil Rights in Mississippi Digital Archive: http://www.lib.usm.edu/legacy/spcol/crda/oh/blackwell.htm

Born March 18, 1933, on a plantation in Lula, Mississippi, Unita Blackwell, like other African Americans living in the South, had few economic and educational choices. She worked as a sharecropper until 1964, when she learned of the Freedom Summer efforts to register black voters. SNCC launched the Freedom Summer project to challenge segregation in the nation's poorest state that had been the most resistant to civil rights efforts. Blackwell became a field worker for SNCC in 1964. She also served as a delegate of the Mississippi Freedom Democratic Party (MFDP) that same year at the Democratic National Convention held in New Jersey. The MFDP offered itself as an alternative to the all-white, segregated Democratic Party of Mississippi. In 1977 she became the first black mayor in Mississippi, elected to serve her home town of Mayersville in Issaquena County, a post she held for 25 years. Mike Garvey interviewed Blackwell in Mayersville on April 21 and May 12,1977.

I came up on plantations, picking cotton . . . and we never had that much. I was reared in a home that people always went to church. They believed in God and that whole thing . . . And so I came up in a school system that even took sides with the lighter children and stuff like this, you know. You was lighter, you look like you got better treatment and that sort of thing. So that was my feeling I had coming up. I was loved by my mother... she would sit and hug me and say, "You know, you is black, but you're honest." I used to didn't know what that meant. And she said, "Be proud you're black."... When the bossman says you go to the fields, everybody went to the fields, schools closed down; the teachers was under every plantation. And everything was run by the plantation, you know. The church, the pastor preached whatever the man wanted to hear, you know...

When the sixties came along, how did you first get involved in the civil rights movement?

You see, they had heard about the Freedom Riders... We had heard the rumor that there's some strange folks down the road. Mr. Henry Sias—he's dead now—I come to find, he belongs to the Masons. And so he had let those guys in his house a year before then. They was in here in '63. That was the forerunners. This group that was coming in, was coming in the next year, which was '64, which, you know, we hadn't heard too much about it, because it was a hush-hush thing. You know what's going on but you don't want to talk about it either; it's best that you don't talk about it because the white folks think you know something about it, you know. And so they said some fellows are down there at his house, and they say they so many people. I told [my neighbor], I said, "Well, I sure hope they come here." She said, "For what?" I said, "Well, Corrine if we need some freedom honey, I just know it, we need some freedom. Cause something is wrong, something is wrong with this world we live in"...

We was going to have the meeting. When we got the word, we got it from a guy that was one of the deacons of the church, "Do not have that civil rights meeting, 'cause them freedom riders, you know, is not going to have nothing in this town..." They would burn that thing down if we had that meeting. And when the deacon got up and told us that we couldn't have no meeting there, we had one. Then he come back and told us again, and said the sheriff said don't have no meeting in that church... Well, we went over there to try to register to vote in 1964, at this courthouse here in Mayersville, Mississippi. The [white] folks was coming through town in their trucks... In that year, more gun racks was coming up in the back of the trucks, was it a psychological thing or fear. They made circles; the white people came in the town and made circles around them...

How was the idea of voting first presented to you?

Yes, this Sunday morning, when this guy said, "God helps those who helps themselves..." And then he went on to describe to us that we had a right to register to vote, and this was our right, and he told us about the amendments. He told us that this [was] the reason why they was here. That we would register to vote, that this is how that all the things that you need, in food, clothing, housing, everything... that the vote was the key. That you would have the say-so, and that you could get those things into your community. And that's the reason why the white people didn't want us to have the vote, whether it was our right, and I heard it; I believed it, and I was ready to move... There was eight of us from this county that volunteered to go try to register to vote... And some got in that first day, others didn't. And this was a continuous thing, cause we was to continue to go out to get people to bring them in, to make sure that we try to register to vote...

I testified before the United States Civil Rights Commission, so I'm down in history as one of the ones that the United States Civil Rights Commission had this hearing [in Jackson] against the State of Mississippi. We filed suits, hearings and so forth for voter registration. Because I could read, I was to interpret... I guess they still have those shots, CBS, NBC. Everybody was there, rolled off every magazine, and all the rest... The State of Mississippi wouldn't even give them a place to have the hearing. So they took the Veteran Hospital, of course it was government, and that's where the hearing went on, in the auditorium. They fixed it all up and made a room to have the hearing. And that was the passing of the 1965 Civil Rights Bill...

When we first started off, you did not pass the [literacy] test [required for voting]. See, that's the reason why we had to have the hearings. Because wasn't anybody passing, and the test was across Mississippi... So I was one of the key witnesses, for the State of Mississippi, against the voter registration situation, that we had to prepare the passage of the 1965 Civil Rights bill.

I was going to ask you, when you went to register, were you afraid? Scared?
Yes, yes. You know I look back over it now and wonder how you got up enough nerve to go, because you just was scared. But it was a kind of fear that I was just going to go on through. I've been through that kind of fear, several times afterwards, but I just look back over it now, and... wonder how you got through it. Because you know your life is on the line. And so we were scared. But the people went anyway; they were scared, but they went on in.

Let me ask you, what was different [for you] in 1964, that had ever been different before? Why did you get involved in this civil rights movement?
Well, see you find yourself into situations, and I laugh about it now. I started off, as I said, I wanted to get in, cause they say if you register to vote, that you could eat and have a decent place to stay. My house was falling on the ground... So when you think about my reasons or something, it's just that for me, what I would like to call ordinary people, [it was] just meeting their needs. It was trying to figure out ways to meet their needs. Because I was just an ordinary sharecropper, and that was it in 1964. Trying to find a way to eat and live, and we was wanting to demand this and that and so on. So when these young people... came in alive, you know. And we was all on the same wavelength, you know. They were talking about doing something for people. And always felt that from the inside, I wanted to do something...

Stokely [Carmichael, noted SNCC organizer] was electrifying; I like to term it that way because he was just a wild, live person. And I had never met men like that. That spoke out, you know, and to talk about white people, to them, you know. And he was inspiring to us. He's wild and he gives you a taste of, it can be done, you know. And that's what he done for us; I know that's what he has done for me... He was a teacher, you know. And you just would sit for hours and listen at Stokely... he would say, "Don't let nobody, no man, take away your right, your right in this country is to register to vote. This is what the amendment says, and this is what we're acting on. We're acting on the law of this land. And if they have lied, they is the one who has lied about the law."

...And then it started to fall into place. I didn't even understand what it was. I was fearful; I was scared, but still I would do it anyway. I kept going anyway, and so then they put me on the staff that summer, because they was looking for people all out in the field. The people who knew the community, who knew the people and would get out and ask [them] to come register to vote. That's how I become on the staff of the Student Nonviolent Coordinating Committee... It was just that whole thinking, you know, of the youth movement, students' movement, you know. And I was truly excited about it...

[After returning from the Democratic National Convention] I was stuck here, with a son getting ready to go to school. And you know, you got to do something. All we wanted was some decent books, and the [county] didn't want to get them, so the only recourse we had was, the lawyer said, desegregate this week. And now if you study law, you will study *Sharkey and Issaquena County Consolidated Line v. Blackwell*. Which at that time, that was my name, I'm Blackwell Wright now. So here I am concerned about my son having decent books to study, you know, and this up-to-date education. Cause see we was always, if our children got any books, they was ten years behind the [white] child that was in the same grade, as far as that's concerned. They just kept them in old stuff, and finally they give them to them. So we end up getting all these people, all these families in Sharkey and Issaquena Counties to sign—I organized that—to sign to desegregate the schools.

And that's when they put a cross in my yard out here. And I called the SNCC office. And all of this is going right after the 1964 convention, you get the picture? And this is '65, '66, all this process is happening...And John Lewis was [SNCC] chairperson, and he sent, you know, folks in to see about them. Stokely and all of them, you know, coming from the other areas of the state; people were coming from everywhere trying to check on violence. Crosses was burning in my yard, and they set one down the road across from Mr. Sias...They was setting them in different places... they sit it right on that corner over there, which is my yard, and we had to hit the floor...

And you know, you'd be surprised of the things that has happened in these towns, and things that we have been into trying to get people registered to vote.

The forms of harassment is unbelievable, it's so childish, that anybody could think up all the pranks that they would do to us. Take the air out of the tires, set us nails across the road, you know, you do that, it's childishness. It's just anything to cut off and intimidate, you know. This is what we've been through. We was afraid to drink water in some towns, and some places we couldn't go in, we had to stay out of... You better be sure you say, "Yas sir," and it just intimidates you, this harassment. So I've been through that quite often and sometimes I was getting arrested every day. One time for thirty days straight...

What they used to think they could do, they would get people like Mr. Barnes...and they thought that they could tell him. And he was the deacon of the church, because people would listen to that. People do have great influences in churches and different things like that. But a movement is bigger than individuals. And they don't know how people get swept into movements. A movement is not always individualized. You have individual leadership and stuff like that. But it can sprout up from anywhere...And they didn't understand that kind of a movement. Cause this movement is bigger than us, bigger than any individual...People like [noted civil rights activist] Mrs. [Fannie Lou] Hamer, I met people from all walks of life, all kinds of people, but she was, as an individual, she was a dramatic person, but she had needs and she was hurted and she had to cry; she was lonesome and all that stuff, but the movement was bigger than her individual thing. And she would teach us that, you know. We got to keep moving...

So, little by little we're coming out. That's the reason why you see me sitting here. Now in a little small town of black and white people, in 1964, I was denied the right to vote, right here, and I'm now mayor, you know...And so that's what I see, this same kind of thing. I'll be dead and gone, and somebody is going to do it, you know, as an individual. And the movement itself is bigger than all of us. It's a fantastic thing, when you look and see in 1964, it was not a person in this county that was black [and] registered to vote.

Postwar Work, Family, and Community

Married women entered the workforce in unprecedented numbers during World War II, and despite expectations that they would return home after the war, a growing number found wage work economically or professionally rewarding. For women of color, the 1950s ideal of the nuclear family, suburban home, and mother at home did not reflect their own economic reality. Opportunities were limited in the 1950s, work was often gender and racially segregated, and women were paid less than men for comparable work. Nonetheless, women found positions in factories, homes, offices, and schools. Women working for wages and at home struggled to redefine gender roles and meet the challenges of caretaking and housework.

Home and community life also changed significantly after the war. In the postwar period the federal government played a critical role in subsidizing new suburbs with roads and freeways and helped millions of middle income and working-class Americans purchase homes with Federal Housing Administration (FHA) loans. However, this wealth generation was directed at white families, since FHA favored new construction and discouraged racial diversity. The quickly assembled houses in Levittown, on Long Island, opened for sale in 1947 as the first planned suburb. Thereafter, suburbs sprouted across the nation, circling major cities and draining jobs and wealth away from the urban core. Cities began a long decline, with employers and white residents moving to the outskirts; by the 1970s, most Americans lived in suburbs. Many Americans in the 1950s and 1960s flocked to the new neighborhoods because they provided affordable housing and new schools for growing families.

Image 13 One-room school in the Hispanic community of Ojo Sarco, New Mexico (Library of Congress).

Questions to Consider: The Moreno and Vahouny interviews featured in this section are unusual in that they come from projects that have deliberately sought to document the ordinary: work life and daily life in the suburbs. How do descriptions of what many might view as mundane represent critical reflections about home, family, and community for social and women's historians?

1. How did these two women approach their family roles after marriage? How did each both embrace and challenge gender expectations for women at the time?
2. In what ways did economic class, race, and location influence the choices women had in education and home and family life?

Negotiating Career and Family in Arizona: Belen Soto Moreno

Source Note: Dr. Gloria Cuadraz, Associate Professor at Arizona State University, joined with the Litchfield Park Historical Society to document the lives of former Mexican-American residents who lived in migrant camps in Litchfield Park between the 1920s and 1970s. A film based on these oral histories, *Voices from the Camps of Litchfield Park*, won a community award in 2006 from WESTMARC, a West Valley business organization. The fifty videotaped oral histories may be accessed at the Chicano Research Collection in the Department of Special Manuscripts and Archives at Arizona State University's Hayden Library.

Born on May 29, 1935, Belen Soto Moreno grew up with five brothers and sisters in Camp 54 near Litchfield, Arizona, where her father worked as an irrigation foreman for Goodyear Farms. As a working-class Mexican American, Moreno struggled to excel in school, attend college, and realize her dream to become an educator. She juggled marriage and family as a substitute teacher in the late 1950s, then taught her own elementary classrooms before she was hired in 1974 to direct the Migrant Program. Moreno later served as the federal programs director, assistant principal, summer school director, and publicity director for the Avondale Elementary School District before she retired in 1999. Gloria Holguin Cuadraz interviewed Moreno on May 31, 2006 in Avondale, Arizona.

What do you remember about your early schooling years? Where did you go to school?

I went to school in Litchfield and like I said we would ride the bus probably about four miles. My first class, we all called it "baby class", it was an Americanization class. There was no kindergarten but all of us that didn't know any English had to go to that class to learn English. And we learned how to read with the primers, *Sally, Dick and Jane*, which were popular at that time. Miss Gomez was my teacher, and my fondest memory that I have is seeing this cute boy drinking water from the water fountain and . . . I really liked him from that day and we became friends through school. And Rudy and I finally ended up getting married in 1959... I think my very first date with him was in high school. My parents didn't let me date. They were very strict. I think our very first, official date was going to a Winter Fantasy Dance at the high school... my dad took me to the high school and when the dance was over, my dad picked me up and took me home.

What do you remember about your fondest teacher?

Well, Miss Gomez was one of the ones that I remember the most because I was so into learning how to read and seeing her work with children, that I wanted to be just like her. I had many excellent teachers... The only kind of things that I was puzzled by was the fact that we couldn't speak Spanish and we would go off, my friends and I we would go off to the edge of the playground, where there were no teachers around or the English speaking kids and we spoke Spanish to our hearts content. You could be spanked and I know a lot of boys that were spanked because they spoke Spanish. Another thing, and I think it was just our shyness maybe, when we took our lunch and it was in a paper sack, we wouldn't eat where the other kids ate. We would go to the side of a building because we didn't want them to see that we had our burritos *de frijoles* or *chorizo* or *huevos*. We were kind of embarrassed, I guess... that we didn't have what they had, the bread, you know...

Were there other memories that you have of school when you think back, what was it like?

...I was very shy and quiet 'cause I thought I wasn't supposed to be smart, you know. The teacher would ask questions and I'd know the answer but I'd keep quiet. As a result of that... I became like a sponge, I absorbed, you know. The saddest thing for me, when I graduated from the elementary school was that a lot of my friends... didn't continue high school, girls or boys. Boys went to work, the girls went to work at home and some of the parents, some of the fathers believed that it was more important for them to provide money for the household or to help the mother at home. I was lucky that my dad believed in education although he only graduated from eighth grade. A lot of his learning was from books and from experience.

So, I was very lucky and then I was even luckier when I was a senior that Miss Ybarra, a teacher who taught Spanish at the school, came into observe us during a Girls League meeting. All the girls in the school belonged to Girls League and we met every so often. All the boys belonged to Boys Alliance and we had meetings on this particular day, our sponsor wasn't there and Miss Ybarra came in to be the official sponsor observer. And after the meeting, she called me over and she talked to me.

She said, "Belen, what are you going to do after you graduate?"

And I said, "Well, I've been taking secretarial classes," I was really good at typing and shorthand and all that. I said, "I'll probably get a job in Phoenix as a secretary and ride the bus in."

She said, "What do you really want to do?"

I said, "What I really want to do is, I want to be a teacher."

"You want to be a teacher?" She took her finger, she pointed at me, she says, "You are going to college and you are going to become a teacher."

And I said, "But Miss Ybarra, my parents can't afford it. They won't let me go." At that time girls only left home when they got married or they went to work but stayed at home.

What year was this?

It was 1954. And she says, "I'll take care of it." She went out to the field where my dad was working and talked to my dad. My dad seemed to be for it but he said, "You have to talk to Malena. She's the one that you have to talk to."

And so, we were having tests one day and I could go home on the early bus and she says, "Don't go home, you wait until the late bus. I'm gonna go talk to your mother," and she did. I don't know what she said to my mother. I never really heard from either one but when I got home my mother was in the kitchen, and she'd been crying, and she says, "*Queres ir al colegio? Deberas queres ir al colegio?*" [Do you want to go to college? Do you really want to go to college?]

"*Si, mama.*"

"*Si deberas, deberas, queres ir, tienes mi bendición.*" [If you really, really want to go, then you shall go. You have my blessings.]

Then we were both crying. And then from then she helped me and then of course, how are we gonna pay for it. You know my father he had five other kids to support and he was a salaried employee but still there wasn't all that money, even though I think tuition was only fifty dollars a semester at that time [laughs]. But Mr. Borg who was the typing teacher called his friend, Melvin T. Hutchinson who was the publicity director at Arizona State College at Flagstaff, now NAU [Northern Arizona University], and talked him into giving me an interview. I went and I interviewed with him and I worked all four years in the publicity office, fifty cents an hour. And I would also sub for... cafeteria workers, I would sub for them. During the summer Boy's State would pay me fifty dollars for one week of typing their newsletter and then I ended up editing the college year book for three years and they also paid me, fifty dollars a month I think it was. So, we made it through. But those two teachers were really, really great and Miss Ybarra is now Dr. Amibisca, my mentor, my friend, my *madrina*...

And then in August, before I went back for my, junior year I think it was, maybe it was my senior year... [my boyfriend Rudy asked] what if he gave me a ring, what would your parents say? I said, "It's not what my parents say, what do I say?"... So I was engaged our senior year and he went off to work at San Manuel at the copper mine while I finished up my year in... college and then I taught one year in Ash Fork and then we got married, in June of 1959.

Did you continue to live in the camps after you were married?

No. After we were married, we were going to live in San Manuel and what happened was, in August there was a strike, at the San Manuel Copper Company and we came home and we stayed with his mother, here on Fifteen East Pacific. And the strike lasted a long time, and by the time the strike was over, I think it was past Christmas, he was working for Goodyear Farms at the Goodyear feed pens and I was teaching. They had asked me to substitute. I started subbing and then they hired me full time, in February... and two weeks after I started my permanent job somebody had a baby and they hired me permanently, the beginning of February. And two weeks after I was hired I found out I was pregnant...

So Rosie was born in October and I didn't teach for that year. Rudy didn't want me to teach. In fact he was upset when I first went and subbed. He said he was supposed to be the bread winner, not me and I said, "I didn't go to college to sit home. I went to college to be a teacher and that's what I'm gonna do... Of course the school, every time we go by there Rudy says, "bread and butter" [laughs], that provided a good living for us. And when I retired I missed the kids, I missed the migrant families, the people I worked with, but I didn't miss the work. Just the people...

There have been stories about [Litchfield] women working while the men were at [the Second World] war. Do you know anything about that?

Some of the women worked out in the fields, somebody had to do the work that the men couldn't do. They worked out in the fields, hoeing and then quite a few of them worked at Goodyear Aircraft, they were called Rosie the Riveter. Rudy's three sisters worked there, Bea and Alice and Mary. Mary retired from there, so did Bea... There were a lot of women that worked there. The women either worked out in the fields, at Goodyear Aircraft, at the Wigwam [Resort] and also helping families, you know, cleaning houses and taking care of children for the families that lived in Litchfield. That's what I remember.

Let me take you back to when you left for college. Can you tell me what that was like for you and where did you live when you were at NAU, what is now NAU.

I was worried about going off to college. I was worrying about what I would wear. My dad used to buy *Seventeen* Magazine for me all the time, and you know *Seventeen* they would always show, this is what the young girl wears to college. And I remember talking to Miss Ybarra, telling her, "You know, my dad, my parents can't afford to buy me those kinds of clothes." And she said, "Don't you worry", she says, "You wear what you have. The important thing is that you keep it clean and that you're always neat and clean. That's the important thing. It doesn't matter what you wear"...

That was a time when it was unusual for someone of Mexican American descent to be going to college.
I was the first one. The first graduate of Litchfield high school to go to college and my dad was very proud of me. But the men that lived in the community, the men that he worked with, criticized him. Why are you letting her go off? She's not going to help you. She's gonna go off. They just thought it was terrible that my parents were letting me go off to college. I was supposed to stay home and work, bring money in for the household... But I know that my dad was really very proud of me. I think if he'd had the opportunity to go on to high school he would have.

Belen, if you were one of the first Mexican-American women to graduate from college then you must have been among the first to be available to work in the schools and in the profession. Can you talk about that a little bit?
When I was working in Ash Fork and I worked there for only one year with second graders, I was the only Hispanic teacher there and I was really welcomed by the staff and the parents. The parents even gave me a bridal shower in one of their homes... For a long time I was the only Hispanic working in Avondale. And whenever they had a Spanish-speaking family go into the office to register, a lot of times they would take me out of the classroom, ask me to go over there and interpret for them, which was a little difficult. And I remember since I was the only bilingual person there, we got a Korean boy and guess who got the Korean boy? I did. And what did I know about Korean?...

The other thing that I remember, being on playground duty. I was working on one side and the children had to cross the street to come over to lunch on the other side. I was watching the children cross the street. This little third grade girl stayed behind, came up to me and she asked me, "Are you Mexican?"

"Yes I am."

"And you're a teacher?"

"Yes I am." I said, "If you want to be a teacher you can be a teacher." She smiled at me as she crossed the street on her way to lunch.

Life in the D.C. Suburbs: Valerie Vahouny

Source Note: The following interview is part of "A Look Back at Braddock District, Fairfax County, Virginia" oral history project, deposited with the Center for History and New Media, George Mason University. A more complete transcript, along with other perspectives on suburban life, is available at the web site http://braddockheritage.org/resources/item/133/.

Like many residents of new suburbs in the 1950s and 1960s, Val Vahouny had fond memories of new household conveniences and neighborhood gatherings and activities. In 1963 she and her family moved to a new home in the original Kings Park development in Fairfax County, Virginia. Like many families at the time, she and her husband first lived in an apartment until their growing family required more space. Vahouny remembers Braddock Road as a two-lane street with no traffic lights and a half-hour commute into the District of Columbia where her husband worked, and a place where her children flourished. Mary Lipsey interviewed Vahouny on June 2, 2005.

Can you tell us what brought you to the Braddock District...?
Well, I grew up in Arlington, and I started raising my family there. And after my husband got his doctorate and we were making a little bit of money, we decided that it was time to try to find a house because we were expecting our third child, and we were living in a two-bedroom apartment. So we knew it was going to be pretty tight. So we looked around Arlington to find a house for our price range, which was about $20,000, and there was nothing to be had... So one Sunday afternoon for the fun of it we started driving around, and we ended up in Kings Park. [We found] the Duke model, which was the split foyer, and the price was $20,000...

So it was like, you can imagine moving from a two-bedroom, one bathroom house or apartment, where I had to take the laundry outside and up the hill and across the street and wait for a washing machine and dryers to do it, to move into this house of our own with our own backyard, and a dishwasher, and my own washer and dryer. It was like heaven.

So you're moving in to a brand new community, okay? What was it like with the types of activities and things like that that the community had?
Well, there weren't very many. The pool was open, and we joined. And since we did move in the summer, it was perfect timing. We went out and met a lot of the people. A lot of our friends came from there... I think at that time [the pool] was the hub of the community and a lot of things happened there. We'd have cookouts. I asked my daughters what they remembered. We'd have competitions between the parents and the children where you'd have to wear all your clothes to swim across the pool, just silly...

They played with their friends after school when we first moved here because there... wasn't anything around. Kings Park was the last community on Braddock Road. After that, it was trees...

As the community expanded, did you get involved in garden clubs, or civic association, or any type of organizations?
Yeah. I personally was in a garden club that was formed pretty quickly after we moved in. The woman that lived behind me was the big organizer, I guess you would say. And I still remember when we met. Some of us had young children, and some of us had older children, and those of us with young children couldn't go to meetings in the daytime, and the others didn't want to go out to meetings at night. So we decided to have two clubs, and I belonged to the evening group. It was called the Chelsea Garden Club. And we did a lot of fundraisers over the

years. As I recall, primarily the money that we raised was used to help landscaping the two elementary schools in Kings Park.

My husband, George, got involved early on when some of the people in the neighborhood noticed how many children were on our block. There were a lot of little kids in Kings Park. And they decided to form a committee and do a little census of their own to calculate how many children were going to be going to Kings Park School. There probably were 10 people, and I can remember them meeting in my rec room. And they went off on their own... They went door to door. How many children do you have? What grades will they be in? And after that, they realized that the projected school rooms were not going to be enough for the children that were already living in Kings Park at that time. And this part I'm not sure about, but I believe they went to the school board and brought it up. And how quickly the school board acted after that, I don't know. But I do know that... soon after the original building was completed, a new section was added on that enclosed what became a courtyard. Originally it was open space at the end. So it became a courtyard. I think they maybe added six school rooms. And my husband became the first PTA president there. And those were exciting times because it was a brand new school and everybody was so excited about it, having your own school and really being involved...

Well, in your community, were there 4th of July celebrations?

...One of the neighbors a couple of streets down from us was the instigator of the 4th of July parade, and she pretty much did it by herself. It was really remarkable. I really got to hand it to her... And she really got this whole thing started and went to the Burke volunteer fire department and asked them if they would have one of their pieces of equipment lead the parade. And ever since then, I think maybe every year... one of the fire engines comes along and leads the parade and blasts their horn, which is a big deal, and then followed by all the children with their bicycles all decorated with the red, white, and blue, and little children being pulled by their fathers on their wagons. It was very special. Afterwards there would be a picnic in the park. They'd have hot dogs for everybody, and I think they still do that...

I really have to say that more than roads and everything, the lifestyle... I think of as being the biggest change since I've moved out here. We moved into this, what we thought was a grand home for us. The houses in Kings Park now are small compared to what's being built now. There were a lot of children. Almost all the mothers that I knew, I didn't know any mother that worked outside of the home. The father had a job that he came home 6 o'clock, ate with his children. And the days were like where you wake up in the morning, you get your kids up from bed. Everybody would sit down and eat breakfast together, and you send the family off to work and to school. And then you would do your chores, your laundry, and your cleaning. And a lot of us with little girls did sewing because that was the only way we could make ends meet. Nowadays I don't think anybody sews clothes for their children anymore.

There was one black and white television in a home...I think there were maybe four television channels...There was no cable, so the pictures were pretty grainy a lot of times, and we had rabbit ears on the television set. Some people later got the antenna on top of the roofs, but not very many people had that. There was, as you said, one car per family, so nobody could get out of the community unless us wives, unless somebody was in a car pool and we could go with them. My husband did not carpool normally. Sometimes somebody would come out and pick him up to go into work if I had to take the children to the doctor or something like that. But ordinarily I didn't have a car. But it didn't seem to matter that much. If we ran out of something, I could call him and he could stop and pick something up in Annandale or in Springfield on his way home, a loaf of bread or whatever we had run out of...

Almost all of us had milk delivered because you couldn't get enough milk into a refrigerator to last you a week, which most of us only shopped at the grocery store once a week. The newspaper was delivered at your door so you didn't have to walk out to the curb. Your mail was delivered at your door. It is still now in places where it was grandfathered or whatever. I never did understand why some places have at the door delivery and some don't.

And utilities were different, too. We had a small refrigerator with a small upper area that was for the freezer things. And so you couldn't get very much into the freezer in advance with a family of five for a week. You'd have to be really careful about what frozen foods you got, so we'd get frozen vegetables. You'd get chicken. Chicken was cheap, so you had a lot of chicken. We had a lot of ground beef because you could stretch that. But it had to fit in that little refrigerator area. Nobody had a freezer, a separate freezer, back in those days. And there was no microwave oven, so you didn't have quick stuff...There was a telephone that sat on the counter or desk...that had a cord to it, unlike today where there's so many...

It was just at the beginning, I think, of what we know as the women's lib. And we would have encouraged our daughters to go to college in any case. But all women, girls, were being told, you can have everything. You can have it all. Go to college, and have a profession, and work. And so girls started doing that, and then they decided, so they were getting their college degrees, and then they were using them for something more than just meeting a man and getting married. So they got their college degrees, and then they wanted also to have a family. So then they were faced with this dilemma, what do you do with the children? So then child care became important for these women to have somebody that they could trust to take care of their children, or quit work, which they didn't want to do because they had now, many of them, really good professional careers...I think that they tried so hard to have everything, and at this point in their lives, they have to hold down their jobs because things have gotten so expensive, everything has gotten expensive. And in order to pay their mortgages and all their utilities and everything, the clothing and everything that they needed for these children, they had to continue working. And it wasn't like when we first moved into Kings Park. People did without. If you couldn't afford it, you just didn't have it. I remember the first year we were there, my husband had to borrow our next door neighbor's lawn mower because we couldn't afford a lawn mower... So thank goodness we had a nice next door neighbor that would let us borrow it. Nowadays people don't do without...

Well, I remember both when John F. Kennedy died, or was shot, and when Martin Luther King was shot. I remember that when Kennedy was shot, it was like, everything changed. Life was simple compared to now—we didn't think so at the time—and peaceful. And to have that happen was just unheard of. And everybody was crying. It was such a horrible time.

If you had to pick your fondest memory of this area, is there one that you could select?

I have to say making the friends that we made. The swimming pool experience was so special back then. We made so many good friends, and all three of our children were involved in swimming and diving, and both my husband and I were officers in the Northern Virginia Swim League. And it was like a big family...

And that's not the family, but I think the memories that they have of what it was like growing up, walking to school. I asked the two that still live here, said what they remember most. Karen said she remembers playing kick ball at night in the street, and I remember boys that lived on Kings Park Drive used to play ball in the street. Nobody ever thought of that. Now, of course, they've got speed bumps, and circles and everything like that. Kids can't play in the street anymore.

FIVE

1965–2000

In the 1960s and 1970s many Americans mobilized to challenge injustice in a variety of social movements. The civil rights, black and brown power, antiwar, Native American, gay, environmental, and women's liberation movements all imagined a different nation that would abolish inequalities and respect the rights of individuals. The bulging baby boom generation expanded their influence in American society by celebrating new music and culture, ways of living, and forms of protest. A new libertine atmosphere allowed men and women to express new gender roles and sexual identities. But by the late 1970s a new conservative movement reacted against these changes in American life and asserted its plans for more limited government and restrictions on abortion and sexual expression. Public reactions to the Vietnam War and Watergate scandal indicated that other limits had been reached as well, largely increasing public cynicism about politics.

Although the United States ended its long war in Vietnam in 1975, the Cold War lingered in immigration policies and in the administration of President Ronald Reagan, who pursued covert actions, especially in Central America, to halt the perceived spread of communism, and expanded military spending and anticommunist rhetoric. But while foreign interventions may have distracted Americans, they increasingly worried about their economic futures. Beginning in the 1970s the four-decades long economic dominance of the United States began to unravel as the country faced an energy crisis, a falling dollar, and increasing competition from Europe and Japan. "Deindustrialization," or the loss of manufacturing jobs, and the end to the welfare state devastated many communities in the country; and the celebrated American middle class began to shrink by the end of the century. Even as the Cold War ended in the early 1990s, new domestic and international threats loomed in an increasingly divided United States.

The ten interviews in this section focus on the challenges facing Americans in the last four decades of the twentieth century. For each of five sub-themes—*social and cultural protest, the gender revolution, the Cold War, migrations, and economic and domestic change*—two oral narratives offer different perspectives about these events and the times. As with other chapters, it was difficult to represent the many points of view and great diversity of experiences in late twentieth century America, but the selections here point to that complexity and variety. Although their voices may sound more familiar since they inhabit the more recent past, the oral histories in this section echo many of the themes that others have raised in this volume. What similarities and differences do you find in the narratives of this section compared to other interview excerpts in the book?

Protest and Social Change

The many social movements of the 1960s and 1970s had a decidedly youthful bent. The largest college generation in United States history participated in civil rights efforts, and then by the mid-1960s they dominated a growing anti-Vietnam War movement. The largest student movement, Students for a Democratic Society (SDS), asserted new youthful power and goals for democratizing society as well as ending imperialistic wars. However, by the late 1960s, young activists became frustrated by the slow pace of change and the brutal response by police and state national guards to demonstrations at the 1968 Chicago Democratic National Convention and Kent State and Jackson State universities in 1970. Some young people turned to more radical organizations like the Weatherman or sought to create alternative communities removed from the mainstream of American life. African Americans, Mexican Americans, Asian Americans, and Native Americans asserted their own political and cultural ideas in new black, brown, yellow, and red power movements. The feminist and gay rights movements also redefined the era by asserting new gender identities and bringing attention to discrimination in the home, workplace, and social arena.

Alongside these social movements emerged new youthful cultural expressions that were not only distinctly different in form but seemed to radically depart from their parents' aspirations and lives. Young people sported new casual dress, "flower power" ideals of peace and love, new communal and collective forms of living and working, and most of all, the music of rock 'n' roll, which bound together young people across race, region, class, and gender.

Questions to Consider: The two narrators below reflect on the events of the late 1960s and early 1970s and how they shaped their own personal development. Note how Casale and Lerner try to recreate the times and explain their youthful thinking, and how in the present they understand their past experiences and actions.

1. What cultural influences from the period shaped the artistic and political development of the two narrators?
2. How does each evaluate his participation in the critical movements and events of the times?
3. What motivated Lerner to participate in SDS and the Weathermen?

Rock 'n' Roll and Cultural Protest: Gerald Vincent "Gerry" Casale

Source Note: With its oral history program, the Experience Music Project|Science Fiction Museum and Hall of Fame (EMP|SFM) in Seattle has created an archive of interviews with the musicians, authors, filmmakers, producers, and other key figures who have shaped American popular music and science fiction. EMP|SFM also uses oral history in its regular Oral History Live! event series, which brings notable music makers, science fiction luminaries and the public together for an intimate curator-hosted interview recorded before a live audience, and in video interviews available online at http://www.empsfm.org/programs/index.asp?categoryID=60.

Gerry Casale, co-founder, with Mark Mothersbaugh, of the rock band Devo, recalls how music of the 1950s and 1960s and the antiwar protests at Kent State University influenced his musical and political development. John Seman, AV Preservationist at EMP|SFM, interviewed Casale on July 13, 2006 at Mutato Musika in Los Angeles for EMP|SFM. A video portion of the interview is available on EMP's website: http://www.empsfm.org/programs/index.asp?articleID=735

The first self-conscious musical memory I have is standing next to one of these huge floor based wooden radios that were typical in homes that a lot of parents had after World War II and through the '50s…And I think I was maybe four. And my mother would turn it to a station during the day that played mostly bad music but there was an hour in the afternoon when they were playing basically hillbilly music. It was Ohio after all. There was a big influx from West Virginia of people that had come from the coal mines and sought work in northeastern Ohio when that failed. So I remember hearing Frankie Laine singing "Night Train." And I couldn't wait for that song, I heard it once and then I couldn't wait to hear it again…And then "Ghost Riders in the Sky." It was Tex Ritter or somebody… those songs just drilled into my brain and gave me a nice foundation for when I first heard Elvis, you know, a few years later.

What kind of influence did Elvis have on you?
For me Elvis was just the right moment, just when you discover pubescence, just when you realize uh gee, I get excited around girls... And Elvis was absolutely not allowed but of course I came from a large extended family and when we would visit... one of my cousins, inevitably somebody had a 45... and heard songs like "Don't Be Cruel" and "Hound Dog." And that was it. It completely transformed me. I was full on preteen rebel, I think I was maybe like 11. And that was it. Elvis was the king for a long time.

But I think that what happened then is that there was an obvious post atomic explosion of cultural change that's been unmatched before or since where every year brought massive amounts of changes in technology and in cultural focus, in look, in information. It was a very short period after that, maybe 2–1/2 years that the Beatles showed up doing "I Want to Hold Your Hand." So there was a whole revolution and shift in that amount of time. And I left Elvis in the dust.

What did the Beatles bring to your musical development?
The Beatles for me probably sealed my interest in making music. Until then I just liked music but I thought I was gonna be an astronaut... When I saw the Beatles I knew what I wanted to do... I watched how everybody responded to them and all the adults hated them and made fun of them and... mainstream kids that came from... families that are the powerful families, the people that run the town, they all hated the Beatles... And all the poor kids and kids that had quote been greasers and outcast kinda kids, and artsy kids, all had the opposite reaction to the Beatles, including me, where all I wanted to do was imitate them... It was a case where an aesthetic was two steps ahead of anybody's consciousness, where you can't even judge it...

That kind of dynamic kept happening. I remember the same thing happening to me the first time I heard Jimi Hendrix... I actually physically saw Jimi Hendrix because by that time I was just old enough to sneak into a concert. And I saw him in Cleveland, Ohio live. And suddenly the Beatles didn't matter. [Laugh] And that was about the time that... my interest in art, in music, my awareness of politics and values or lack thereof, my strong—I guess for want of a better word—hatred of illegitimate authority all came together.

And I think it wasn't long after that that I started playing music... I had to teach myself, for two obvious reasons that most kids didn't get music lessons unless they had parents with money... most parents that didn't have money also disregarded that as any kind of valid pursuit... They wanted them to go get a factory job... We just formed a cover band like every teenager does... covering mostly Rolling Stones kind of songs because they were easy to play and I'd grown up heavily influenced by blues and R&B. That's what the AM radio stations in northeastern Ohio played mostly and a lot of them came out of Detroit... And we loved that kind of music... It took the English to bring it back and make kids listen to the stuff that was theirs because of the segregated culture and the... whitewashed squeaky clean milk white culture that pervaded at that time...

And in college [Kent State] then I kind of drifted to visual art... And at the same time... I was in the middle of the firestorm of basically a civil war in America... And the people that were anti-war and the people that were concerned about the direction of a kind of a corporate feudal industrial complex, were very well informed and very articulate about it...

So when you come to the really important defining moment at Kent State University that changed my life forever and ultimately sent me back to music and creating Devo, were the killings by the National Guard of the four students over the anti-war protest. Nixon decided on May 3rd 1970 that he would expand the [Vietnam] war into Cambodia, and they did it without an act of Congress and this was very upsetting to everybody back then. They actually believed in the Constitution and... the separation of powers. They thought he had to get an okay. And he just did it, executive power...

So on May 4th, Monday, the students called an impromptu rally at noon, to protest the expansion of the war. But over the weekend anticipating student unrest the National Guard moved in, hidden in the heating plant inside the university, unbeknownst to the students. Had jeeps parked about three miles out of town and were ready to go.

And so the governor, at noon, declared a limited form of martial law... and he forbade protest. He made that automatically by definition illegal that day, so that whatever happened the National Guard had then the rationale to do what they did.

Now you gotta remember the students protesting were 18 and 19 and the National Guardsmen were 18 and 19. That was the condition I grew up in, in my formative years from just... being a kind of passive live-let-live kind of pseudo hippie to a fully aware person who had to strike out against hideous illegitimate authority. And I was there that day. And I had become friends with two of the four students who were about to die, Jeffrey Miller and Allison Krause...

And we were all kind of being herded by the National Guard who cut off our escape route over the front of the campus so we had to keep going back towards the football field. And then just like a B movie, a second phalanx of them appear coming out of the heating plant and now they've got everybody boxed in, so everyone starts running for the student parking lot.

And that's when they knelt, the first row knelt, the second row stood and... they fired. And nobody thought they had live ammunition. Certainly no one even could guess that. The bayonets were scary enough. The tear gas was bad enough but nobody thought about actual bullets. And I still remember the crack of the rifles and everything and not knowing what the hell, nobody knew what it was.

And so this massive human animal confusion, like when Kennedy was assassinated and everybody's looking around. It sounds like a backfire. And then suddenly there's that moment like in a bad auto accident or like in the stylizations of a Scorsese film like *Raging Bull* where everything goes into slow motion. Sound blows away. You don't hear the birds anymore, the wind, the trees. And some horrible feeling in your gut is... emanating out of your whole body as you realize somebody's laying there with blood coming out of 'em.

There's smoke everywhere. Everybody's frozen and then back to live action. Screaming, yelling, screaming chaos. And you don't know what's going on and it turns out the person 50 feet away from me laying face down on the sidewalk was Allison Krause. And the guy down like 100 feet down the hill on the, on the driveway where the famous picture of the girl screaming towards the sky over him, kneeling over him, that was Jeffrey Miller. And I found that out and at the same time we were being herded like cattle and made to sit on the grass at gunpoint and we sat there for 2–1/2 hours till they figured out what to do with us. They marched us off campus single file through a line of National Guardsmen, closed the campus, declared... I guess full curfew and martial law in the city for the next five days... And I can't... find an explanation here verbally right now to tell you how much that changed me. But let's just say it was no more Mr. Nice Guy. Especially when the papers came out the next day with the headline "Students Hurt Guardsmen."

The town sheriff deputized about 50 guys and they were driving around... with shotguns hanging out their windows. Empowered, convinced that the students had shot at guardsmen... Obviously that turns out just like with the weapons of mass destruction today, there were none. No, no student had a gun. No student hurt a guardsman. The most any of us did or the braver ones ran up with wet rags over their faces and tried to throw the teargas back, usually at the detriment to themselves and nobody else...

From there out I cut my hair [laugh], I developed a much more militant kind of art aesthetic, and it got quickly transferred to playing music... Obviously [Mark Mothersbaugh and I] were responding in a health[y] artistic way to the kind of things that were actually nauseating us... Your creative response to that is to analyze what it is about it that is freaking you out and use that creatively to make a statement. And we were doing then the same thing at night in the basement with the music. And these two things kinda came together. And so then we decided consciously I think somewhere around 1973 to try to create a band called Devo. And Devo would be an audio-visual band because [laugh] Mark and I both naively believed in all the magazine articles we were reading about the coming revolution of Laserdiscs.

Radical Protest—SDS and the Weatherman: Jonathan Lerner

Source Note: This narrative, and the interview in the next section with Warren Smith, comes from the American Century Project (www.americancenturyproject.

org) at St. Andrew's Episcopal School in Potomac, Maryland. High school students there have assembled one of the largest archived pre-collegiate oral history projects in the country, available online at www.mdch.org.

Jonathan Lerner grew up in a middle-class neighborhood in Chevy Chase, Maryland, and attended Antioch College in Ohio in the late 1960s. He dropped out to pursue acting and dancing in New York, where he joined Students for a Democratic Society (SDS), the leading student organization in the country. He worked on the SDS staff in New York, Washington, DC, and Chicago, and in 1969 helped the Weatherman faction take over and ultimately dissolve SDS. He remained in the group until it fell apart in the mid-1970s. Here he describes his role in the organizations and how tensions within the movements contributed to their demise. Courtney Ivins interviewed Lerner at Emory University in Atlanta, Georgia, on December 5, 2004.

In junior high and high school living in Washington, the presence of the Civil Rights movement and then the anti-war movement was very visible. There were always the marches, and picket lines, and things like that at the White House. My friends and I at school participated in those things, because that just seemed like the thing to do and they were happening, and it was partly because it was fascinating, and it was electrifying, and it was fun, and it also felt right. So . . . as a teenager it was hard not to have political consciousness if you were paying attention to what was happening right in the city you lived in . . .

What made you decide, when you were at Antioch, to join SDS?

I never actually joined at that time; I joined later. I wasn't really interested in being in an organization and dealing with ideology and theory. I mean, I felt politics viscerally, and in terms of this just innate sense of what's right and what's wrong in the world. But the idea of talking about it and planning strategy and being an organizer didn't – I was happy to be an artist who was political, to the extent that I even thought of it that way. It just seemed like the normal thing to do. But I had become very good friends with a guy named Jeff Jones, who was very involved in the SDS chapter there . . . But Jeff and I both quit school at the same time and coincidentally both moved to New York, and I did it to continue to do theater work which I had been doing. He did it to run the New York SDS office . . . There were a lot of Antioch people who were going to New York, and he kept trying to get me involved in different organizing projects and eventually sort of talked me into joining the staff. The way he did it was to say, "we need you to organize guerrilla theater groups at all of our campus chapters and be a teacher of guerrilla theater," which I did for about five minutes, and that wasn't really what was needed. What was really needed was someone to run the office and write leaflets and organize demonstrations, and so I ended up doing those things. So I was really in SDS in a formal sense after I was at Antioch . . .

There was a national office of SDS that was in Chicago, and then there were regional offices that were in half a dozen cities around the country, and then, in some places, there wasn't really an office but there were individual people who would be called "campus travelers," who might have responsibilities for a state, for traveling around working with students at different campuses... That's how I found myself to be a writer, through my writing in the radical press. So I did a lot of that, and I was in SDS on the staff for about three years – from '67 to the end of 1969—when the organization sort of fell apart...

What made you decide, and other future Weatherman members decide, that SDS was ineffective as an organization?

I think our rage and our anger and our impatience, our sort of insistence that we really knew best what could happen. 'Cause the thing about SDS was, it was a big, genuinely democratic organization. It was big and loose and messy. We had a couple of national conferences every year, and the big one in the summer that like 2,000 people would come to, and I mean anybody who wanted to stand up with a petition, or call for any crazy idea of what to do, it was wide open, which was sort of wonderful. It was all this ferment, and we thought there was kind of a place for anybody.

But in... those last years of the 60's, political tensions and polarization within the country and even within the Left were really accelerating. We all began to feel really desperate because there had been these years of peaceful protest and petitioning and trying, in 1968, to get a peace candidate in the Democratic Party, and there were these increasingly huge anti-war mobilizations, half a million people several times a year in New York and Washington, and the war only got more intense. The racial polarization in the country was getting much more intense. There were riots in cities. In those summers, the Black Panthers emerged, and other really militant black groups emerged. There was a lot of repression. The Panthers were having shoot outs with the police... and of course they were always outnumbered and always ended up being killed.

It was this sense that all of these kind of polite and legalistic things we were trying to do weren't working. And we felt so angry and outraged and desperate about the war and the racial situation... the polarization was also replicating itself within SDS, so that by the end what I was describing how big and wonderful and... democratic, sort of pleasantly anarchic, the conferences had once been, they were then very hostile. There were factions where the people who were your friends six months ago now were your enemies... because you had some difference on what we all should be doing for the next six months. Should the main thing be to organize a huge, national mobilization in Washington and get everyone in the country to come there, or should we have decentralized action on every campus?... Everybody really still wanted to end the war, but we were very young, so our passions were taking over. And so now this organization – the beauty of it had once been how open and loose it was – now it just seemed sort of useless... that you couldn't really get anything done. And we, the people who became the Weathermen, just sort of said... never mind, this is bullshit, we don't need this anymore, and we eventually just sort of... took what we wanted from it, and let it die eventually.

Could you explain how that transition occurred in 1969?

The last national convention was in June of '69 in Chicago. By this time, there were three main internal factions and... some of these people had been our friends and lovers just recently, you know, but we came down differently on political positions... And one of the big issues was about working class, factory organizing versus youth culture organizing. It was the classic Marxist-Leftist thing about organizing in unions and in factory situations, which was both of the other factions were more on that side, versus our thing, which was more this kind of exuberant youth culture, rock n' roll and drugs and street kids and hippies and stuff, idea that that's where our energy should go and that that's where the more potentially revolutionary people were. We sort of looked at factory workers and said, you know, they're all busy makin' payments on their motor homes and stuff, they don't care, they've been bought off... they're living a privileged life. Because, although they're workers, they're workers here in the United States, and they don't care about our colonial exploitation of other economies and things.

So that was basically the issue that was the split. It happened in stages that happened very quickly. [After the Weatherman faction maneuvered to take control of SDS at the convention] by the fall, when normally in other years SDS organizers would fan out across the country because students were coming back to school... we didn't care about that. We were busy organizing suicidal street demonstrations and thinking about how to make bombs, and basically by January or February we just closed the door and walked away and just left it. The whole apparatus of the organization, the membership lists, the fact that there was a centralized place, the fact that there was a weekly newspaper, a network of organizers, we just trashed the whole thing...

How did you feel about the [Weatherman] bombings?

At the time I thought they were very exciting... Our theory about them was that they would reveal who the enemy was, because we were bombing things like international corporations, and the Pentagon, and the U.S. Capitol, and police stations, and things like that... at the time, I thought they were great. I don't really feel that way now. I'm proud of the fact that, aside from the three people of our own that died [making a bomb] in the [March 6, 1970 Greenwich Village] townhouse explosion, no one was actually hurt in one of our bombings...

What kind of problems arose within the group that eventually tore it apart?

The outside context was that the war had ended in '75, and of course, therefore, the anti-war movement petered away. So the idea that we had been providing some kind of symbolic leadership for a movement, well, now there was no movement... I think also individually, it's very hard living underground.

It's not really fun . . . People probably missed seeing their families. Probably a lot of people wondered . . . "I was supposed to be a doctor, and I could be a doctor in a free clinic, and now here I'm nothing, you know, and having no effect." And with the war ended, then there became this issue of what to do, what should we be doing to justify our existence? . . . And just the whole thing within the period of about a few months completely split apart in the most vicious, resentful, mean, awful, series of people switching sides and blaming each other, and it was really sort of a nightmare. And then it was over within, let's see, Hard Times Conference was February of '76 . . . well, I was out of it by May, and I think the whole thing had split apart by the end of the summer. So it ate itself alive, really is what happened . . . I think that we helped destroy the Left in this country . . . weaken it, by our eager participation in sectarianism.

The Gender Revolution and its Backlash

By the mid-1960s, the increasing numbers of women in the workplace and the impetus of the African American civil rights movement led many women to call for full equality in American society. Dissatisfied with their secondary roles in the civil rights and student anti-war movements, young women recognized the need for a new feminist movement. Many women who joined groups such as

Image 14 Demonstration in favor of equal rights for women, Washington, DC (Library of Congress).

the National Organization of Women (NOW) stressed the need for equal rights and believed this could be achieved through legislation and the courts. Younger women's liberationists believed that equality could only occur once private lives were transformed, and they focused energies on consciousness-raising, challenging family roles, respecting sexual identities and difference, and creating institutions that directly addressed women's concerns such as reproductive rights, health and child care, and racial justice.

On June 27, 1969, the New York police raid of a gay bar in Greenwich Village, the Stonewall Inn, provoked an uprising that launched the gay liberation movement. Homosexual men and women across the country, especially in urban centers like New York, San Francisco, and Houston, encouraged gays and lesbians to "come out," declare their sexual identities and demand the end to discriminatory treatment. Gradually, through the 1970s, states began to decriminalize homosexual acts between consenting adults.

But by the mid-1970s, in reaction to the era of protest and social change, a new conservative movement emerged to roll back government programs and changes in traditional gender and family roles. In 1972 Congress and a majority of states enthusiastically endorsed the Equal Rights Amendment, but by the end of the decade, the anti-ERA movement successfully halted ratification in the necessary final states. The 1973 Supreme Court *Roe v. Wade* decision legalizing abortion galvanized religious groups to fight to restrict women's access to abortions at the state level and to end federal funding of abortions for poor and military women.

Questions to Consider: In this section, one narrator is pushing against gender roles and restrictions, and the other is struggling to retain traditional family roles. How does each explain his or her position? Also, each tries to clarify "what happened" at the significant events of the 1969 Stonewall riots and the 1977 International Women's Year conferences. How do you assess their versions of events?

The Dawning of the Gay Rights Movement: Warren Allen Smith

Warren Allen Smith grew up in Iowa and was drafted into the US Army in 1942. After his service in the European theater of the war, he earned his MA in English at Columbia University, and then taught at the Bentley School in New York and New Canaan High School in Connecticut. With his partner of forty years, Fernando Vargas, he also managed a recording studio, Variety Recording. Here he describes his participation in the Stonewall Riots of 1969 and the event's significance for the gay rights movement. Among other activities, for five years Smith led the annual Gay Parade in New York. Stiliana Dimkova interviewed Smith on December 22, 2003, in New York, for the American Century Project of St. Andrew's Episcopal School.

Did you ever experience any discrimination in the army, was it different being a homosexual in the army?

Well, first of all, nobody in my company knew the meaning of homosexual. I didn't call myself homosexual. I had a girlfriend in college... before I was in the army. I didn't really know what it meant to be a homosexual. I never read about sex very much and in the army... we were kept busy every minute. I didn't really have homosexual experiences.... I did one night, at the Rheims Cathedral, that's where all the kings were crowned, and it was an old Cathedral and it was so old it was just ruined, and one night I was just curious and I walked in there and there were two men having sex, and that was really the first time I saw men having sex. And the funny thing was that the enlisted man was on top and the other was on the tilt, and you would think it might be the other way around. That, I guess, was the introduction to me that there was more than just playing around with somebody. You could do things that I had not heard about before.

I know you did not come out at one particular time, but when did your family realize you were gay?

Ok, well when I met [Fernando Vargas] that was in 1948, 1 recall I then got my masters in 1949, and taught at a private school. During that time, yes we lived together but in those days to be homosexual was to have a psychiatric problem, you were sick. He and I, we never felt that way at all, and I think it's funny because we were not into religion, honestly... people who were into religion were always talking about sin, we were talking about pleasure. He had been raised a Catholic, I had been raised a Methodist, we both left that, and my interest is more in literature and his interest is more in electrical engineering. That's why... we started a studio in 1961 together, and I was the business person... because I had learned in the army how to do all these things. So, we complemented each other...

And the faculty by the way, in both schools that I taught... the faculty never brought up the subject of gay, I don't ever remember. I may have suspected that one of the Phys Ed lady teachers was what we called a dyke, but at any rate we just never talked about it. I do remember being an English teacher and I required lots of writing and there were some kids who would write about having trouble with their parents because they caught them masturbating or something like that, and I never really advised them. I particularly took students out on Wednesday nights, and took them to dinner and took them to the studio. So they got to see what I did, but I didn't tell them about Fernando or anything like that. But I had a good time teaching and I think it was partly because I stayed in the closet...

Historian Eric Foner called the 1960's the "Rights Revolution;" where do the gay rights fit in the larger fight for civil rights, women's rights and students' rights?

Well, I think it was a key part, but I think also the blacks were a model... they refused to sit in the back of the bus. Well, at Stonewall, that was something similar for the gays. For the first time the gays started to fight back, there wasn't really any organized movement really... So when I left that particular time in June, and went to the Village really just to get a beer, it was like a happening because there were these people fighting the police but there was no organized movement. Once gays organized, yes, there would be specific directions, you know at a certain night appear at a certain place and carry plaques, but to answer your question, prior to '69, I don't remember any [organized movement]...

It was just that in one particular night, when the police came to be paid off, there was a problem, in this particular bar...There are different versions. The version that makes most sense to me, because I became involved in two of the Stonewall veterans groups...I think the cops went in [the bar] and they were a little pushy. And they pushed one drag queen and if it wasn't she, it was some kind of a little struggle in there and then it was like a happening then everybody jumped in. The first thing you knew, the cops had to call for reinforcements...There are allegedly 3000 people who were in that bar that night, but the place couldn't hold more than fifty or so, so many of the versions never happened, and many of the theses as to why it happened are so varied that I don't think I am capable of even evaluating them. To me it was a happening, it just happened. It had nothing to do with Judy Garland having died, it had nothing to do with...I think two people rubbed a cop the wrong way, he reacted, they reacted, those of us on the street, I am talking about the second night, I was there the second night, third night and the fifth night.

Let me go back, what do you remember when you first heard about it, June 27th, that night, what do you remember?

Ok, it was maybe just a word of mouth, you know practically nothing in the newspapers...It was just another fight. But, when I went to Pedora's Restaurant, I heard..."Boy did you know what happened last night?" so then I went over and here it was again. They were redoing it...I heard about it at Pedora's Restaurant...a known gay restaurant where all the waiters were gay and it was a place where you would feel safe. There were different bars where you could feel safe. There was Mary's on 8th Street, and there were several others, but the Stonewall Inn was one of the worst, it was the dirtiest. When you went in, you had to sign in and of course, everybody signed a fake name, Frank Sinatra was signed ten times on a page. I am exaggerating but people would sign as some famous person. At any rate, what I remember was that really was a big problem, one of the waiters at Pedora's was put into this police wagon, they called it a paddy wagon, and even to this day he doesn't really talk about it, he doesn't want to remember it, I don't know why because he is openly gay...

But the second night to me it was more like a happening, wow they are doing it again, and I was across the street and there were like twenty, thirty of us there, and we saw the cops coming out, bringing in people, and it was only natural to say "let them go," and they called the cops pigs in those days, and of course they would come over and grab you and say "did you call me a pig?" and then they would put you in the paddy wagon too. I was across the street and there was a garbage can and so a person that I didn't know...next to me, we just agreed, let's throw this and make things worse. So we carried it a little bit and then he set fire to the paper that was in it, and we threw it, and immediately I saw a cop running toward me and then I could imagine a headline in the morning paper "a public school teacher caught throwing garbage can" and I ran like mad, and they didn't catch the other guy either...but it was fun. It was like a food fight in high school [laughs]. But that was the second night...So I was curious and I had gone down every night hoping to see more. I didn't go back in the place, I just stayed outside...

What do you remember about the nights that followed and the things that were published in the newspapers?

Ok, now the second night, the reporters did come in then, and the stories were far more complete. The individuals that I interviewed, that were in the Stonewall Veterans, even they had different versions of what happened...

I don't think the *New York Times* would give it much coverage. Basically it was not a big deal in June of '69. What happened was that in many people's eyes this was the first time on record that a group of gays rejected the subservient, and that was easy to publicize. Once that was publicized there were a lot of people that became involved. So again, although I was in the Stonewall Veterans Group, I couldn't go back to Connecticut and brag about it and remember this association. It was a time where [it] paid to be closeted, you just didn't dare come out...

On the second night for example, word got out to the other gay bars as well, "hey there's trouble at Stonewall" and then they'd empty out and go over and now the police had instead of dozens they had hundreds, so it was a difficult time for the police...They were carrying out whatever the mayor of the city made them do. So for all I knew the man who chased me might have been gay, I don't know, he just carried out the mayor's orders...

It was a dangerous time; it really was a dangerous time for anybody to be out; people today have no idea how bad it was. On the other hand it was good in that you could have sex every night, you could go to a bar, pick somebody up, take them home, and they'd give you their phone number, it was always a fake number, and you always went with different people. I'm not saying that everyone did this but the good thing was if you got syphilis and you just went to the doctor and you just got some treatments you were cured. If you had gonorrhea, the doctor had some treatments and you were cured; it's not like today. Today if you have sex once that could be the time that kills you...It's just that there wasn't AIDS, there wasn't HIV. So the theory was that if you get sick you can get cured.

What does Stonewall symbolize to you?

Well, originally it symbolized a dirty, ugly place where they charged too much for the spectators, it was unattractive, it was no place for a pick up. Today, it has become a symbol of the place for human rights. So when I got involved with the

Stonewall Veterans our first problem was how do you know that somebody was a veteran? So the first thing I did was interview them and I put it on the Web, and I found that some people had been at the Stonewall before that particular week but they weren't there that week...

The legacy of Stonewall is that the idea of humans being capable of different kinds of sexual expression has now gone around the world... So there will always be gays no matter what, it's just a biological factor. Whether or not they are acceptable is something else. But that's where Stonewall is important in that it has symbolized... that there are enough people who have made the point that it is now being recognized as a distinct possibility.

The Conservative Women's Movement: Kathryn (Kay) King Regan

Source Note: The interview is part of the Washington Women's History Consortium (WHC) Oral History Project of the Washington State Historical Society that collected interviews with 27 Washington women involved in the July 1977 Washington State International Women's Year Conference for Women, held in Ellensburg. The conference, along with the International Women's Year conference held in Houston, is remembered as a dramatic and emotional confrontation between feminists and conservative women from the religious right. Full transcriptions are available on the WHC website: http://www.washingtonwomenshistory.org/themes/womensrights/oHistProj.aspx

Kay Regan grew up in the mill town of Raymond, Washington, and attended Washington State University in Pullman. She married Joe Regan on his return from service in World War II, and they settled in Seattle and raised five children and five foster children. Regan was active in her Catholic Church and in local and statewide Republican Party politics. She served on the first Seattle Women's Commission and was elected as a delegate to the International Women's Year (IWY) Ellensburg Coordinating Committee, and there elected as a delegate to IWY Houston. Regan remained politically active after the conferences, serving as delegate to the 1980 White House Conference on Families, as a Washington State delegate to national Republican Conventions, and running for state office. In the oral history excerpt below, she talks about her experiences as a conservative, in opposition to many positions such as the Equal Rights Amendment, lesbian and abortion rights. She reflects on how it felt to be in the minority at the Ellensburg and Houston conferences, and how feminists helped push conservative women to form a new movement to protest equal rights and abortion. Mildred Andrews interviewed Regan on February 22, 2007 in Kirkland, Washington.

I'd like to know something about what your affiliations and networks were in the '60s and '70s?

I was appointed by Mayor Wes Uhlman to the Seattle Women's Commission. And that was the first city women's commission in the nation. And then other cities had women's commissions after we did... So we spent many meetings just trying to agree on some kind of an agenda. We had nothing to follow, at all, because we'd been the first women's commission.

Now there were three or four gals on there who had been involved in radical feminist stuff. But they knew a lot about what was going on. At least they had some literature about what was happening, and they would bring those things up as possibly we could get into this or that or the other thing, and do these things that would help women get equal opportunity, help them in their jobs, help them understand that they have value, all these kinds of things. So I learned a lot... Because I really did not know what was happening in the world of just women. Nothing in college prepared me for that...

We would take assignments for the next meeting and... so I had to go to the library and try to find information, and there wasn't much, because it was so new. The women's movement was just starting... But I read lots of papers... about Bella Abzug, for instance. And I thought, she's got some good points, but she's not going about it in a very feminine way. To me, you could do these things, but still be a feminine woman. But she wasn't. She wasn't my kind of example for what I wanted the women's commission to be, myself. But there were these three gals on there that were very feminist, and very anti-man.

So you could see, we had two black women that were kind of like me, that wanted to go slowly and understand, wanted families to be part of the discussion... And then after a year or so, we'd call each other on the phone. We'd help set the agenda... we would know what we were talking about, a little bit... And then there were two others that represented unions on there... we didn't think alike on some issues, but we had a lot in common, like love of our families... So after a year, we came a little bit prepared, and I felt better about the whole thing... Then after we began talking about it and realizing yeah, there's good things we can do here, and let's do them, and let's stick with these good things that we agree on, and quit arguing, then it worked out great. Then I enjoyed it a lot...

I'd been involved in Republican politics since 1962, when I started helping Barry Goldwater get recognized. And in 1964, we nominated him, and you know the rest of the story. He didn't make it. But that set the stage for us to work for Ronald Reagan, then. But in 1964 was the first year I was elected by the Washington State Republican Party to be a national delegate. That was an honor. It always is... And then I was elected five times since. So six times I've been a national delegate. And I've worked hard to get there. You don't get there by sitting at home...

When I first got on the Women's Commission, I thought, you radical feminists don't even know what some of us women have done, without thinking that we had to fight the men to get there. I didn't have to fight the men to get my job, or whatever. I never felt like I was in competition, and I used to feel bad that these women felt that we should fight our way to the top. I thought, we don't have to. Get your education, get your smarts, learn how to respectfully debate, know what you're doing. You don't have to fight. But I didn't say that.

I was going to ask how you viewed your role in the home, how you viewed women's role in the home and in society at the time of the conference, and whether you saw a need for change.
Well, I was a home mother, but I was a substitute teacher, and sometimes I worked at the Bon Marche at Christmas time at night. But I didn't want to leave the kids alone, you see, so I didn't take full time jobs. So, my chosen role as a wife and mother was to stay home, after we had kids... There was nobody telling me I should... They were so darling, and such fun to have around. Who wanted somebody else to have that fun? I took part time jobs and nighttime jobs here and there, just to bring in extra money...

How did you become interested and involved in the Ellensburg conference?
Being a part of the Seattle Women's Commission, I think all of us on the commission were elected. I forget how many delegates each county got... And of course I wanted to go to that, because I was very interested in it, and I wanted to do what I could there...

All I could do was pray that there were a lot of other pro-family people there... I just didn't want to get a whole crowd of people that didn't like me because I was pro-family...

So I got there, and there were a whole lot of people there. And I thought jeepers, where did they come from?... More and more people came into the room and sat around the periphery of the room, listening in on the meeting. This was the meeting before the thing started. And I realized these people, when I'd say something about agenda items, they seemed to clap or like what I said. And I thought whoa, there's some people here that think like I do...

Now you said it was, well, tumultuous, is that a good word?
Well, some of the time, yes. Because whenever the issue of life came up, and of course, I'd always stand up for life against abortion, and boy, I would get it. Oh! I had to develop a thick skin. Because the crowd, they had a crowd there that were not delegates... if I said something like that, all hell would break loose. And this gallery would just scream at me... It was very nerve wracking. [laughs] Luckily, though... the Mormon Church had sent some of their people. I didn't know where they came from. I never saw them before. I thought, oh, thank you, Lord, for these people that seem to be clapping when I say something. Because that's all you want is... you feel like somebody cares about what you're saying...

There were [conservative] delegates at Houston that came from the Southern states. Somebody called me before we went to Houston and said, "If you can get there a day early, we're going to have a meeting at such and such a place the night before." And I thought, okay... Well, and at that meeting were a lot of these pro-family, mostly Mormon women... And they were running that meeting the night before, talking about strategy... They said, "You'll know us tomorrow. We'll have yellow ribbons. And you meet with any of us, and we'll give you one."

So as soon as I got there, I looked around for yellow ribbons... but our delegation from Washington state was in the front. I looked around and I didn't see a yellow ribbon in the place... But then I got up and walked around, and it was a huge auditorium where it was held... In the way back, all the Southern states that were pro-life, those were all yellow ribbons. And I thought okay, I'm wearing my ribbon, even if I'm the only one in the front of the room that's got it. [laughs] So I did. Because there were people in the room who felt like I did. And I thought, I'm not going to give up on my issue, when I've got some other people helping out.

So when they voted for the abortion plank, I'll never forget that. I can't explain it. This whole upstairs area was full of people... the shouting was guttural, it was deep, it was, to me, out of the pits of hell. It just made me shake all clear to my bones, it was so awful... They were yelling in approval of their voting it down... I sat there and cried. Not because it went down. I knew it would. I knew that we couldn't win it. That was a given. But it was that reaction. Oh my God. I'll never forget, as long as I live...

In your opinion, what was the significance, the overriding significance of both Ellensburg and Houston?

...The significance to me, personally was, when I sit and think of these things during these times, I must get more people involved in knowing what's happening here. Because people are not understanding that this is... going to have a terrible influence on families. It's going to encourage people not to get married. And that's what they talked about, too, this old hat, this marriage business. And I knew enough and studied enough to know that families are so much better off with a mom and a dad. The kids grow up much better, statistically; it isn't just an opinion. They always grow up better with an intact family. So what's it going to do to the entire social milieu of our family if all these things are accepted? It had a great impact on me.

So I thought the significance of the state convention, for the amount of publicity it got... a lot of people were awakened by it, and saying, whoa, I think we ought to get involved and do something, and they started telling me that. And I thought praise God, maybe this is what we need for a wake up call. Because a lot of us just stay in our communities and do our thing, and raise our kids, and go to their Scouts and all this stuff, but we don't know what's really happening. So it awakened a lot of people. That was the significance to me. And then when Houston came, they really were awakened, because a lot more people saw that... A lot of us that were involved in that got a lot more people involved in politics, by giving speeches wherever we could, and so on...

It might have been that the radical feminists thought they were doing a great, wonderful thing, but I think they were ultimately the losers. Because this sleeping giant of American women were awakened to say, "Hey, get out of our house here and get cracking, because we're more than just mothers. We're human beings and part of this universe that need to have a voice in what's happening to our country." So I think it had great significance.

Cold War Warriors

By the mid-1960s the Cold War began to have less prominence in American life. Film, television, and print media broke the McCarthy period's blacklist and aired more diverse viewpoints; social movements struggled for equality; and protests around the world against the logic of nuclear power and the Vietnam War questioned the very nature of the struggle between the United States and Soviet Union. Yet Cold War principles continued to dominate U.S. foreign policy in this period. The Vietnam War preoccupied the nation for over a decade. Presidents Johnson and Nixon engaged the United States more deeply even as it became clear that the Vietnamese communists would not surrender. The age of the typical U.S. soldier averaged nineteen, and because the draft gave deferments to college students, most G.I.s were poor or working class. The youth culture of the 1960s and early 1970s pervaded the military, and many G.I.s smoked marijuana, listened to rock music, and wore peace symbols. Some increasingly defied orders from their commanders. Meanwhile, a growing anti-war movement at home increasingly clashed with governmental authorities. The United States signed the Paris Peace Agreement in January 1973 and began withdrawing troops in March. In April 1975 the war ended as North Vietnamese communists united the southern half of the small country.

In the 1980s, President Reagan revived Cold War fears, calling the Soviet Union the "evil empire" and making such rhetoric the centerpiece of his foreign policy. Declaring the "Vietnam syndrome" over, he asserted the U.S. right to intervene anywhere in the world to combat communism, and increased support for anti-communist military dictatorships and resistance movements in Latin America. His administration accelerated spending on nuclear and other weapons systems, even as a growing anti-nuclear or "Freeze" movement garnered unprecedented support in the United States and abroad.

Questions to Consider: Each of the following two narrators holds a different understanding of the U.S. role in the Cold War. Compare these two accounts, one about attitudes held in the 1960s, and the other from a more contemporary perspective after the end of the Cold War.

1. What do you learn about the life of a Vietnam War soldier based on Taylor's account? What do you glean from the interview about attitudes in the United States toward the war? And among soldiers in Vietnam?
2. Why did Zabarte become concerned about the effects of nuclear weapons testing in Nevada? How did his cultural traditions and beliefs influence his perspectives?

Vietnam War Soldiers: Dave Taylor

Source Note: The interview comes from the extensive oral history archive at the Vietnam Center and Archive at Texas Tech University. The Oral History Project (OHP) records and preserves the recollections and experiences of all who were involved in the wars of Southeast Asia, including American veterans, former allies and enemies of the United States, anti-war protesters, government employees, and veterans' family members. Some full transcripts, including the following, are available on the project website http://www.vietnam.ttu.edu/oralhistory/interviews/browse/index.php.

Dave Taylor, originally from Philadelphia, Pennsylvania, joined the U.S. Army after his three brothers served in Vietnam. Taylor enrolled in Officer Candidate School at Ft. Benning, Georgia, and became a tactical officer in the 62nd Company. In Vietnam he was an Infantry Officer with C Co., 5/46, 198th Light Infantry Brigade, American Division from February until June 1969. On June 3, 1969, he was wounded in action (for a second time) and evacuated to Japan and eventually back to the United .States. He later served in the U.S. Army Reserve between 1972 and 1993. Here Taylor describes his motivations for joining the service and his experiences on the ground in Vietnam. Richard Burks Verrone interviewed Taylor in Medina, Ohio, by telephone on April 5 and 8, 2005, from Lubbock, Texas.

I went to a junior college '66 and early '67. And all during that time, the anti-war movement was really building, and... it did not deter me. I knew that [joining the military was] something I wanted to do. And when I finished my... Associate's degree, I decided I was tired of school and I really wanted to go in the Army... If I could not get accepted into the Officer Candidate School program, I did not want to be stuck with a three-year enlistment. So I went down to the local draft board and volunteered for the draft, and the lady there said well, I can go on and complete my four years of college because they were getting enough people in the Army in my district that I was not going to be drafted. And I replied, "You don't understand. I do want to be drafted ..." And so the next month I was drafted, and in basic training I applied for Officer Candidate School or OCS, and I was accepted...

My two years in [Peirce] Junior College were kind of interesting because we were at the height of the antiwar movement and the junior college was in Philadelphia, across the street from the Philadelphia College of Art... And compared to the protestors in Berkeley, California, the protestors and the students at the Philadelphia College of Art were very mild and tame, although I think they probably thought they were radical. So we saw that and felt that every day, and a lot of people were searching their souls as to which way to go on this, and while I enjoyed tremendously the folk music—I was very much into folk music and that kind of thing—I could never embrace some of the sentiment behind it—kind of had a socialist tint to it as far as I could see...

What did you think of the Vietnam War at the time... especially when the actual shooting war started in 1965 when we had ground troops first there?
I believed in the thinking at the time, the Domino Theory and that we had to stop the spread of communism and these wars of national liberation, which would be the means to spread communism. I believed in that... And also, I did believe there was enough of a component of the South Vietnamese wanting to be free that we should be there to help them. Now hindsight in that area, I think that that probably deserves a lot more introspection on my part, but I do think that the feeling at the time of the Domino Theory and the spread of communism was reason enough to go over there...

I was drafted, and since I lived in southern New Jersey, I went to Ft. Dix, New Jersey for my basic training... About ninety-five, ninety-six percent of the trainees were National Guardsmen who were getting their basic and advanced individual training and then going back to their National Guard units. They would not stay on active duty. The balance were RA, that is to say people who enlisted on their own to go into the Army and they chose what specialty they wanted to get into. I was the only draftee in my basic training company, and I took the training more seriously than anyone else. In fact, when we would line up across each other for things like the pugil pit, where we'd bat each other and everything, people did not want to face me, and I'm not a big person... because I took everything seriously, and the Guardsmen had a bad attitude. They didn't want to be there, but they knew that that was their ticket not to have to get drafted and go to Vietnam. And what was interesting to me is even the people who enlisted themselves, they didn't particularly want to be there either, but they knew that they had desk jobs that were waiting for them...

I went to Ft. McClellan, Alabama... for people that were bound for OCS... And already some of the people who were supposed to be going OCS were starting to have second thoughts... so some of them were able to bargain themselves out of OCS and in exchange get an assignment in Germany. So I could see some were getting a little weak-kneed, but there was no doubt in my mind what I wanted to do... And I say that not as someone who was a warmonger. I say that as someone who believed we had a patriotic duty to be in Vietnam and also someone who knew that this was the war of his lifetime... I had to witness this; I had to experience this myself because this was part of our times. And I just felt compelled to go and see what it was all about...

We did get to Cam Ranh Bay, and as I'm sure many people have told you the first images when those doors open up and the hot blast of air came up to meet us, it was just something I was not prepared for. It was hot. Very hot. And as soon as we got off the plane, some other people got on... They were waiting in line. They looked tired, they looked worn. I could tell they were young, but they looked old. And the other image I have in Cam Ranh Bay is when the buses came up to pick us up, they had wire mesh over the windows, and that just hit me that, 'Ok, this is for real.' If they found it necessary to do that in a very big base like Cam Ranh Bay, this was for real...When we arrived, the briefer said, 'You are here at the most secure base in South Vietnam,' and then the next day, we get rocketed...

We were all packed, we had received jungle fatigues and everything else, so we were kind of like...'Let's get on with it, we're here, let's get started.' So, I was happy to get out of there....We flew up to Chu Lai, again flying in very hot [weather]. There we got picked up by two-and-a-half ton trucks. I remember Chu Lai, the smell. The smell of burning wood, the smell in some cases of incense, the smell of rotting fish, that kind of thing. The smells were much more apparent...

I was confident, and when I got my unit, my platoon, we had a sit down and I told them that we were not going to do things stupid. We were not going to get on line and charge; we were not going to do dumb things. There was a reason why we had indirect fire support, and I intend to use it. But, I said at the same time, we are not going to avoid the enemy. At that point in time, you know, some units...they're supposed to be out on patrol, and they would say they're searching and avoiding...

Dave, your initial impression of the morale. What was that like?
When I got to Charlie Company, the morale seemed ok. The men just seemed very tired, low-key...And I did not see [discipline problems] until oh, maybe a month after I was with the battalion. Then I could start to see and feel a little bit of that inside the battalion firebase on LZ Gator, and it mostly had to do with support soldiers who did not go to the field...And you could see some of that building up, the antiwar resentment. They did their jobs, but every chance they got, they would kind of congregate together and most probably sneak a marijuana here and there and smoke that. That kind of thing. So I did start to see some of that...

What was it like those first days going out? It was your very first patrol in Vietnam.
Well, the first patrol...I looked at my radio operator who was down on the ground. I said, 'What was that?' He looked at me and he said, 'Uh, sir, they're shooting at us ...' It was just that one little incident that got my head on straight, and from that point on, I was in the war...

We carried about fifty pounds in our rucksacks. Mostly ammunition [and water]. Not too much food. It was so hot, we didn't eat that much. And we were also fortunate, every other day we would get a meal brought in at noon. And so we would stop, put in a perimeter, and have a good meal from the mess hall...

Another image I have of operating in that valley is that there were mines and booby traps, not as bad as out on the Batangan Peninsula, but there were some. And of course the villagers pretty much knew where they were. They had to straddle both sides of the fence to deal with the Viet Cong that might come through now and then and certainly deal with the South Vietnamese Army and the American forces...And so I picked up something that my sergeants told me about. When we were walking through an area, if we would see a villager out in the field, we would have him walk in front of us. Particularly if we had to walk on a trail to get someplace. And so we did make the villager walk in front of us. The two times I did that, they did not resist. And then they would walk in front of us for a while until we started getting out of the immediate area, and then we would let them go because in Asia, most villagers did not know too much beyond their immediate area...

Truthfully, I rarely encountered the enemy. When I did, they were up close and personal. But...the weapon of the enemy that we feared the most that we had the most contact with were the mines and booby traps...After our time in the Rocket Valley, we went to the Batangan Peninsula out on LZ Minuteman, which was north of the Pinkville area along the coast. This is a firebase that was built early in 1969 during Operation RUSSELL BEACH, and the civilians were relocated just outside of LZ Minuteman in a refugee village. And so the mission on LZ Minuteman was to protect the refugees. And so we spent a considerable amount of time out there in the spring of 1969, patrolling the area out there on the Batangan Peninsula. It was very heavily laced with mines and booby traps. Even inside of LZ Minuteman...on a few occasions when the firebase would not be occupied, the Viet Cong snuck up and they put mines and booby traps inside the perimeter...

Did you see a marked difference in the post-Tet [1968 Viet Cong and North Vietnamese Army offensive] era? You weren't there before, but can you draw any comparisons as to what it was before the Tet and then you patrolling in this area after Tet?

Yes, only from the experience my men relate to me. They were very, very frustrated because during Tet and before Tet, when you would encounter the Viet Cong, you would encounter them in some group of some size where you could bring your fire power to bear. You could not do that anymore. Not in our area of South Vietnam. So the vets were very chagrined that we couldn't see the enemy, yet we were losing people, we were losing arms, legs, in some cases lives from mines and booby traps, and there was no way to get back at the enemy...It made me very nervous and it made me more determined on managing my men. When we did patrolling on the Batangan Peninsula, we had to be very, very careful. Absolutely you did not go on any trails and the men did not need to be told that. But, the problem was if you were walking along and you saw a hedgerow of bushes in front of you, the men would naturally want to go through the natural opening in the hedgerow because it was so hot. They had heavy loads. And it was up to me to make sure that the point man would not do that, that we would cut our own way through the hedgerow. And men would get upset because it meant getting scratched and bruised and everything else, but it was the safe way to go [to avoid mines in the natural openings]...

The Nuclear Cold War and Its Environmental Consequences: Ian Dominic Zabarte

Source Note: The interview is one of 192 oral histories collected for the Nevada Test Site Oral History Project at the University of Nevada, Las Vegas (UNLV). The project includes a wide range of narrators who were affiliated with or affected by the Nevada Test Site during the era of Cold War nuclear testing, including: national laboratory scientists and engineers; labor trades and support personnel; cabinet-level officials, military personnel and corporate executives; Native American tribal and spiritual leaders; peace activists and protesters; and Nevada ranchers, families and communities downwind of the test site. Interview transcripts, documents and photographs are housed in UNLV Lied Library's Department of Special Collections. Searchable transcripts, selected audio and video clips, scanned photographs and images are available on the website: http://digital.library.unlv.edu/ntsohp/

Ian Dominic Zabarte, a member of the Duckwater Shoshone Tribe, became alarmed at the health and environmental effects of nuclear testing when he returned to his reservation in the early 1980s. He joined other tribal members, anti-nuclear and environmental groups to question the impacts of the nearby federal Nevada Test Site—65 miles north of Las Vegas—and the proposed Yucca Mountain nuclear waste repository. Between 1951 and 1992, 1021 nuclear detonations took place at the Nevada Test Site—100 in the atmosphere and 921 explosions underground. Zabarte participated in educational activities, hearings, protests, and several lawsuits against the United States Department of Energy, including the National Resources Defense Council [NRDC] case won in the late 1990s to force the Department to make available information to communities around its weapons sites. During the 1990s Zabarte served on the boards of directors of Nevada Desert Experience and Citizen Alert, and currently serves on the board of the Native Community Action Council. Mary Palevsky interviewed Zabarte on April 4, 2007, in Tecopa, California. A full transcript is available on the NTSOHP website http://digital.library.unlv.edu/ntsohp/.

My mother is Shoshone and growing up [in the 1960s and 1970s] I knew I was Indian... We lived in Pacifica [California] as a kid. And I grew up like most American baby boomers at that time; lunch was a bologna sandwich and a bowl of Campbell's soup with a glass of Kool-Aid, you know, and that's the way it was, growing up...

And growing up as a kid, I mean I always knew where home was... Duckwater [Indian Reservation, Nevada]—we always went every summer... And my father being an immigrant... appreciated [my mother] and native people... and going to powwows and things in the Bay Area. Then he was involved in supporting the 1971 [American Indian Movement] Alcatraz [Island] takeover. Of course my uncle Adam Nordwall in Fallon [Nevada] was really big involved in that takeover anyway, so there was a lot of support, if not real understanding or knowledge on my father's part. He just wasn't an Indian and never grew up that way. And so the upbringing I had, there was opportunities and those are the things that never went away, whereas five years of Catholic boarding school [in California] didn't really penetrate, you know. It never grabbed me. I was more rebellious of that than anything...

And at some point I decided, I need to get out of this place...I worked with my father in San Francisco for two years. He was a salesman for a wholesale tool distributing company. And that was about the first time I started to...become cognizant of war and the war machine, because back at that time, early '80s, that company got a contract, to refit the USS New Jersey battleship...So I was just a delivery guy and delivery driver. But...my vague familiarity with them and the whole area put together the foundations for really understanding today how they support what happens at the Nevada Test Site, and a much larger national laboratory system.

But really how I became involved in this is after going back to the reservation and hearing sonic booms and living in a place where I was able to be free. You can look out there and go there, without fences and without anybody disturbing you. That was freedom to me, that was knowing how to live off the land, you know, going hunting. And knowing this place all my life...And when I came back to the reservation, I think I was eighteen or nineteen...and my uncle had cancer and he passed away, and then my grandfather [Raymond Graham] passed away in '86, a couple of years later...And that's when I started going to council meetings. Some of the people on the rez says, Hey, come on, let's go to a council meeting. OK. So I went to the Western Shoshone National Council meeting, and that was with a lot of really what we call traditional people, the elders...And for two years I didn't say anything because I didn't know anything, so I didn't begin saying anything until 1986, I believe. And I just started becoming more aware of what was happening...the stories of people and the talk of people and seeing these jets overflying the reservation...

When I went back to the reservation, at least I knew what there was, and I could live off the land...And that is where our morals and spirituality is rooted. It's in the land, in our sense of place, in our identity and being. And it's not just a house. I ask people all the time, I say...Where's home? Oh, it's in L.A. Where's your homeland? What are you talking about? Whereas most native people, it doesn't matter where they're at, you can ask them those same questions and they can tell you right back to where they come from and their ancestors. And that's important...

I would like to get back to why I was on the reservation and how I got involved in nukes...Like I said, my uncle died of...a throat cancer which isn't one of the primary cancers [compensable per programs for test site related illnesses]. My aunts and the rest of the family and everyone there knew he was a kid in 1951, playing in this white ash. And there's all kinds of those stories. People saw the [atomic bomb] flash and they saw the clouds come and saw the people sick the next day, or their gardens dead; other people talk about the sagebrush around Duckwater used to be ten feet high and now it's one-and-two-foot stubble... A lot of stories like that. So, you know, those were talked about and I kept hearing it at the national council. And at home, then my grandfather passed away from—he had a heart attack but my later learning is that that was potentially brought on by the stress to his immune system... And then other Shoshone, such as Joe Sanchez Jr., I think he was thirty-something when he passed away, but he was actively involved in Citizen Alert Native American program, and these are the people that inspired me to know more and it was the death and loss of these people that flamed the passion for me to do something about it... Then I became aware of the Project Shoal site, outside of Fallon [Naval Air Station]—weapons, a lot of weapons, a lot of bombs. Dr. [Richard] Bargan was a rural doctor that used to fly in and out with his airplane, and we'd go out to those bombing ranges, Bravo 19, Bravo 20, to protest the bombing. It's just a big mess out there, craters everywhere...

And so when I bring it up to the people on the reservation, in about '85,'86—who are also my relatives, that have fought hard to get what little there was there, from no electricity to getting electricity in '76, so when we had electricity, then we could put in a well to pump water and have running water and telephones and all of those types of things—and when I bring this nukes up, it was still very fragile. There was still a lot of racism and oppression evident and there was a little bit of backlash from the people in the community that have worked hard to try to get these things in, and they said, Do you really want to raise those issues? And for me, coming from outside of the community, I said, Yeah, it's not right. It's not right. Of course I didn't have to fight through all that racism that they did, growing up with the boarding schools, my aunts and uncles and cousins, so that was foreign to me...

So the problem is that we have been adversely impacted by the testing of weapons of mass destruction, and we are being victimized again in a different way—being told this is good for us because we all get electricity and it's in the grid and we all benefit from it... When we haven't seen the benefits yet, we're being told that we're to... bear all of the burden of the threats and hazard. So when we look at nuclear waste coming from all these seventy-five sites with 115 reactors at them, that stream of waste to come into Shoshone treaty territory... as it enters our country and comes to Yucca Mountain. That is unacceptable...

Now, you were talking on the phone and you mentioned also this morning, and you're obviously touching on it now, this notion of genocide and continuation of genocide, so help me understand that better.

When I began going to meetings regarding onsite tours, regarding Yucca Mountain, we were misled by the researchers. They had developed a study and they were funded by the Department of Energy... They came to Shoshone communities and interviewed Shoshone and they came across as real nice and they would say, Come on over here to this meeting we're having and we'll pay your travel... except we didn't really understand what they were doing, and they were vague about that. They said it was about... the Nevada Test Site... and that's when I started to learn more about the test site and we went down there... A year or two of doing these things, I began to become aware...

Let me interrupt you for a second. When you say you begin to understand what's happening, what's occurring to you? What insight are you having about what's happening?

That these researchers were facilitating the projects being conducted by the Department of Energy and we were being used to support them being able to do what they do. So when our people were told that we're protecting these burials or we're protecting these funerary objects or we're protecting the plants and the animals by going there, that was not what we were doing. We were actually helping the Department of Energy... to continue to make roads, to continue to place buildings, to continue to disturb our things...

After a couple of years of [the researcher] doing this study, he said, Well, you have to do something. Here's what the tribe over here did in Utah or whatever, in that project. Do you want us to cover it over with cement, or should we just let them bulldoze it? You know, this kind of pressure to make a decision, or should we just avoid it and just mark it or not mark it? And so he made the proposals of what our options and alternatives should be... And so at that time I was ostracized because my elders are saying, Well, what should we do? We have to do something... And I said, We don't do that... It's the United States government brokering a solution for the commercial nuclear industry's waste problem, for the profit of the nuclear industry that we don't even benefit from—it effects genocide because the destruction of our people through the use of cultural triage... the forced choice decision-making by an ethnic group in response to a development project...

Yes, my roots are planted from here to the Snake [River]. They're planted in the rivers with the fish, they're planted in this alkali with the various plants and the birds, and it's not rooted in the bombs, it's not rooted in the casinos, it's not rooted in those kinds of things. Our values go a lot deeper than that, a thousand generations here, and I think a lot of Americans are set adrift and they're lost and... they're looking for something authentic and they see that in Native Americans. Used to be a time in America when they seek to find it in their car, what they drive, what their house looks like, even if it's unsustainable... and now we have a market culture which is not making life better for human beings, but it's about making more money than can possibly be spent for more Americans, and not taking care of the poor and not making life better for people...

When I talk about not being antinuclear, it really comes down to realizing that nuclear weapons and nuclear waste and nuclear technology exist and it's on the land, it's out there; I will have to deal with it, and so will everybody else. So creating anti-and pro-nuclear positions is not helpful, it doesn't facilitate the dialogue, and it would handicap me and anybody else who tries to deal fairly and rationally with the problem . . . We know that our communities are threatened, we know that things aren't right, and we don't have to be a rocket scientist or a nuclear physicist to know these things.

Cold War Migrations

Following on the heels of historic new civil rights legislation, in 1965 Congress altered legislation that had since the 1920s severely restricted immigration through national-origins quotas. Now, instead of favoring northern European immigrants, the new legislation allowed approximately 7 million immigrants, mostly from Latin America and Asia, to enter the United States during the 1970s. In 1970, 88 percent of Americans categorized themselves as "white." By the end of the decade, partly due to immigration, only 83 percent of Americans considered themselves white. New places— cities in the South and West; and California, rather than industrial cities of the Northeast— became the leading destinations for the immigrants of this era. The percentage of immigrants would continue to grow through the rest of the century, making the United States a more diverse nation.

U.S. immigration policies favored refugees fleeing communism in Cuba, Southeast Asia, and Eastern Europe. After 1975, when South Vietnam fell to the communist forces, many Vietnamese and Hmong supporters of the American military emigrated to the United States and formed sizable expatriate communities. Private and federal refugee assistance programs helped settle the immigrants in communities. The United States was less welcoming, however, to refugees from repressive regimes in countries that it supported, such as Haiti, El Salvador, and Guatemala. Often facing deportation and brutal reprisals when sent home, these migrants often crossed the U.S. border illegally, seeking aid from relatives, churches, and associations such as the Sanctuary Movement. The numbers of illegal Mexican immigrants also sharply increased after 1976, when Congress passed new legislation to establish annual quotas for Western Hemisphere countries.

Questions to Consider:

1. What circumstances led to migrations of people from Southeast Asian and Central American countries to the U.S.?
2. What support networks existed to assist refugees?
3. Because Bo Thao was a child when she immigrated to the U.S., how does she qualify her memories of particular events?
4. How does Ochoa-Krueger see the plight of Central American political refugees and Mexican economic immigrants as somewhat linked?

Image 15 Hmong girls playing a traditional game of ball-tossing, December 2005 (Wikipedia Commons).

"Born a Hmong Daughter": Bo Thao

Source Note: The interview is one of 18 collected for the Hmong Women's (*Hmoob Thaj Yeeb)* Oral History Project, which chronicled the cross-generational contributions and experiences of Hmong women with ties to Minnesota. Members of the Hmong Women's Action Team, a group of Hmong women community leaders and activists, interviewed each other and their mothers and grandmothers, and in one case a daughter. The interviews are in the collections of the Minnesota Historical Society.

Bo Thao was born in 1974 in Luang Phrabang, Laos, just before the communist takeover of that country as the United States lost its war in Southeast Asia. Thao and her Hmong family fled Laos and lived in refugee camps in Thailand for two-and-a-half years before immigrating to the United States in December 1979. Because the Hmong supported American troops during the Vietnam War, they gained refugee status and many were resettled in American cities. The Twin Cities in Minnesota became home to one of the largest Hmong communities in the country, and many Hmong who were originally resettled in other areas chose to move there to be close to relatives and cultural institutions. Thao discusses coming of age in the United States and negotiating expectations of Hmong and American cultures. MayKao Hang interviewed Thao in St. Paul on January 17, 2000.

What is your religious affiliation?
When we first came, we were sponsored by the churches, so when we arrived here, my parents went to church. My parents were even baptized. However, as time passed they attended church less and eventually stopped going to church . . . When my siblings and I got older my parents told us that it was our choice. They said they took us when we were little, but when we grow up we could decide whether or not we wanted to attend church. So, when I was in college I stopped going. Now I don't practice either traditional or Christianity. For younger Hmong persons, such as myself, practicing the old ways is difficult, because we don't know enough. Of course when my parents held ceremonies with shamans or had soul calling ceremonies (*hu plig*) I helped, but I was only there as an observer. If I were to fully practice animism today I don't think I could do it. I don't know enough. As for going to church, I don't go either. I don't know what I should be practicing, so I don't do either . . .

When you were a child, what were your duties at home?
I think, because I am a daughter, I was taught what most Hmong girls were taught. For example, cleaning the house, and getting up to cook breakfast. When I was too little to know better, they would tell me to do whatever my mother did. Like learning how to do the handiworks (*paj ntaub*). My mother and older women would thread the needle, and give it to me to play with, and eventually I learned . . .

These are things that my parents were taught are roles for girls. They were taught this way, so in their minds they did not think girls could go far or achieve much. They believed that if you were a girl you had to be skilled in these things in order for someone to marry you. When I returned home from school they would say, "Oh, come and cook first." You know—they never told me to do my homework first. In second or third grade, they wanted us to go and learn how to dance, because that was pretty and it was what all girls did. [Laughs]

What are some social activities that you remember from when you were a child?
See, I was already six years old when we arrived in this country. The things that I did for fun were jump rope with rubber bands and playing rocks. You know, things like that. Those were Hmong games. When I went to school Caucasian children were different. They played differently, so I tried to learn their games too. I went roller-skating and things like that. When I was with my Hmong friends, I played Hmong games, but when I was with my American friends, they didn't play those games . . . We first arrived in Chicago when many Hmong families were also arriving there, so we had many relatives, and I played with their children.

What were your aspirations as a child? What did you think you wanted to do or be when you grew up?
When I was little, my parents could not have seen the future, so they only taught me what they knew . . . For a Hmong girl, the ultimate goal is to be married.

That's what I thought my future would be, and I really didn't think beyond that... When I got into high school, that's when I became more serious about what I wanted to be. I began realizing that I had many opportunities, and could be a lot more than what I saw.

Our family has never had a girl who received a higher education degree. Not only that, the sons who have tried also failed to graduate, so our close relatives were not hopeful that any sons or daughters could accomplish this task. They didn't even talk about it at all. I never heard any talk of college except in school. My friends and I would talk about it, and I would think, "Oh yes, I could do that."

I was fortunate; because when I was in high school I had a really good group of Hmong girl friends. It seemed as though every one was very ambitious, and we would always talk about this and that about the future. That was odd, [laughs] because there had never been a group of Hmong girls who talked about these dreams for the future.

I try to be respectful, because I know that the Hmong people have not had these roles in the past. Unmarried daughters have not participated in these processes before. We are a new group in America. They don't know what to do with us. They don't know if they should be happy that we've attained our education, or sad that we're not married yet. [Laughs]...

This is relevant to Laos and here. What did women do to support the families?
I think back in Laos, the community lived an agrarian culture, so everybody had to help each other out. Families had to work hard in the fields, and women played an important necessary role in doing household chores... Even in this country, I think women work outside the home, because everything is money. If you depend on just one person's income, it's often not possible. I think the thing that is different is that women now work hard to help make money.

Hmong women have accomplished a lot since first arriving in this country. After being in the U.S. for about two or three months, my parents started working, but during the summer my mother still gardened. She did not get any money for doing that, but it was a way to bring extra food... to help the family. She planted vegetables, so that she did not have to buy them. My father worked, and he didn't help her out much with the gardening. They both worked, but on the weekends, my mother still farmed to support our family...

I know that you came when you were six, so just tell me whatever you can remember... of the refugee experience. Do you remember how you decided to leave Laos during the war, and how was that decision made?
...Actually, I don't remember a lot about Laos, because when the country was at war and fell to communism, I was only three years old. I've only heard my mother talking about it. She says we were one of the last families to leave the village, because at that time my grandfather and grandmother were very old, and they

did not want to leave. So, my parents stayed behind as long as they could...All their children were still very little—ages four, three, two and one...My father joined the guerrilla fighters (*cob fab*), and often left my mother home alone with the children.

That made it hard for my mother, because she could not just leave Laos... She says that when our family fled Laos, someone was paid to carry my younger sister. My older sister and I walked, while she carried my brother. It was rainy most of the time. God, the rain and cold! I just remember little things...

What do you remember about the refugee camps?

...I just remember the very poor living conditions. Everybody lived in tight quarters. It was always very hot. When the food rations came, I remember being so excited, and always tagging along with my parents to get the food...Like I said, I remember very little. I remember going to school for only one week. Then my younger sister got really sick, the elders were occupied with being worried about her failing health, so they did not pay attention to whether or not we were going to school. So, we stopped going. My sister got very sick, and eventually she passed away...

Can you tell me about how you came to America and what was it like? How did your family decide to come to United States?

At that time my dad's younger brother, my uncle was already in the U.S. He came in 1976, and lived in Chicago. Then in 1978, my dad's old brother also came to the U.S., so they kept telling my dad to apply to come here. A younger uncle and my dad were the two brothers remaining in Thailand. My uncles who were already in America kept writing, asking my dad to come. Finally, my uncle and my dad decided to come. Two American families sponsored us.

My memory of coming to the U.S. is limited. All I remember is getting on the bus—the big bus. I remember seeing my grandma. The whole memory is similar to all the videos that you see of Hmong people coming to America. That's exactly what it was like, because we got on the bus, and had no idea where we were going. I see my grandparents crying, and I questioned myself, "Why are they crying?" We were so happy, because we've never been on a bus before, but my parents and grandparents are crying...

I realize that even though I've avoided being Hmong when I was younger, I am still very much impacted by my relatives and my community. I can't ever run away from it, so I try to make the best of the situation.

After college when I was thinking about graduate school, I told my parents that I was going to continue school in California. I applied to a graduate school there, and went to visit it. When I returned from my visit, I noticed many of our relatives were over at our house. I figured they were there to talk about some cousin's problems as usual, and thought nothing of it. In the past they came to talk about my younger sister, because she was the black sheep in the family. When

I got home they said, "We've come here to talk to you." I couldn't figure it out. [Laughs] "Why?" They said, "We heard that you are planning to go to school far away. Is that true?" I answered, "Yes." I just came back from my visit to the school. They told me, "You cannot go," and I was stunned.

What do you mean I can't go? My uncle just said, "Well, because you are a girl. We are worried that if you go far away you may get sick, and there will be no one to take care of you." They just said that, but their reasoning was that I am a single woman, and if I go there everybody will say bad things about our family.

I was 21. I couldn't believe that they couldn't be happy and supportive of my decision to continue my education. Rather they were concerned that I was going to have a bad reputation for being far away from home. [Laughs] These are times that make me think that, in general, people don't realize that because I was born a Hmong daughter, I have to live with all those conditions. Only if I really push myself, can I overcome those barriers.

Sanctuary for Central American Refugees: Ninfa Ochoa Krueger

Source Note: The interview is one of a series titled *Oral Memoirs of the Sanctuary Movement*, which includes interviews with twenty-eight persons who participated in various aspects of church-sponsored aid to Central American refugees in the period 1980–1990. Since 1970, the Baylor University Institute for Oral History has collected and transcribed approximately 4,500 oral history interview recordings on a wide variety of topics; over 2,000 of these interviews are currently available for public access.

Ninfa Krueger's experiences working for the American Friends Service Committee in Chile with her husband, a United Church of Christ minister, made her aware of political violence in Central America and helped her understand the plight of refugees once she returned to her home in south Texas. She co-founded and became director of BARCA (Border Association for Refugees from Central America), which is a community-based effort to provide direct, basic aid to refugees in the Rio Grande Valley area. Jaclyn Jeffrey interviewed Krueger on January 17, 1987, in Edinburg, Texas.

I am in this [Sanctuary Movement], because I grew up here, and I know that prejudices and the racism, the separatism, that exists here between two cultures. We are in a situation here that is very similar to Latin America. We are one of the richest areas in the country, and yet per capita income is one of the lowest... And one of the things is that immigration affects all of us. I have been involved here locally with organizations that were trying to bring about this type of change, whether it be political or non-political. I've participated in La Raza Unida party... I participated in the Political Association for Spanish-speaking Organizations [PASSO], which was a perfectly legal thing to get involved in. We had the marches and all, yes, in support of the farm workers, you know, but we also had legal processes that would bring about change...

What I want is for the local community to become aware that a [refugee] problem exists and to seek a solution *locally*. Like, I was involved in the original formation of Mujeres Unidas, Women Together, which is a shelter for battered women. The fear we had was a very high incidence of battering, and the community was not involved in this, so I got involved. When I left it was well-established and it was acceptable in the community. All these local organizations with these nice ladies got involved, you know, like the Jaycees and Rotary Clubs and all those . . . prominent, established organizations got involved . . .

Now, I was involved in the original founding of BARCA, because churches— and Anglos work closely with churches—because I lived in Chile, and I traveled through Guatemala and Panama. So, when people were talking about oppression and dying, the possibility of dying and torture over there, I realized this is true. It wasn't something that you read about and you don't quite believe the words, maybe yes or maybe no. But the community and the Immigration Service were throwing the Salvadorans in the same bag with Mexicans . . . [both as] illegal aliens [fleeing economic conditions when the Salvadorans were escaping political violence] . . .

Those of us who came together at first [in the Sanctuary movement] were people who had worked in Latin America as missionaries, primarily. Missionaries are non-political, but they do see oppression. And here is an opportunity where, thanks to the freedoms we have, we can express ourselves and not fear the consequences. So, we saw that as a good opportunity. We also saw that there has always been abuse on the part of the border patrol. If we can get the community involved in this, the abuses will stop in this area. And it has in this area. [We] have the lowest physical abuse of people being apprehended by the border patrol . . . and that is primarily because BARCA originally started working with the Protestant churches . . . When a Protestant minister says something, he is viewed probably as a Republican, a very conservative person, but he is genuinely concerned about human needs, you know. So, the immigration system tends to pay a little bit more attention when the Anglo minister goes before the authorities and says, this is what's happening now . . . Yet [ministers] see the frustration themselves when we ask, will you take this person to the immigration service and try to get him or her permission to leave to go to Wyoming or wherever, and they are met with a closed door . . .

I think that the religious perspective here is not so much the Sanctuary Movement, like the movement has come to be known, that it is a political statement, but it is a feeling of responding to a need of a certain people who happen to cross into our community from another country . . .

Yes. Let's back up a little bit. When did you first realize that there was a problem with these Central American refugees coming over here without any help?

I knew that there were problems in El Salvador way back in '77 because we were in Chile at that time, and the Latin American press does a lot more coverage in

Latin America about situations than the U.S. press... So in '78 and '79 when people were talking about the [violence], we knew it was true. The actual organizational effort to respond was around mid '80, the actual meetings that were taking place to form a structured response. Then we got incorporated in September of '81 as an organization, as a non-profit organization...

BARCA was started, surprisingly enough, by a Lutheran pastor and a Mormon bishop [Ralph Baumgardner and Chad Richardson]. So, it was not started as a means of protest or a political statement but the opportunity for response to a need. And so right away, when we incorporated... those who were actually identifying with BARCA—we [decided that we] would not do anything illegal... One of our biggest functions is to be the advocates, to go to the immigration authorities to say: We want [this refugee] processed, and can you issue an Immigration and Nationality Act form 210, which is what our preference is because that gives them permission to go anywhere.

So, that is really where the original BARCA people come from and, also, BARCA people are really people out in the community. We don't have a little core, like Refugio [del Rio Grande, a church-run refugee camp in the Valley] has a place and they have paid staff and they are there, you know. And Proyecto [Libertad, a legal assistance organization for refugees] has the same thing, you know; they are there. Whereas, what we do is we draw in from the community... If I get a call from a refugee, say, in Brownsville, I have a little support group in Brownsville that I can call and say, "Can you take this person to Immigration Service for this, and this is what you say." That is what we are about, and so we are visible in the community...

As conservative as we are viewed by other organizations such as Proyecto and Rio Grande Defense Committee and Refugio and all those—[one particular conservative denomination] felt that we were still too radical... It was primarily the newsletter that they were objecting to, not our ministry and not me... They ended up saying that they would not give me [a donation]... They wanted me not to mention anything in my newsletter that would reflect any anti-administration feelings about foreign policy toward Central America... and that's where the conflict with me was. You can criticize the local border patrol and the local immigration but don't criticize President Reagan, was really what it amounted to... And the fact is that there is very little border patrol abuse here, and I feel that our organization has a lot to do with that... I felt I'm not going to have that much to criticize out here if that's what I'm allowed to do, but there's a lot to criticize about why people are coming, and so I was just not willing to do that...

Does [your approach to work within the system] cause some conflict with the people who are coming down here from different parts of the country?

You have to make a choice: Do you want [to raise consciousness]? Do you want to educate the community, or do you want to protest? Okay. One is the one big splash on the six o'clock news and you might divide the community; and the other, the educational, you have to tone down your speeches and whatever, but it may be a more long-lasting thing... Like two years ago we decided that we were going to do a demonstration at the detention facility and everybody thought it was a great idea. I said, "But we have to get the permits. We have to do it legally." They decided, Okay, we'll do it legally... But it was a long process. It took us about two months to get the permit, but we did it right. And we had a lot of ministers who showed up. Only about a hundred people showed up... and I told the border patrol chief, half of them were probably undercover agents. (laughs) But nevertheless, we got the people out there. We got the county commissioners to discuss this publicly, to agree to the permit... For certain people it would have been preferable that we go in there and get arrested and make a big splash on the six o'clock news. See? But after the six o'clock news, what? Whereas with the county commissioners, you know, they did a lot for us. And the county judge even went and talked at our rally...

Now, some people would say that what you are doing is treating the symptoms of the disease and the people who want national attention are going after the cure, which is a change in U.S. foreign policy. How would you respond to that?
Okay. I'm not talking refugees; I'm talking community. I'm talking about any one of us. We're an 81 percent Hispanic community here. I can be stopped at the airport. I can be stopped by immigration authorities in the middle of the street and this and that and the other. Mexicans historically have been beaten, abused, whatever, and nobody responded. Nobody cared anywhere what happened to the Mexicans. So what cure are we talking about? If I know that these national church bodies or national organizations or whatever are addressing a foreign policy in Central America, great. *I* want to address a symptom *here,* and if we change the symptom here, we're changing the community here, and we're changing it to the extent where there is no beating of Mexicans or Central Americans. And there is a very cautious, healthy respect about stopping Hispanics just because they're Hispanics, see. So, why should I with my extremely limited resources spend all my energies aggravating somebody when with these same limited funds and energy I can address a long-term cure in this community. So, I don't care about being criticized by organizations, by groups, or by the immigration service... And if I happen to have a perfect tool, because churches are responding more to a refugee concern, great, but at the time when I'm addressing a concern of the refugees, I want to address a total concern. I don't want a church to give food only to a refugee; I want it to give food to any undocumented person who comes to that door. See? I want them to address a need of the farm workers just like a refugee or Mexican. I want them to address a need of a kid in elementary school who is being discriminated against and not given food stamps or whatever, you know. I want a response to a total community here. That's what I want.

Economic Change and New Domestic Challenges

Beginning in the mid 1970s high energy prices, inflation and debt associated with the Vietnam War, and recession weakened the American economy. The nation's position in the world also declined, as Europe and Japan became leading economic competitors. Workers and their advocates faced difficult obstacles, including stagflation, deindustrialization, and rising employer strength. Declining industrial jobs hurt workers as well as their unions, reducing the political clout they had enjoyed since the 1930s. Beginning in the 1980s, the celebration of wealth, profits, and commerce dominated much of American life through the rest of the century. The nation moved toward greater inequality, with the rich growing richer and the middle class shrinking.

Amidst economic decline, Americans faced other worrisome challenges, including growing homelessness, drug abuse, and threats of international and domestic terrorism. In the morning of April 19, 1995, Gulf War I veteran-turned-anti-government-activist Timothy McVeigh detonated a homemade bomb at the south entrance of the Alfred P. Murrah Federal Office Building in Oklahoma City. The blast reduced a nine-story building into a pile of rubble, killed 168 people, injured over 500, and left psychological scars on survivors. It was, at the time, the largest act of domestic terrorism in the nation's history.

Questions to Consider: The following two accounts deal with trauma to communities. One narrative describes economic change, a long process that gradually diminished workforces and community health; the other account recalls a more sudden, surprising, and violent attack. In each case, how did workers and communities respond to these distressing events?

Shrinking Jobs in the Industrial Economy: Kenneth Hill

Kenneth Hill joined the United Auto Workers (UAW) when he began working at the Kokomo, Indiana, Chrysler transmission plant in 1966, just after he graduated from high school. He eventually became president of UAW Local 685. He speaks about his motivations for becoming active in the union and the pressures on unions and workers as the nation's industrial plants faced new economic crises in the 1970s and "deindustrialized" in the 1980s. Jane Armstrong and Timothy Borden interviewed Hill on July 10, 1996, for the Indiana Labor History Project. The interview is deposited with the Center for the Study of History and Memory at Indiana University.

We didn't know anything of a global economy in the '60s. It was never even dreamed of. First of all, transportation was very restricted. You know, you couldn't move materials from Taiwan to the United States and back, and if you did, the workmanship and things of this nature were a joke. Things that were made in Japan were junk, just absolute junk…

After I graduated [from high school] in January of 1966, I immediately went to Chrysler, went to work, and I worked about ten months prior to being drafted and spending two years in the military. I can honestly say I didn't think that I would ever come back. I didn't really like the work, I didn't think I'd return. I thought, "Well, I'll go back and maybe finish my education or do something else." There was a lot of factors that changed that…

To be honest, I was laying in a rice paddy [in Vietnam] one night as scared I've probably ever been in my life, and I thought, you know, as bad as I hated that factory, if I ever end up back, I don't think I'll ever complain again. You know, as bad as it smelled, and as dirty as it was, and as noisy, it wasn't as bad as this. And, so, when I came back, I said, you know, "That job is there, I have the right to go back to it." I went back, and I've never left, and I've never regretted it. It's been good to me, good to my family…The plant was expanding very rapidly through the sixties…It was the last place on earth I thought I wanted to be, but it provided a paycheck…

What else do you recall about the work force there? Mostly men, mostly women?
At the time I went in the [transmission facility], there was only two women left. Those two women had been there since World War II when the men were taken out [of] the plant, you know, to go to war, they put a lot of women into the plant. They were the only two that remained…They had considerable amount of seniority by that point in time. So what they did prior to that, I don't know, but they had reasonably light duty, what I consider light duty jobs, but their seniority had gotten. I don't think anybody just gave it to them…

Now, I know eventually you were elected president of Local 685, could you trace out how that happened? Was there an event that spurred you to get more involved?
Believe it or not, it was a series of things that led me to be an active participant in the union or an officer in the union. Everybody eventually has a bad supervisor. And I had a supervisor who was a bully, an absolute bully. He bullied everybody, he said, "I may not be right, but I'm still boss." And it led to a, just an intolerable situation, and I got the feeling that the only way I could survive the situation was to become more and more active, and I ran for a chief steward's position, and eventually a committeeman's position, and then vice-president, and eventually ended up president of the local union. But I did not start out with any ambition, didn't know where I'd end up.

When you look to the union leadership at that time…how were things going…was the union strong, then?
Well, obviously the union was strong because every contract it appeared that we did better, much better. You know, raises and things like this came in leaps and bounds, but, as I said, during the '60s, obviously, things were economically different, and it was much easier for unions to negotiate…You knew that something was going to come in the contract that improved either your economic status or your leisure time. Those seemed to be the two things, and, naturally,

everybody was looking forward to retirement. On the first day they walked in there, everybody lived for that day they could walk out and retire.

Do you recall when people's expectations changed or the union itself, or Chrysler itself changed in '73, '74 with the energy crisis, did that change the picture?

Well, it absolutely changed it. Chrysler was not prepared for the energy crisis. Their cars were huge gas guzzler cars, and naturally we saw huge numbers of auto workers dislocated. In fact, if you remember those days, it actually depleted our sub-funds, it depleted the unemployment compensation, but for having people in the White House that could extend the unemployment benefits, they would have been people in really dire straits. You know?...

In 1979, [Chrysler] went through an era when it appeared that the corporation would not survive as an independent entity. And it changed the attitude of not only the management, but the employees, it was a survival mode. Everybody worked towards a survival. Concessionary contracts were negotiated which either gave back wages, or at least we didn't get raises that were geared into the next contract...There was a hundred and sixty thousand Chrysler employees at that time, and it amounted to about a billion and a half dollars which gave a Chrysler the cash flow that it needed for new product development, and consequently they were able to survive.

And, you know, in the U.A.W. where they played an important role during this period of time, Chrysler didn't have a political machine. They had never been involved in the politics of the country before. So consequently when they needed the loan guarantees, they didn't know how to go about it or to go to, and the U.A.W. had to lead the fight...We had a good relationship with the Carter administration, and we were able to go to Washington, D.C. and generate the support. Now, Chrysler had gone out and hired Lee Iacocca who's a very dynamic salesman [and who]...along with Doug Fraser from the U.A.W., finally educated the American people to say, "You're not looking at 160,000 auto workers if Chrysler goes under, you better multiply that by five, maybe ten, because of the people who make the tires, the people who make the plastics, the steel workers, and the guy at the filling station...who gets unemployed." Finally, you find out there may be as many as a million and half people dislocated if Chrysler no longer builds automobiles. And the investment of loan guarantees was a very small investment for the American people.

When the future of Chrysler looked, we'll say uncertain, around '79, '80 before the bail-out, can you describe the feeling in the community?

Well, half of the people disappeared during that era. Now, some were given incentives to retire, but many of them just literally lost their job. They were laid-off greater than what the contract could cover them for. Consequently, they lost their opportunity. We went from some six thousand people down to twenty nine hundred people in a matter of two years, and these people did not ever come back into the industry.

So everybody from that point on knew that we were very precarious, and it didn't make any difference, if Chrysler didn't survive, nobody survived. You know, we would all have to start over again. So all efforts were geared towards making that survival. Thus, out of this came your product quality improvement program, your joint activities and things that make doing business more economical and more efficient...

It was extremely bleak, you know, there was several things that had to happen. We had to start a crisis center. The resources, the social resources of the community was very, very strained. And it's still trying to recover... You know, the community rallied as best as it could, but it was one of many communities around the country. Every community, it seemed like, suffered, but you have to remember the steel industry took a terrible beating at the same time, the textile industry in the South, you know, it was just everywhere, and there was no way to compensate, and we haven't compensated to this day from that. Now, you're talking just in Kokomo, it did better, because we also had a big GM presence in Kokomo at that time...

You might not have been here for the '60s and the early '70s, but you could sell anything you built. It didn't matter whether it got home, there was people waiting in line to buy an automobile. The capacity was not as great, we didn't have any foreign cars, in any large numbers sold. So if you wanted a car, you had to wait for Ford, GM, or Chrysler to build the thing. And the baby boomers had come of age. So consequently, if you could build a car, you could sell it, and why build quality into it, if you don't have to?

Do you think that made it a little difficult to change the culture there when most management and labor sectors were a little suspicious, saying, "Well, for years, we've been told to get the numbers out instead of thinking about quality—"

...It was difficult to change on both sides. First of all, the union found itself in a new position of almost being co-managers. Well, certainly, if you're going to stand over here and tell a person that the union along with the company demands that you build a quality product. Now, we've never been in that position. We'd always left management with the sole right to say, "Hey, this is good enough or not good enough." And now we have got initiatives into the thing that says, "This is the quality standard that we demand in the thing." And we found ourselves in a new position.

We also had supervisors over here who said that they had always been the boss, undisputed as to whether this was good enough or whether a guy could refuse a machine that was running obviously bad parts. He had the right to say, "I'm not going to do that. I'm not going to put myself out of a job. Now, you get somebody over here to fix it." That brought, you know, conflict. And we're still struggling with that...

One reason that the [out]sourcing issue is so great, because if you source it away, you're going to lose. If you allow them to go build it, either in another, for less money in another part of the country, or out of the country off-shore, there's less revenue. Consequently, there's less to negotiate for collective bargaining, and there'll be less people paid...

Certainly, labor has to take a responsibility in it. But we have to hold the companies accountable. You know, you're asking something from us, you're asking us to really jeopardize ourselves to a degree as we have to take almost a management role in the several of the things that we do in our jointly administered programs...And if we're going to do that, because you can't dictate it, you know, I'm going to tell you, you can beat somebody until they're blue and still not make them put their heart in it. You know, the only way you're going to do that is to get somebody from the inside whether it's the union, and normally it is the union, and the constituency or the membership itself going in and saying, "Guys we've got to do that. We have got to do that. It's for the good of everybody."

Why should we improve the profitability of a corporation if they're going to [take] the profits and run down to Mexico and build a plant with it. Tell me why, why you would do that? You know, the only incentive is, we know that they have to make a profit, when they make the profit, then we have to be able to stand strong and fast and say, "If you don't reinvest that profit, or you try to take this out of this country, or out of this area, we're going to stop you. We will do what they did in Dayton, Ohio, what they did in Kokomo, Indiana, what they have done in numerous places across this country is try to protect the industrial base that we have in this country."

Domestic Terrorism and the Oklahoma City Bombing: Hal McKnight

In the aftermath of September 11, 2001, and the terrorist destruction of the World Trade Towers in New York City, few Americans remembered that just six years earlier, another domestic act of terrorism had destroyed a federal building in Oklahoma City and shattered the lives of many people. Local businessman Hal McKnight recalled the scene after the blast and the heroic efforts of rescue workers and volunteers. As owner of the bicycle shop Wheeler Dealer, McKnight immediately volunteered his labor and organizational skills to assist with those efforts. Rodger Harris interviewed McKnight on June 14, 1995, in Oklahoma City for the Oklahoma Historical Society.

So what was your initial recollection of the building being bombed?

Well, like most people in Oklahoma City, I felt the shock of the blast and heard it. I was home. I live about seven miles north of the federal building. And, of course, did not know at the time what it was. I was upstairs in my—I have a porch area. I went out—tried to go out—to see what it was, but the physics of the blast had slammed my door shut so hard that I had to later use a screwdriver to open it...And, it was very like today, a very clear, crisp day which allowed the energy to expand, mainly to the north...Everyone in this part of the world felt the connection once we found out what it was. I turned the TV on, saw with

Image 16 Oklahoma City Bombing (Federal Emergency Management Agency).

horror what had actually happened. Wanted to help. Wanted to get involved. I made several phone calls to the Red Cross. Made several phone calls to Larry Jones ministry—Feed the Children. I guess a couple days had passed after that Wednesday, so it made it Friday or Saturday. I decided—it was a rainy, cold day—I decided that I would just go down in the area and see if I could get involved. I had received a phone call from Lt. Gov. Mary Fallin, who said she had heard that they were needing volunteers at a supply dump by the Red Cross at 8th and Harvey. So, I went down there and... people were bringing all kinds of donations and dropping them at that intersection. You could not drive in, they had pretty heavy security at that point. So, for the majority of that morning and into the afternoon, I assisted with a wheelbarrow in picking up supplies. People were bringing a lot of rain jackets and stuff for the people working in the area.

Now, did you think you would need some kind of identification at that point?

No. At that point they said, "You are only allowed to go from the One Bell Place to that intersection and back ..." Somewhere... in the range of about 3:00 p.m., a lady... asked if I would help her load her golf cart. She was going inside the perimeter, inside to the building, as it turned out—taking supplies in there as a runner for Red Cross. I helped her several times. And, after several trips in, she asked... "I had a guy who was helping and he is just too exhausted. Would you ride in with us to help unload this stuff?" Some of it was pretty heavy equipment—sledge hammers and such... "We will take you to the FBI and get you clearance ..." She vouched for me and I went through questioning at the old PubCo Building and got an FBI clearance badge. We immediately went in... and went directly to ATF headquarters and dropped a load of stuff there... east of the Murrah Building on 5th Street...

It was rainy and overcast—I had not really gotten a look at the building until that point. I was really surprised that a building that had received so much damage on the south side, paradoxically, was not that damaged. We then came around, entered the building from the west into the old freight dock... That was operation center. FEMA were headquartered there. Rescue teams were headquartered there. All the fire fighters were headquartered there and had their chiefs coordinating activities from there, as well as a Red Cross station that had been set up with supplies to hand out goods to the fire fighters and rescue workers as they would enter the building or tear a pair of gloves and had to come back and get some. They were short handed... Early on, they were using the crew actually in the building, 24 hours a day, 250 people working inside the debris...

So, as the crews would come on, they would come by and get respirators, would get headlights, etc.... So that's when it started for me—there at rescue supply at ground zero. It was extremely hectic, extremely busy. The people that were working there had been working long, long hours. Some without rest. I worked until about 4 or 5 a.m. Then went home and slept a couple of hours, ate a breakfast and came back the next day...

I tried to focus early on just what we were doing and not that we were in the building. Somewhere right about sunset, in the afterglow of sunset, I walked over to the Post Office, which was across the street there at 5th and Harvey... I had gone over to get a load of flashlights... I went over and as I came back it was a very impactual [sic] visual to see the incredible destruction first hand of what had happened from the blast. And it was raining. It was sort of very surrealistic—they had generators and lights there on the building so that the work could continue through the night. In the rain, it did not look real. I am sure, seeing for the first time like many others, it was hard for the brain to compute what had actually happened—physical destruction of that was just unbelievable.

That next day, we were in the situation where we were in need of certain parts, equipment parts, blades for saws, different kinds of screwdrivers, cutting situations, all kinds of tools... I think a lot of these companies around Oklahoma just donated goods. The reality the first night came to form very quickly, when we unloaded a series of large boxes that contained jaws of life tools. I'm not sure from whence they came, but, very high dollar, very expensive tools being used in the building. On equipment such as that—the procedure was that we would check those out... Items like gloves, respirators, headlights, flashlights—since we had not the lights to attach to the helmets, we were... duct-taping on flashlights to helmets... those things would be given away. We were in a constant state of running out of things and then trying to get them. The next day I set up lines of supply to different places, to the Post Office, to be able to call by phone rather than go over and get those items, and to the area at 8th and Harvey, where I had initially started...

People had come from different places and like myself had ended up there and were working around the clock and were burning out. You can only do that for so long. I decided that someone needs to set up a volunteer pool and a work schedule so that we have it organized. We don't want to have too many or too few. I guess that was the third day of my involvement—is when I did that... I came in and set up three 8-hour work shifts at rescue supply there at the Murrah Building. Our first shift would run from midnight to 8:00 a.m., from 8:00 a.m. to 4:00 p.m., from 4.00 p.m. to midnight... I also then got a list of the people that had been working—the veterans, so to speak... who would be in charge of each work shift... I would run into people that I knew... and said, "I need help, if you would get properly badged." I called almost every friend and acquaintance that I had asking, "Do you want to be involved?" ... Like myself, so many people wanted to work, wanted to volunteer, make a difference, do whatever they could, give blood, etc. And, we had a real need for people to work...

Incredible acts of heroism... the rescue workers, the people with the dogs, the seek and search folks, the fire fighters—there were fire fighters from all over the United States... They were going in without, amazing, without any concern for their own lives. Going into the building and doing work that was very tedious, very dangerous work and trying, early on, to find any survivors, anyone that might be caught in the rubble and alive. After a period of time, realizing that the chances were very, very slim on that, removing the bodies...

At one time they determined to put American flags on all the floors that had been cleared. They started at the top and worked down. So we would rig up flags with the post on them so they could be attached and extend out from the building to the north. I personally put on, I cannot tell you how many, American flags on the cranes. So as the cranes would lift up equipment and personnel there was an American flag there. Donations came from—our equipment would come to the Red Cross from all sources, as well as from Feed the Children. It would end up at our station where we would hand it out. American flag bandanas were extremely popular...There was a memorial at one point where all the workers wore an American flag bandana as an ascot. There was a lot of pride in the work we did. I have tremendous pride in the people that I worked next to—for the dedication and the commitment and for how well we did what we did...

There were letters from school kids that would filter in to us, mainly from Oklahoma but also from out of the state showing support, and love, and prayers. We put those right behind our work station on the concrete wall, right behind us, so that as these [rescue workers] would come in...it would look like they had been out in a dust storm, and they would look up and they would see these bright colored hand prints and coloring and stuff on cards and letters from kids and a light would come back to their face. It was real powerful...I prayed early on just to be used any way that I could and, I think, this was all divine guidance. I think God moved me to this position to do what I could do, as well as a lot of other people to do what they could do. When I first went down there and realized I was in the thick of this and that it was going to go on for many hours and many days, as it did, that a lot of the questions that haunt us all, I would be able to answer from just the exposure and experience of being there. I still don't have answers to those questions.

What are some of the questions?

Why another human being would do this. Why an American would do this to Americans. Why someone would do this hideous situation that would take the lives of totally innocent men, women, and especially children. No idea why...I cannot use enough imagination and creativity to think, why people would do this to people here in the United States...

The Red Cross would send psychologists and psychiatrists by to see how things were going and to talk to us. That was one of the questions—"How are you dealing with your anger?" Which is presumed that by dealing with this situation, to see this and to work with this, yes that is a natural—anger—it is a disgust...There was a lot of pride in what was going on and the work that was going on...even though, people, I'm sure, were dealing with a lot of emotional challenges. The focus was tremendous. That was being exhibited by the people supporting and working.

APPENDIX

How to Conduct an Oral History Interview: A Quick Guide

Oral history interviewing seems straightforward, but a good interview has a lot of preparation behind it. We encourage you to review suggestions in the bibliography to learn from the advice of experienced oral historians before undertaking your own. The list of tips below should help you get started.

Before you begin, think through your oral history project from beginning to end. What is the purpose of the interview? Will it be biographical or focused on a particular topic or event? How will you find narrators? How will you use the interview? Where will it be archived? In consultation with the archive, you will need a legal release form for the narrator's signature to allow you and others to use it.

Do your research. The best interviews are based on background research. Find out as much as you can about your narrator, the topics and historical period to be discussed. Develop an outline or list of topics to cover in the interview

Contact your prospective narrator and explain the nature of the project. The first thing your narrator will likely ask you is "Why do you want to interview me?" You need to have a thoughtful and complete answer, including how the interview will be used and where it will eventually be stored: in an archive, a publication, or on the Internet.

Understand your recording equipment and try to produce the best sound quality possible. Whether you are using a tape recorder or digital equipment, practice beforehand until you are comfortable with using it. Be sure you have the ability to record for 2 to 3 hours, and use an external microphone.

Understand your obligations to the narrator. Become familiar with the Oral History Association Evaluation Guidelines, available at http://www.oralhistory.org/network/mw/index.php/Evaluation_Guide. Among other guidelines, always treat narrators with respect, and do not pressure them to speak about matters that are uncomfortable to them. Ask for and obtain written consent (a legal release form) for the recording at the end of the interview.

Keep your promises. Show up for the interview at the agreed time. Sign for and return any borrowed materials. Keep any oral promises, such as saying you will stay in touch or provide a copy of the interview. Be sure, in oral or written presentations, to give credit to the narrator.

Practice. An oral history interview is not a conversation, nor is it the kind of interview we often see on television, where the interviewer conducts a brisk question/answer session according to a prearranged script. In contrast, emphasize the narrator's story; your role as the interviewer is simply to ask initial and follow-up questions. Most narrators expect either a conversation or a TV-like interview, so it may take a while for them to realize that they are in charge. The techniques to put your narrator at ease may not come naturally to you. Practice with friends or relatives beforehand, with the following goals in mind:

- Think about how to ask questions to put the narrator at ease and in charge.
- Elicit fuller reminiscences by asking open-ended questions rather than ones that can be answered by yes or no. For example, questions like "How were your teachers?" or "tell me what a school day was like" will likely generate a richer response than the question, "Did you attend school?"
- Ask brief questions, one at a time.
- Listen carefully and avoid interrupting. Jot down questions or topics that come to mind while the narrator is speaking, and return to them when there is a lull in the interview.
- Do not worry about silences. Sometimes a narrator is collecting her or his thoughts and will have more to say if we remain quiet.
- Don't argue, even if provoked. Parry a request for your opinion with a statement that the purpose of the interview is to explore the narrator's life and opinions.
- Limit the interview to about 2 hours maximum, unless the narrator clearly wants to go on longer.
- Schedule a follow-up interview if necessary. It is very tiring to remember and to listen carefully!
- By the end of the interview you should have a clear life chronology and a sense of the historical changes of which your narrator was a part. Wait until the end of the interview to look at photographs and scrapbooks.
- Conclude by saying something like you have enjoyed hearing about an interesting life. If you plan subsequent interviews, say briefly what they will be about.
- Label the interview and create backup copies (on tapes, discs, or hard drives) and create finding aids to the interview, which might include an index, summary, or transcript.

Select Bibliography

There are numerous guides to oral history, and the following include extensive bibliographies that can lead you to more sources about interview techniques, recording equipment, preservation, and uses and interpretation of oral history.

Charlton, Thomas L., Lois E. Myers, and Rebecca Sharpless, eds. *Handbook of Oral History.* New York: Altamira Press, 2006.

Dunaway, David K., and Willa K. Baum, eds. *Oral History: An Interdisciplinary Anthology.* Walnut Creek, CA: Altamira, 1996.

Frisch, Michael. *A Shared Authority: Essays on the Craft and Meaning of Oral and Public History.* Albany: State University of New York Press, 1990.

Grele, Ronald J., ed. *Envelopes of Sound: The Art of Oral History.* New York, Praeger, 1991.

Hamilton, Paula, and Linda Shopes, eds. *Oral History and Public Memories.* Philadelphia: Temple University Press, 2008.

Ives, Edward D. *The Tape-Recorded Interview: A Manual for Fieldworkers in Folklore and Oral History.* Knoxville: University of Tennessee Press, 1995.

———. *An Oral Historian's Work.* [Video]. Blue Hills Falls, ME: Northeast Historic Film, 1988.

Perks, Robert, and Alistair Thompson, eds. *The Oral History Reader.* Second ed. London: Routledge, 2006.

Portelli, Alessandro. *The Battle of Valle Giulia: Oral History and the Art of Dialogue.* Madison: University of Wisconsin Press, 1997.

Ritchie, Donald. *Doing Oral History: A Practical Guide.* New York: Oxford, 2003.

Schneider, William. *Project Jukebox: Where Oral History and Technology Come Together.* Anchorage: University of Alaska Press, 1992.

Thompson, Paul. *The Voice of the Past: Oral History.* New York: Oxford University Press, 2000.

Yow, Valerie Raleigh. *Recording Oral History: A Practical Guide for Social Scientists.* Thousand Oaks, CA: Sage 1994.

Oral History Association Pamphlets

The Oral History Association offers many resources, including short and accessible pamphlets to address your questions about oral history. Contact the OHA at http://www.oralhistory.org/

Barnickel, Linda. *Oral History for the Family Historian: A Basic Guide* (2006).

Mercier, Laurie, and Madeline Buckendorf. *Using Oral History in Community History Projects* (2007).
Neuenschwander, John A. *Oral History and the Law* (2002). Third edition.
Wood, Linda P. *Oral History Projects in Your Classroom* (2001).

Websites

There are hundreds of valuable websites featuring oral history, too numerous to mention here and whose web addresses are likely to change. The following are suggestions to get you started in surveying the rich resources, guides, and model projects available online.

In addition to its "Oral History Evaluation Guidelines," the Oral History Association links to dozens of projects and programs across the country that offer online digital recordings, guides to oral history collections, curriculum materials, and more. Refer to the OHA Wiki at http://www.oralhistory.org/network/mw/index.php/Main_Page

Baylor University Institute for Oral History. "Oral History Workshop on the Web." http://www.baylor.edu/oral_history/index.php?id=23560
H-OralHist http://www.h-net.org/~oralhist/. The discussion listserv includes a searchable archive on topics ranging from equipment to ethics.
Mercier, Laurie, ed. "Using and Interpreting Oral History Interviews." Columbia River Basin Ethnic History Archive (2003). http://www.vancouver.wsu.edu/crbeha/tutorials/int_oh.htm
Portelli, Alessandro, and Charles Hardy III, "I Can Almost See the Lights of Home: A Field Trip to Harlan County, Kentucky." *Journal of MultiMedia History* vol. 2 (1992). http://www.albany.edu/jmmh/vol2no1/lights.html
Shopes, Linda. "Making Sense of Oral History." *History Matters: The U.S. Survey Course on the Web*, February 2002. http://historymatters.gmu.edu/mse/oral/

LaVergne, TN USA
02 March 2011

218471LV00003B/17/P